Evidence-Based Practices in Behavioral Health

Series editor

Nirbhay N. Singh, Medical College of Georgia, Augusta University, Augusta, GA, USA

More information about this series at http://www.springer.com/series/11863

Marjorie H. Charlop • Russell Lang
Mandy Rispoli

Play and Social Skills for Children with Autism Spectrum Disorder

Springer

Marjorie H. Charlop
Psychology Department
Claremont McKenna College
Claremont, CA, USA

Russell Lang
Texas State University College of Education
San Marcos, TX, USA

Mandy Rispoli
Department of Educational Studies
Purdue University
West Lafayette, IN, USA

ISSN 2366-6013 ISSN 2366-6021 (electronic)
Evidence-Based Practices in Behavioral Health
ISBN 978-3-030-10213-5 ISBN 978-3-319-72500-0 (eBook)
https://doi.org/10.1007/978-3-319-72500-0

Printed on acid-free paper

This Springer imprint is published by Springer Nature
The registered company is Springer International Publishing AG
The registered company address is: Gewerbestrasse 11, 6330 Cham, Switzerland

We dedicate, with love, to our children, Kaitlin Charlop Christy, Emerson Lang, and James and Luke Rispoli. To the children with autism spectrum disorder whom we have learned so much from, we hope that this body of work brings joyful engagement in play with friends.

Thanks also to Benjamin Thomas, Jenna Gilder, Nataly Lim, Catharine Lory, and Soyeon Kim for their special contributions to this book. Finally, thank you to countless other students for your research over the years at The Claremont Autism Center and Texas State's Clinic for Autism Research, Evaluation and Support (CARES). You have all contributed so much to this book, our careers, and the lives of many.

Preface

There are precious few advantages to getting old. But one of them is perspective, specifically a perspective that allows one to fully enjoy the sheer beauty of progress. For me, reading this book allowed me the pleasure of just such a perspective. I have been in the ASD field for a half century, and in that time I have been a witness to the enormous advances that have been made in the field of ASD treatment, many of which are so elegantly presented in the present book.

Back when I first entered the field as an undergraduate student at UCLA, we were faced with trying to teach children with ASD, and since many had written off these children as "uneducable," we knew we had our work cut out for us. How very excited and delighted we were when, via the application of learning theory, we were able to teach these children simple behaviors such as verbal and nonverbal imitation, object labels, social greetings, simple play skills, etc. Most often using food reinforcers and a highly regimented discrete trial intervention, we were gradually able to teach limited, albeit important, behavioral repertoires. This was groundbreaking stuff followed by accolades from others—along with the subsequent realization that this early work had some profound limitations in terms of overall generalization of treatment effects. Back then we knew so much less about not only the nature of ASD but also which behaviors to teach, how to teach them, and what to expect in terms of developmental/functional sequence and collateral effects. Then, as applied behavior analysis as a science was maturing and coming into its own, so was our ability to understand ASD as well as curricular issues and intervention effects. In turn, this has allowed us to affect more substantial and comprehensive treatment gains in these children. This progress has been dependent upon many years of systematic, well-designed, focused research conducted by many laboratories and clinics in the United States and abroad.

The material presented here by Charlop, Lang, and Rispoli is informed by many, many years of research in the areas of teaching social and play skills to children with ASD. Since play and social skills are areas of renowned deficit for this population, they have been strong foci for research and these authors use well the results of this research to present the latest proven treatment strategies. This book provides we readers with just the right information to allow us to understand the ASD social and play deficits, appreciate the relevant research, and comprehend the latest intervention strategies and how to use these strategies to teach social and play skills, all this in one neat well-written and entertaining package.

This is not a "how-to" book of cookbook recipes for designing play and social skill interventions. If that is what the reader is looking for, I suggest they look elsewhere. And good luck. As someone who has taught behavioral intervention strategies for 45 years, I can say that such cookbook strategies are unlikely to be effective since they rarely provide generalized, or generalizable, teaching skills. The key to acquiring generalized skills that allow one to work successfully with a variety of individual children and to adapt and alter treatments as needed is an understanding of the underlying theory and principles of the strategies one is employing. This is just the kind of information the reader of this book is getting. First, the authors provide historical perspectives of the treatment described. This is important for giving readers (practitioners, researchers, families, students) the crucial context of the development of the field. Then the authors carefully and clearly present the theoretical bases of the strategies themselves. Then there is the presentation of the specific strategies. These are not only explained in the text, but there are many very helpful charts and tables to further present the material.

Overall this is a delightful book that is useful and practical and includes the context and rationale to enrich readers' understanding of important concepts regarding the teaching of social and play skills. We are no longer teaching simple skills and repertoires as we did all those years. How far we have come!

San Diego, CA, USA Laura Schreibman

Contents

1 More Than Just Fun and Games: Definition, Development, and Intervention for Children's Play and Social Skills 1
Typical Social and Play Development 3
Typical Play Skill Development 3
Typical Social Skill Development 7
Social and Play Behavior in Children with Autism Spectrum Disorder 8
Play and Social Skills Can Be Taught 11
Talk, Talk, and Talk Some More! 12
Be Responsive to Verbalizations and Communicative Gestures! 12
Summary Points 13
References 13

2 New Is Not Always Improved: Evidence-Based Practice in Play and Social Skills Intervention 17
Brief History of the Evidence-Based Practice Movement 19
Identifying Evidence-Based Practices for Children with ASD 20
National Professional Development Center on Autism Spectrum Disorders 22
National Autism Center's National Standards Project 26
Autism Evidence-based Practice Review Group 27
Summary of Three Evidence-Based Practice Reviews 27
Factors that Influence Treatment Selection 28
Summary Points 30
References 30

3 All Children Can Play: Prompting and Modeling Procedures to Teach Play to Children with Autism Spectrum Disorder 33
Why Teach Play? 33
A Behavioral Approach to Play 34
Creating Play Programs for Children with ASD 34

Types of Play with Toys . . . 35
Exploratory and Functional Play with Toys . . . 35
Imaginative and Pretend Play with Toys. . . . 36
Categories of Pretend Play . . . 36
Solitary and Pretend Play . . . 36
Associative and Cooperative Play. . . . 37
Group Play and Games with Rules . . . 37
How to Teach Play . . . 38
What to Choose. . . . 38
Child-Preferred Toys, Activities, and Play Partners . . . 38
General Prompting Procedures . . . 42
Play Interventions . . . 43
Imitation to Teach Functional Play . . . 43
Independent Activities. . . . 44
Cooperative Play . . . 46
Group Play . . . 47
Middle School-Aged and High School-Aged Children . . . 48
Conclusion . . . 49
References. . . . 49

4 Keeping It Real: Naturalistic Teaching Strategies (NaTS) for Play and Social Skills with Children with Autism Spectrum Disorder . . . 53
Three Basic Components of NaTS . . . 54
Motivation. . . . 55
Enhancing Generalization. . . . 58
Specific Naturalistic Strategies that Work Well for Teaching Play. . . . 61
Natural Language Paradigm (NLP) . . . 61
Pivotal Response Training . . . 62
Self-management . . . 64
Milieu Teaching Strategies . . . 65
Mand-Model . . . 65
Multiple Incidental Teaching Sessions (MITS) . . . 66
Conclusion . . . 67
References. . . . 68

5 Lights, Camera, Action! Teaching Play and Social Skills to Children with Autism Spectrum Disorder Through Video Modeling . . . 71
Background Rationale for Video Modeling . . . 71
Visual Learning and ASD. . . . 72
Visual Strategies and Video Modeling . . . 73
Video Modeling . . . 74
Empirical Support. . . . 76
How to Do Video Modeling . . . 81
Video Modeling Readiness . . . 81
Choose a Target Behavior. . . . 82
Operationally Define Target Behavior . . . 83

Task Analysis 84
Script 86
Models 86
Scene Setup 87
Filming 88
Intervention 89
Conclusion 90
References 91

6 Visualizing Success: Visual Schedules and Script Strategies for Teaching Play and Social Skills 95
Background 95
Modalities of Presentation of Intervention 96
Visual Activity Schedules 97
Scripts 97
How to Do Scripts 100
Conclusion 104
References 104

7 Want to Play? Peer-Mediated Intervention for Young Children with Autism Spectrum Disorder 107
Background and Theoretical Constructs 107
PMI Improves Outcomes for Children with ASD 110
Peer Training 112
PMI Strategies 114
How to Implement Peer-Mediated Interventions 117
Planning 117
References 123

8 The Power of Parents: Parent-Implemented Interventions for Young Children with Autism 129
Background and Theoretical Constructs 130
Family-Centered Approach 130
Early Intervention 131
Promoting Generalization and Maintenance of Learning 131
Brief Literature Review 132
Types of Parent-Implemented Interventions 132
Teaching and Supporting Parents to Implement Interventions 134
Training Structure 134
Training Duration 136
Training Procedures 136
Additional Considerations 137
Parent-Implemented Intervention Improves Child Outcomes 138
Social Communication 138
How to Use Parent-Implemented Intervention (Fig. 8.1) 141

Evaluating the Fit of Parent-Implemented Intervention with Individual Families 141
Selecting Child Outcomes. 142
Identifying Routines 142
Training Parents 144
Coaching Parents 147
Conclusion 148
References. 148

9 Conclusion: Play and Social Skills as Behavioral Cusps. 155
Treatment Without Play and Social Skills 156
The Case of Jake 156
The Case of Richard 157
Developmental Trajectories and Behavioral Cusps 158
Go to Preschool and Prevent Crime!. 158
Behavioral Cusps of Play and Social Skills 159
Treatment with Play and Social Skills 160
Conclusion 162
References. 162

Index. 163

About the Authors

Marjorie H. Charlop has dedicated her life's work to helping children with autism and their families. She is a professor of psychology at Claremont McKenna College and director of the Claremont Autism Center, her research and treatment center for children with ASD and their families. As a licensed psychologist, she also maintains a private practice and consultation services. Dr. Charlop has hundreds of professional conference presentations and publications in the field of autism and has been invited to provide workshops and lectures around the globe. Her book *Naturalistic and Incidental Teaching Strategies for Children with Autism Spectrum Disorder* is in its second edition. She has served as an associate editor and on editorial boards on numerous behavioral-, autism-, and education-related journals. Dr. Charlop's research areas focus on the treatment of communication, motivation, social skills, and behavior problems. Using technology is among her newer research interests. Parent collaboration and education is among her primary area of practice.

Russell Lang is an associate professor of special education at Texas State University and a board-certified behavior analyst—doctoral level. Dr. Lang is also the executive director of Texas State University's Autism Treatment Clinic. He earned a doctoral degree in special education with an emphasis in autism and developmental disabilities from the University of Texas at Austin and completed a postdoctoral researcher position at the University of California in Santa Barbara. His primary research interests include teaching play and leisure skills, assistive technology, and the treatment of problematic behaviors in individuals with autism spectrum disorders. He is an associate editor of the *Journal of Child and Family Studies* and the *Journal of Developmental and Physical Disabilities*.

Mandy Rispoli is an associate professor of special education at Purdue University and a board-certified behavior analyst—doctoral level. Dr. Rispoli is the co-director of the Purdue Autism Network. Dr. Rispoli's research focuses on function-based assessment and interventions for challenging behavior in young children with autism spectrum disorder and on teacher professional development in the area of challenging behavior.

Chapter 1
More Than Just Fun and Games: Definition, Development, and Intervention for Children's Play and Social Skills

All children can play and everyone needs friends. Play and social interaction provide a natural and powerful context for ongoing learning and development throughout childhood. The importance of skill acquisition in these areas has consistently been recognized by practitioners and researchers in the fields of education, developmental psychology, applied behavior analysis (ABA), and other related disciplines for decades (e.g., Bijou & Baer, 1961; Lifter, Foster-Sandra, Arzamarski, Briesch, & McClure, 2011; Lifter, Mason, & Barton, 2011; Lovaas, Baer, & Bijou, 1965; Piaget, 1962; Vygotsky, 1933). This widespread and long-standing recognition is due to a robust body of research linking proficiency in play and social skills to physical, intellectual, and emotional functioning as well as research demonstrating that interventions that improve children's play and social skills may also occasion collateral gains in other areas such as language, academics, and motor skill development (Elkind, 2007; Lifter et al., 2011; Ozonoff et al., 2008; Pierucci, Barber, Gilpin, Crisler, & Klinger, 2015; Singer & Lythcott, 2004). For example, even the simple forms of social interaction and play that occur in the first year of life such as shaking a rattle, pushing over a block tower, and batting at a hanging crib mobile require children to practice emerging motor skills (e.g., coordination of arm movements to bat the mobile) and early problem-solving strategies (e.g., obtaining an out-of-reach rattle by pulling the blanket the rattle rests on). Learning opportunities continue to arise in the context of play and social interaction throughout childhood, and increasingly complex behaviors such as sharing, turn-taking, and social problem solving become necessary for children to interact and play with one another.

When social and play behaviors are reinforced, they become more likely to occur again (see Fig. 1.1 for notes on reinforcement). An increase in early play and social behavior sets the stage for novel learning opportunities later in childhood. For example, a child who learns to share toys is more likely to be approached by peers and more likely to play in close proximity to peers (Hine & Wolery, 2006). More time spent playing near other children may then result in more opportunities to observe and imitate play behaviors and more opportunities for peer-to-peer social

M.H. Charlop et al., *Play and Social Skills for Children with Autism Spectrum Disorder*, Evidence-Based Practices in Behavioral Health,
https://doi.org/10.1007/978-3-319-72500-0_1

Fig. 1.1 Notes on reinforcement

What is "reinforcement" and why is it important?

- Reinforcement has occurred when the consequence of a behavior increases the likelihood of that behavior occurring again.
- For example, if a child smiles at mom (behavior) and, upon seeing the smile, mom hugs the child (consequence), the hug can be considered a form of reinforcement if the child smiles more often because of the hug.
- Reinforcers can be social or non-social.
- Social reinforcers (sometimes referred to as "socially-mediated") involve interaction with another person; for example, receiving praise and physical affection.
- Non-social reinforcers (sometimes referred to as "automatic") involve consequences that are not dependent on other people. For example, a child who continues to spin a top because they enjoy the visual stimulation of watching the top spin may be experiencing automatic reinforcement.
- Because reinforcement increases the occurrence of behaviors, it is an essential component of many interventions designed to teach social and play skills.
- Subsequent chapters will provide additional details on the use of reinforcement within specific intervention approaches.

interaction. Observation, imitation, and peer-to-peer interaction facilitate the acquisition of even more social and play skills, and the learning process continues (DeQuinzio, Townsend, Sturmey, & Poulson, 2007; Gonsiorowski, Williamson, & Robins, 2016; Ingersoll & Schreibman, 2006; Robinson, Anderson, Porter, Hart, & Wouden-Miller, 2003). The ongoing process of using newly acquired skills that create novel opportunities to acquire additional skills has been suggested to be one of the primary drivers of child development (Bijou & Baer, 1961). Although the exact mechanisms and associations between early social and play behavior and ongoing child development are not yet fully understood (Lillard et al., 2013), there is virtually no debate: quality play and social interaction are foundational to healthy child development (Kagan & Lowenstein, 2004).

Unfortunately, children with autism spectrum disorders (ASD) often experience deficits and abnormalities in the development of social and play skills (e.g., Carter, Davis, Klin, & Volkmar, 2005). Given the importance of these domains, it is not surprising that a great deal of intervention research aimed at teaching children with ASD target play and social behaviors has been conducted (e.g., Flynn & Healy, 2012; Lang et al., 2009). The interventions with the most supporting scientific evidence are the focus of the majority of this book. However, before describing how play and social skills can be taught, this initial chapter first provides an overview of the sequence, and time frame-specific play and social skills are observed in typical developing children. Knowledge of typical play and social development is important because play and social interventions for children with ASD tend to be more effective when the target behavior (i.e., the specific skill being taught) is developmentally appropriate for the child (Lifter, Ellis, Cannon, & Anderson, 2005). Next, specific deficits and other abnormalities associated with the social and play skills of children with ASD are identified, defined, and discussed. Emphasis is placed on the play and social skills most often targeted in intervention research (Matson & Wilkins, 2007). Finally, before subsequent chapters discuss more specialized interventions, this chapter concludes with two simple recommendations appropriate for parents and early childcare professionals who aim to support the development of social and play skills in children with or without ASD.

Typical Social and Play Development

Child development typically proceeds in a predictable sequence with specific skills and behaviors observed at roughly the same time of life across children. To illustrate a typical developmental sequence, consider motor skill development as an example. Specifically, children first learn to lift their head and then to use their arms to push up from the ground. Next, they learn to crawl, and crawling is typically replaced by walking all before 24 months of age. This sequence and the approximate time of life specific motor skills emerge are consistent across a large majority of typical developing children. In a manner comparable to motor skill development, children's play and social repertoires also tend to develop in a predictable sequence with key social and play behaviors emerging around the same age across children. Table 1.1 provides an overview of the developmental milestones related to play and social skills that are typically reached in the first 5 years of life.

Typical Play Skill Development

Because researchers across multiple fields have addressed a variety of research questions related to play using dissimilar research methods, numerous definitions and categorical systems (taxonomies) of play have been developed. Lifter et al. (2011) conducted a comprehensive review of the various taxonomical approaches to classifying and defining play behaviors and noted that most conceptualizations emphasize either (a) the appearance (topography) of the play behavior—that which can be directly observed (e.g., stacking blocks or rolling a toy car)—or (b) the underlining cognitive processes and constructs assumed necessary for a specific form of play, which are not readily observable. The latter, for example, is evident in definitions of pretend play that emphasize the symbolic representation and pretense

Table 1.1 Social and play skills observed in typical development

Birth–2 months	Tends to look toward faces
	Imitates some facial expressions
	Orientates or looks toward the sound of voices
2–4 months	Smiles and makes eye contact at short distances
	Plays with their own feet and hands by wiggling, rubbing, and grabbing
4–6 months	Imitates a wider range of facial expressions
	Recognizes familiar people at a distance
	Coos, babbles, and begins to imitate the intonation and pace of speech
	Seeks out affection (e.g., raises arms in an effort to be picked up and snuggled)
	Reaches for and grasps toys (e.g., batting at a hanging mobile)
	Can hold and shake toys (e.g., make noise with a rattle)
6–9 months	Distinguishes between familiar people and strangers (e.g., behaves differently with mom than unknown person)
	Plays with a variety of toys but has favorite toys
	Responds to voices by making sounds
	Uses gestures to communicate (e.g., reaches hand toward desired object while looking at the adult capable of reaching the object)
	Plays simple social games (e.g., peek-a-boo)
9–12 months	Responds to simple spoken requests (e.g., come here)
	Joint attention is well established
	Uses toys in a variety of ways
	Hands objects to people to initiate play (e.g., brings dad the blanket in an effort to start a round of peek-a-boo)
	Uses two or more toys together (e.g., banging blocks together)
12–18 months	Simple pretend play (e.g., doll drinks from empty cup)
	Scribbles with crayons
	Pulls toys on a string
2 years	Seeks out and plays near or around but not directly with other children (i.e., parallel play)
	Points to pictures in books
	Knows names of familiar people
	Plays simple make-believe games
	Stacks blocks and builds block structures
	Physical activity play involving items (e.g., kicks and throws balls)
3 years	Shows affection, concern, and empathy to friends (e.g., kiss another person's "boo-boo")
	Takes turns in games
	Back-and-forth conversation
	Completes simple non-interlocking puzzles
	Pretend play involves multiple toys (dolls and doll houses) and more complex themes
4–5 years	Prefers to play with other children
	Plays board or card games
	Plans games and activities ahead of time
	Concerned with whether friends like them

Table 1.2 Developmental sequence of play behavior

Approximate age range observed	Type of play	Definition and example topography
0–6+ months	Sensorimotor play	Exploring the environment by touching and mouthing objects. For example, putting hands or objects in mouth and rubbing hand on a bumpy wall
3–9+ months	Object exploration play	Seeing an object, reaching for that object, and then manually or orally manipulating the object
4–12+ months	Simple functional play	Engaging with objects (toys) in the manner intended, for example, pressing buttons on a light-up toy and shaking a rattle
8–12+ months	Relational or combination functional play	Making two or more objects interact or combine in some way, for example, stacking blocks
9–18+ months	Functional or pre-symbolic play	Using a toy in a way consistent with what the toy represents, for example, putting sand in the bucket of a toy dump truck
12–18+ months	Symbolic, imaginative, or pretend play	Using an object as if it were a different object (e.g., a book as a race car ramp); acting as though an object has an attribute it lacks (e.g., a toy oven imagined to be hot); or an object or person that is not present is imagined to be there or an event that did not occur to have occurred (e.g., a dragon is attacking the castle but no item represents the dragon)
18–24+ months	Dramatic or self-pretend play	Pretending to be someone or something else, for example, pretending to be a superhero or animal
24 months to 3 years	Parallel play	Playing alongside another child but not directly interacting with the other child
2.5 years to 4 years+	Associative play or early cooperative play	Seeking out other children to play with, has clear preferences for play partners but may still require adult support for more than brief play interactions
4 years+	Cooperative play	Playing with other children unassisted; able to identify friends and shows concern for whether or not other children like them

assumed necessary for a child to imagine that one object is another object (e.g., pretending a broom is a guitar) or that an object has properties it does not actually possess (e.g., pretending a broom can fly).

Lifter et al. (2011) astutely point out that both perspectives, whether focused on play topography or the underling cognitive processes (referred to as the behavioral and constructivist paradigms, respectively), have contributed to our understanding of play and to the identification of effective approaches to teaching play. Table 1.2 overviews the categories and definitions of play appearing the most often in intervention research aimed at improving play. An approximate age range during which each form of play may be observed in typical child development is also provided. However, due to differences in how play is defined or measured across research studies, there is no single agreed-upon taxonomy for play in the scientific literature.

As such, Table 1.2 is intended only to provide a sampling of various play taxonomies and multiple theoretical underpinnings (Barton, 2010; Belsky & Most, 1981; Lifter et al., 2011; Malone, 1997; McCune, 1998; Rutherford & Rogers, 2003).

As previously noted, play provides a naturally reinforcing context for children to practice emerging motor, communication, social, problem-solving, and other essential skills throughout childhood (Freeman & Kasari, 2013; Warreyn, Paelt, & Roeyers, 2014; White et al., 2011). Beginning very early in life, infants learn about the appearance, taste, and feel of objects during sensorimotor play. Natural reinforcement contingencies involving stimulation (automatic reinforcement; Fig. 1.1) obtained from sensorimotor play likely contribute to learning to reach, grasp, and crawl. Later in childhood, most children begin to engage in functional play wherein they imitate others (often parents) by using toys that resemble real objects in a manner consistent with the objects' function, for example, feeding a doll with a toy bottle (Lang et al., 2009). The extent to which functional play is reinforced by socially mediated contingencies such as praise (e.g., "Wow, you're feeding your baby just like Momma does!"), some form of nonsocial automatic reinforcement that does not rely on input from others, or a combination of socially mediated and automatic reinforcement is not clear. Regardless of the reinforcement contingencies involved, functional play clearly provides children opportunities to imitate the behavior of others and provides parents, caregivers, and interventionists with opportunities to model developmentally and contextually appropriate skills and language (Freeman & Kasari, 2013; Pierucci, 2016).

By the time most children are 4 years old, they will have started engaging in symbolic and pretend play that involves imagining that an object is a different object, that a missing object is present, and/or that objects or people have attributes they actually lack. Further, toddlers will integrate these skills in various ways such that characters, events, and toys fit together within a play scheme. The acquisition of pretend play skills is truly an awesome achievement in early childhood! Consider, for example, the remarkably complex repertoire of skills and cognitive processes that must be involved when a child pretends a hairbrush is a microphone and that the living room couch is a stage as they sing to a crowd of stuffed animals and dolls.

In terms of the acquisition of advanced abstract thinking, problem-solving, and other sophisticated cognitive skills, the role of pretend play is currently a subject of debate. Specifically, it remains unclear whether pretend play is (a) an essential and irreplaceable experience that drives ongoing cognitive development, (b) one of many potential mechanisms or contexts capable of facilitating more advanced cognitive skills, or (c) merely the result of already having acquired these skills through some other means (Kasari, Chang, & Patteson, 2013; Lillard et al., 2013). Regardless, including sociodramatic and pretend play activities within a "playful curriculum" designed for young school-age children has been repeatedly demonstrated to be associated with improvements in sustained focus, recall (memory), and the ability to adjust to changes in routines and environments (e.g., Diamond, Barnett, Thomas, & Munro, 2007; Paley, 2005).

Typical Social Skill Development

In a seminal experiment, Meltzoff and Moore (1977, 1989) demonstrated that infants have the capacity to imitate some facial expressions as early as the 12th day of life. Whether this initial imitation ability is innate (a type of reflex) or a skill the child has somehow already learned is not yet clear. Either way, the presence of the ability suggests that infants are able to recognize that they are separate beings from other people and, at only weeks old, already have a tendency to attend to other people's faces. Clearly, these must be among the earliest and most foundational of all social skills! Over the next few months of life, babies learn that their actions (behaviors) influence other people and that specific behaviors and people are associated with specific social consequences, many of which are reinforcing. For example, infants learn that crying often results in reinforcement in the form of the parent bringing food, warm hugs, and dry diapers. These early infant-parent social interactions set the stage for other important social skills including more complex forms of communication (Bijou & Baer, 1961).

Children tend to begin demonstrating a desire to play with other children around 3 years of age by attempting to initiate social interactions or by responding to the social initiations of other children more frequently (Coplan & Arbeau, 2009; Hay, Caplan, & Nash, 2009; McElwain, Ogolsky, Engle, Holland, & Mitchell, 2016). While adults are more likely to compensate for a child's social deficits by scaffolding the complexity of the interaction or prompting the appropriate social response, social interactions with peers are more likely to require the child to independently adjust their own social behavior to repair or avoid social problems and communication breakdowns. These more complicated requirements for successful peer interaction, therefore, provide both the motivation and context to learn more nuanced social skills such as negotiation, perspective-taking, cooperation, and sharing (McElwain et al., 2016).

There are a number of specific social behaviors that have been the focus of research, and summary of that large body of literature is complicated by the input of multiple disciplines, each with unique approaches and perspectives. Most notably, as with play, social behavior has been studied from both the behavioral and constructivist research traditions. Research from the behavioral (operant) paradigm has focused on observable characteristics of social behaviors and on the reinforcement contingencies involved in social interactions, while constructivist or developmental researchers have tended to focus on the biological and cognitive underpinnings of social behavior and on taxonomical systems for temperament and attachment (Matson & Wilkins, 2007; McElwain et al., 2016). Table 1.3 is intended to provide a representative overview of the social skills found most often in intervention research and provides definitions and examples drawn from both developmental and behavioral sources (Sticher, Randolph, Gage, & Schmidt, 2007; Watkins et al., 2015; Whalon, Conroy, Martinez, & Werch, 2015; White, Keonig, & Scahill, 2007).

So far this chapter has provided an overview of typical play and social skill development and described how play and social interaction may facilitate ongoing

Table 1.3 Definitions and examples of social skills frequently targeted in intervention research

Social skill	Definition and example	Importance
Eye contact	Focusing gaze on another person's eyes	Eye contact facilitates the expression of emotion and the accurate identification of another person's emotions (Senju & Johnson, 2009)
Imitation	After observing the behavior of another person, the observer engages in the same behavior that was observed, for example, a child goes down a slide after watching another child use the slide	Imitation is fundamental to the acquisition of speech and is a primary mechanism for learning a variety of skills across domains (Heimann, Nordqvist, Strid, Almrot, & Tjus, 2016)
Joint attention	Coordinated attention between two people wherein a person looks at another person's eyes and then follows their eye gaze to observe the same object or event, for example, a child looks at mother's eyes and then follows her gaze as it shifts to look at a toy across the room	Joint attention has been linked to receptive and expressive language proficiency, social initiations, and imitation and may be essential during symbolic play involving two children (White et al., 2011)
Social response	A response to a social initiation, for example, agreeing to join a game after being invited to play by another child	Responding to social initiations is necessary for social interaction and engagement (Matson & Wilkins, 2007)
Social initiation	An effort to begin a social interaction with another person, for example, tapping someone on the shoulder and asking "do you want to play?"	The ability to initiate social interactions affords a child more opportunities for social interaction and forming friendships (Grosberg & Charlop, 2014)
Engagement and turn-taking in communication	Two people interacting in an ongoing conversation, manipulating the same items (e.g., working together to build a block tower), or other forms of ongoing interaction that typically involve communication, turn-taking, eye contact, and joint attention	Engagement is necessary for friendship and provides a context to learn more advanced skills (Koegel, Vernon, Koegel, Koegel, & Paullin, 2012)

skill acquisition throughout childhood. In the next section, the characteristics of children with ASD are discussed with a focus on social and play behaviors.

Social and Play Behavior in Children with Autism Spectrum Disorder

The fifth edition of the American Psychiatric Association *Diagnostic and Statistical Manual of Mental Disorders* (APA, 2013) provides diagnostic criteria for ASD that includes (a) restricted and/or repetitive behavior involving motor movements (e.g., flapping hands), use of objects (e.g., spinning objects like a top), and/or speech (e.g., repetitive vocal sounds) and (b) persistent deficits in social communication and/or social interaction. There has been a focus on the social behavior of children with ASD since autistic disorder was first described (Kanner, 1943). In fact, even the term "autism" is derived from the Greek word for "self" and was used because children in early studies were thought to be absorbed within themselves—favoring social isolation over social interaction. Perhaps some children with ASD prefer social isolation, but a large body of more recent research indicates that most children with ASD desire social interaction, friendships, and other relationships. It is a mistake to assume that the social skill deficits observed in a person with ASD indicate aversion to social interaction or a disinterest in social relationships. In fact, many people with ASD seek out social interactions and sincerely cherish their social relationships. Simply being unskilled in social interaction does not mean that a child has no desire for social interaction. The social characteristics commonly associated with ASD include deficits or abnormalities in (a) eye contact, (b) initiating and/or responding to social interactions, (c) emotional reciprocity, (d) speech, (e) joint attention, and (f) use and interpretation of facial expressions and gestures (APA, 2013; Matson & Wilkins, 2007).

Unlike social deficits, abnormalities in play are not required for an ASD diagnosis. However, the diagnostic criterion involving restricted and repetitive patterns of behavior is often first observed during play, and, like social behavior, atypical play has been discussed since autistic disorder was first described (Kanner, 1943). Understandably, given play's connection to healthy child development and its potential to facilitate development in other areas, the play behavior of children with ASD has received notable research attention. The most commonly reported play abnormalities in children with ASD involve spending less time engaged in parallel and cooperative play and demonstrating less variability or diversity in play involving toys or other objects. For example, in his original description of children with autistic disorder, Kanner noted the tendency to play in isolation and to demonstrate a rigid "insistence on sameness" when given the opportunity to play. As examples of this rigidity, Kanner described play that involved repeatedly spinning a block on its corner always pointing the block in the same direction, repetitious counting objects, and arranging toys in a straight line. These and other examples of restrictive and repetitive play have also been observed in more recent studies. For example, Ozonoff and colleagues (2008) compared the object-exploration play of children with and without ASD and reported that children with ASD displayed significantly more spinning, rotating, and unusual visual exploration of objects.

These restrictive and repetitive play behaviors likely displace learning opportunities that could facilitate the acquisition of skills in other domains. For example, instead of building a block castle with a friend, a child with ASD may line the blocks up in a straight line and become upset if another child approaches or tries to touch the block line. Similarly, a child with ASD may insist on playing the same game in the same way every time, which likely limits opportunities for new experiences and may drive away potential playmates. Over time, this type of isolated and repetitive play is likely detrimental in a variety of ways. For example, Ozonoff et al. (2008) reported that the more restrictive and repetitive a child's object-exploration play behaviors were at 12 months of age, the more severe their social skill deficits and cognitive delays were at 3 years.

Additional play deficits associated with ASD include spending less time engaged in the imaginative or pretend play that has been linked to cognitive development (Kasari et al., 2013; Wing, Gould, Yeates, & Brierley, 1977) and a reduced tendency to observe and imitate the play of other children (Rogers, Young, Cook, Giolzetti, & Ozonoff, 2008). Although delayed or abnormal play development is not emphasized to the same extent in ASD diagnostic criteria as the presence of social skill abnormalities, the potential adverse impact of play deficits on development is considerable.

Despite the pervasive nature of ASD's symptoms, it is important to note that symptom severity varies a great deal across individuals. For example, some children with ASD reach spoken language milestones at the same age as children of typical development (e.g., first words around 12 months and complete sentences at 3 years), but others do not acquire spoken language at all. Heterogeneity in the ASD population is also evident in domains not directly related to the diagnostic criteria. For example, some children with ASD have an intellectual disability, while others demonstrate average and even far above average intellectual functioning. Similarly, challenging behavior (e.g., self-injury) and comorbid mental illness (e.g., anxiety disorder) range from severe to absent in children with ASD. All of these factors certainly impact a child's social and play behavior and illustrate the diversity of the ASD population. Table 1.4 provides a brief list of the common social and play deficits reported in ASD but should be considered in light of this diversity.

The severity of ASD symptomology is categorized according to the level of support the child requires for daily functioning. The *Diagnostic and Statistical Manual of Mental Disorders* (APA, 2013) describes three support levels ranging from "requiring support" to "requiring very substantial support." In terms of social skills, children that require very substantial support may present with a complete absence

Table 1.4 Social and play characteristics associated with autism spectrum disorder

Characteristics of ASD related to social and play skills
Deficits in social-emotional reciprocity
Difficulty with back-and-forth conversation
Failure to initiate or respond to social interactions
Abnormalities in eye contact, use of gestures, and body language
Difficulty interpreting the meaning of other people's gestures and body language
Unusual facial expressions
Difficulty fostering and sustaining friendships
Failure to adjust behavior based on social contexts
Difficulties engaging in imaginative play
Using toys to engage in stereotyped or repetitive behaviors that do not resemble typical play behaviors
Inflexible adherence to routines, insistence on sameness
Interests in items or activities that are too intense and/or too limited

of speech, no demonstrated ability to initiate or respond to social interactions, and intense rituals and repetitive forms of behavior that, when interrupted or redirected by caregivers, cause notable distress and challenging behavior (e.g., tantrums and aggression). On the other end of the continuum, children may initiate or respond to social situations in unusual or awkward ways and fixate on a specific toy or play routine. Although they may develop speech and some play and social skills, children on this end of autism spectrum will still require support and are still likely to benefit from systematic play and social skill intervention. Given the importance of social and play skills in early childhood, it is not surprising that parents of children with ASD often rate these skills among their top intervention priorities for their children regardless of their child's level of functioning (Pituch et al., 2011).

Play and Social Skills Can Be Taught

The terms "development" and "emerge" seem to suggest a passive process wherein the social and play behaviors first observed in early childhood arise simply as a result of nature (e.g., genetics and physiology). Conversely, referring to play and social behaviors as "skills" that can be "acquired," "learned," or "mastered" suggests a more active process wherein skills do not emerge unless they are nurtured through interactions. The relative influences of nature and nurture on human behavior is a long-standing debate in the field of psychology. There is no doubt that child development in any domain is influenced by nature. For example, genetic mutations can certainly disrupt and delay the emergence of specific developmental milestones. However, it is important to recognize that a child's environment and their history of interacting with others (nurture) also influence the acquisition of skills and it is widely accepted that both nature and nurture influence social and play behavior. For example, consider two children: one a perfectly healthy child without any illness or developmental disability (sufficient nature) neglected in an orphanage (suboptimal nurture) and another child with a genetic disorder (suboptimal nature) raised by attentive parents in an enriched environment (sufficient nurture). Although these two children may display similar social and play skill deficits, the primary cause of deficits may be very different.

Regardless of the cause of deficits, because we have little control of nature (e.g., genetics, biology, and physiology), and treatments based on nature (e.g., medication) for ASD have not been demonstrated to be sufficiently effective, most efforts to ameliorate the social and play deficits in children with ASD have focused on nurture. Specifically, these interventions involve changing the way people interact with the child and/or the arrangement or quality of the child's immediate environment. More precisely, nurture-based (behavioral) interventions involve teaching social and play skills by systematically considering how people prompt and reinforce target social and play behaviors and by arranging environments to be supportive of skill development. Although it is true that ASD is likely caused by one or more biological factors, it is a mistake to assume that deficits attributed to nature cannot be remediated by nurturing skills with behavioral interventions. All children, regardless of their nature, can learn to engage in some form of play and social interaction.

Specific research-based teaching procedures and intervention packages designed for children with ASD will be discussed in subsequent chapters. Those interventions require careful planning and training to implement correctly. However, even without specialized training, there are some simple strategies parents and early childcare providers can employ to nurture children's social and play skills. Two of these strategies are discussed briefly.

Talk, Talk, and Talk Some More!

The more spoken language a child hears during early childhood the better. Hart and Risley (1995) collected longitudinal data in the homes of 42 families with young children from a variety of socioeconomic classes and reported an astonishing association between the amount parents talked around their children and the children's achievements later in life. Specifically, the more words children heard before 3 years of age, the larger their vocabularies and higher their IQ scores were throughout childhood. Further, the children who heard a lot of words before age 3 were more successful in school at 9 years of age. Hart and Risley's study focused on typical developing children; however, similar results have been reported in studies focused on the amount of speech heard by young children with ASD in the first few years of life (Perryman et al., 2013).

Parents and early childcare providers should talk to children as much and often as possible. Reading aloud, singing, and other similar activities should help increase the number of words a child hears. Some parents verbally narrate their actions while caring for their baby as a way to model language, for example, a mother saying "Momma's changing your diaper" while changing the child's diaper. This approach, sometimes referred to as linguistic mapping, may be particularly beneficial when parents talk about the child's current focus of attention, for example, commenting upon the toy a child is manipulating or providing the name of an item the child is reaching for (Perryman et al., 2013; Siller & Sigman, 2008). Attempting to establish joint attention (see Table 1.3) and then talking about whatever the child is focused on is a potentially powerful approach to supporting language and social skill development (Hancock, Ledbetter-Cho, Lang, & Howell, 2016).

Be Responsive to Verbalizations and Communicative Gestures!

Children begin making vocalizations early in life by babbling, cooing, and squealing. Letting the child know that they were heard by responding to these early vocalizations may help teach basic skills that underlie more complex communication and social skills. Ideally, these responses should be related to what the child is experiencing at that moment. For example, if a child squeals after knocking over a block tower, a caregiver could be responsive by commenting "blocks crashed!". Similarly, when a child reaches for an object that is out of reach and then looks to a parent for help, the child's reach and glance should be considered an effort to communicate. These gestural forms of communication also create an opportunity for caregivers to facilitate skill development. Specifically, because the caregiver knows what the child wants (whatever is being reached for), this is an opportunity for the caregiver to model the appropriate language (e.g., "bottle please") and then give the bottle. The natural reinforcement contingency of providing the bottle following the child's communicative gesture (reaching for bottle while looking at parent) can increase the child's likelihood of trying to communicate in the future. The parent's modeling of the verbal request ("bottle please") helps teach the child how to make that request verbally. This type of responsivity to a child's early-in-life vocalizations and gestures supports social skill acquisition and language development (Hancock et al., 2016).

Summary Points

- Like motor skill development, play and social development in typical childhood has a predictable trajectory wherein skills are acquired in approximately the same sequence and at roughly the same time of life across children.
- The acquisition of early social and play skills can lead to opportunities for children to learn even more skills.
- Many foundational skills essential for healthy development across many domains of functioning can be acquired in the context of play and social interaction.
- Unfortunately, the social and play deficits associated with ASD may interrupt or impede this developmental process.
- Even though ASD may be caused by one or more biological (nature) factors, intervention involving changes to how people interact with the child and other aspects of the child's environment can remediate those skill deficits.
- All children can learn.
- Parents and caregivers can support play and social development by talking to and around children, playing with children, and being responsive to children's early social and play behaviors.

References

American Psychiatric Association. (2013). *Diagnostic and statistical manual of mental disorders: DSM-5*. Washington, DC: American Psychiatric Association.

Barton, E. E. (2010). Development of a taxonomy of pretend play for children with disabilities. *Infants & Young Children*, *23*, 247–261.

Belsky, J., & Most, R. K. (1981). From exploration to play: A cross-sectional study of infant free play. *Developmental Psychology, 17*, 630–639.

Bijou, S. W., & Baer, D. M. (1961). *The nature of developmental theory. Child development, Vol. 1: A systematic and empirical theory*. East Norwalk, CT: Appleton-Century-Crofts.

Carter, A. S., Davis, N. O., Klin, A., & Volkmar, F. R. (2005). Social development in autism. In F. R. Volkmar, R. Paul, A. Klin, & D. Cohen (Eds.), *Handbook of autism and pervasive developmental disorders: Vol. 1. Diagnosis, development, neurobiology, and behavior*. Hoboken, NJ: Wiley.

Coplan, R. J., & Arbeau, K. A. (2009). Peer interactions and play in early childhood. In K. H. Rubin, W. M. Bukowski, & B. Laursen (Eds.), *Handbook of peer interactions, relationships, and groups* (pp. 143–161). New York, NY: The Guilford Press.

DeQuinzio, J. A., Townsend, D. B., Sturmey, P., & Poulson, C. L. (2007). Generalized imitation of facial models by children with autism. *Journal of Applied Behavior Analysis, 40*, 755–759.

Diamond, A., Barnett, W. S., Thomas, J., & Munro, S. (2007). Preschool program improves cognitive control. *Science, 318*, 1387–1388.

Elkind, D. (2007). *The power of play: How spontaneous imaginative activities lead to happier, healthier children*. Cambridge, MA: Da Capo Press.

Flynn, L., & Healy, O. (2012). A review of treatments for deficits in social skills and self-help skills in autism spectrum disorder. *Research in Autism Spectrum Disorders, 6*, 431–441.

Freeman, S., & Kasari, C. (2013). Parent-child interactions in autism: Characteristics of play. *Autism, 17*, 147–161.

Gonsiorowski, A., Williamson, R. A., & Robins, D. L. (2016). Brief report: Imitation of object-directed acts in young children with autism spectrum disorders. *Journal of Autism and Developmental Disorders, 46*, 691–697.

Grosberg, D., & Charlop, M. (2014). Teaching persistence in social initiation bids to children with autism through a portable video modeling intervention (PVMI). *Journal of Developmental and Physical Disabilities, 26*, 527–541.

Hancock, T., Ledbetter-Cho, K., Lang, R., & Howell, A. (2016). Enhanced milieu teaching. In R. Lang, T. Hancock, & N. N. Singh (Eds.), *Evidenced-based practice in early intervention for children with autism*. New York, NY: Springer.

Hart, B., & Risley, T. (1995). *Meaningful differences in the everyday experience of young american children*. Baltimore, MD: Brookes.

Hay, D. F., Caplan, M., & Nash, A. (2009). The beginnings of peer relations. In *Handbook of peer interactions, relationships, and groups* (pp. 121–142). New York, NY: The Guilford Press.

Heimann, M., Nordqvist, E., Strid, K., Almrot, C. J., & Tjus, T. (2016). Children with autism respond differently to spontaneous, elicited and deferred imitation. *Journal of Intellectual Disability Research, 60*, 491–501.

Hine, J. F., & Wolery, M. (2006). Using point-of-view video modeling to teach play to preschoolers with autism. *Topics in Early Childhood Special Education, 26*, 83–93.

Ingersoll, B., & Schreibman, L. (2006). Teaching reciprocal imitation skills to young children with autism using a naturalistic behavioral approach: Effects on language, pretend play, and joint attention. *Journal of Autism & Developmental Disorders, 36*, 487–505.

Kagan, S. L., & Lowenstein, A. E. (2004). School readiness and children's play: Contemporary oxymoron or compatible opinion? In E. Zigler, D. Singer, & S. Bishop-Josef (Eds.), *Children's play: The roots of reading* (pp. 59–76). Washington, DC: Zero to Three Press.

Kanner, L. (1943). Autistic disturbances of affective contact. *Nervous Child, 2*, 217–250.

Kasari, C., Chang, Y., & Patteson, S. (2013). Pretending to play or playing to pretend: The case of Autism. *American Journal of Play, 6*, 124–135.

Koegel, L. K., Vernon, T. W., Koegel, R. L., Koegel, B. L., & Paullin, A. W. (2012). Improving social engagement and initiations between children with autism spectrum disorder and their peers in inclusive settings. *Journal of Positive Behavior Interventions, 14*, 220–227.

Lang, R., Machalicek, W., O'Reilly, M. F., Sigafoos, J., Rispoli, M. J., Shogren, K., & Regester, A. (2009). Review of interventions to increase functional and symbolic play in children with autism. *Education and Training in Developmental Disabilities, 44*, 481–492.

Lifter, K., Ellis, J., Cannon, B., & Anderson, S. R. (2005). Developmental specificity in targeting and teaching play activities to children with pervasive developmental disorders. *Journal of Early Intervention, 27*, 247–267.

Lifter, K., Foster-Sandra, S., Arzamarski, C., Briesch, J., & McClure, E. (2011). Overview of play: Its uses and importance in early intervention/early childhood special education. *Infants & Young Children, 24*, 225–245.

Lifter, K., Mason, E. J., & Barton, E. E. (2011). Children's play: Where we have been and where we could go. *Journal of Early Intervention., 33*, 281–297.

Lillard, A. S., Lerner, M. D., Hopkins, E. J., Dore, R. A., Smith, E. D., & Palmquist, C. M. (2013). The impact of pretend play on children's development: A review of the evidence. *Psychological Bulletin, 139*, 1–34.

Lovaas, O. I., Baer, D. M., & Bijou, S. W. (1965). Experimental procedures for analyzing the interaction of symbolic social stimuli and children's behavior. *Child Development, 36*, 237–247.

Malone, M. D. (1997). Preschoolers' categorical and sequential toy play: Change over time. *Journal of Early Intervention, 21*, 45–61.

Matson, J. L., & Wilkins, J. (2007). A critical review of assessment targets and methods for social skills excesses and deficits for children with autism spectrum disorders. *Research in Autism Spectrum Disorders, 1*, 28–37.

McCune, L. (1998). Immediate and ultimate functions of physical activity play. *Child Development, 69*, 601–603.

McElwain, N. L., Ogolsky, B. G., Engle, J. M., Holland, A. S., & Mitchell, E. T. (2016). Child–child similarity on attachment and temperament as predictors of positive interaction during acquaintanceship at age 3. *Developmental Psychology, 52*, 1394–1408.

Meltzoff, A., & Moore, M. (1977). Imitation of facial and manual gestures by human neonates. *Science, 198*, 75–78.

Meltzoff, A. N., & Moore, M. K. (1989). Imitation in newborn infants: Exploring the range of gestures imitated and the underlying mechanisms. *Developmental Psychology, 25*, 954–962.

Ozonoff, S., Macari, S., Young, G. S., Goldring, S., Thompson, M., & Rogers, S. J. (2008). Atypical object exploration at 12 months of age is associated with autism in a prospective sample. *Autism, 12*, 457–472.

Paley, V. G. (2005). *A child's work: The importance of fantasy play*. Chicago, IL: University of Chicago Press.

Perryman, T. Y., Carter, A. S., Messinger, D. S., Stone, W. L., Ivanescu, A. E., & Yoder, P. J. (2013). Parental child-directed speech as a predictor of receptive language in children with autism symptomology. *Journal of Autism and Developmental Disorders, 43*, 1983–1987.

Piaget, J. (1962). *Play, dreams, and imitation in childhood*. New York, NY: Norton.

Pierucci, J. M. (2016). Mothers' scaffolding techniques used during play in toddlers with autism spectrum disorder. *Journal of Developmental and Physical Disabilities, 28*, 217–235.

Pierucci, J. M., Barber, A. B., Gilpin, A. T., Crisler, M. E., & Klinger, L. G. (2015). Play assessments and developmental skills in young children with autism spectrum disorders. *Focus on Autism and Other Developmental Disabilities, 30*, 35–43.

Pituch, K. A., Green, V. A., Didden, R., Lang, R., O'Reilly, M. F., Lancioni, G. E., & Sigafoos, J. (2011). Parent reported treatment priorities for children with autism spectrum disorders. *Research in Autism Spectrum Disorders, 5*, 135–143.

Robinson, C. C., Anderson, G. T., Porter, C. L., Hart, C. H., & Wouden-Miller, M. (2003). Sequential transition patterns of preschoolers' social interactions during child-initiated play: Is parallel-aware play a bidirectional bridge to other play states? *Early Childhood Research Quarterly, 18*, 3–21.

Rogers, S. J., Young, G. S., Cook, I., Giolzetti, A., & Ozonoff, S. (2008). Deferred and imitation in regressive and early onset autism. *Journal of Child Psychology and Psychiatry, 49*, 449–457.

Rutherford, M. D., & Rogers, S. J. (2003). Cognitive underpinnings of pretend play in autism. *Journal of Autism and Developmental Disorders, 33*, 289–302.

Senju, A., & Johnson, M. H. (2009). The eye contact effect: Mechanisms and development. *Trends in Cognitive Sciences, 13*, 127–134.

Siller, M., & Sigman, M. (2008). Modeling longitudinal change in the language abilities of children with autism: Parent behaviors and child characteristics as predictors of change. *Developmental Psychology, 44*, 1691–1704.

Singer, J. L., & Lythcott, M. A. (2004). Fostering school achievement and creativity through sociodramatic play in the classroom. In E. Zigler, D. Singer, & S. Bishop-Josef (Eds.), *Children's play: The roots of reading* (pp. 77–93). Washington, DC: Zero to Three Press.

Sticher, J. P., Randolph, J., Gage, N., & Schmidt, C. (2007). A review pf recommended social competency programs for students with autism spectrum disorders. *Exceptionality, 15*, 219–232.

Vygotsky, L. S. (1933). Play and its role in the mental development of the child. In J. Bruner, A. Jolly, & S. Slyva (Eds.), *Play: Its role in development and evolution*. New York, NY: Basic Books.

Warreyn, P., Paelt, S. V. D., & Roeyers, H. (2014). Social-communicative abilities as treatment goals for preschool children with autism spectrum disorder: The importance of imitation, joint attention, and play. *Developmental Medicine & Child Neurology, 56*, 712–716.

Watkins, L., O'Reilly, M., Kuhn, M., Gevarter, C., Lancioni, G., Sigafoos, J., & Lang, R. (2015). A review of peer-mediated social interaction interventions for students with autism in inclusive settings. *Journal of Autism and Developmental Disorders, 45*, 1070–1083.

Whalon, K. J., Conroy, M. A., Martinez, J. R., & Werch, B. L. (2015). School-based peer-related social competence interventions for children with autism spectrum disorder: A meta-analysis and descriptive review of single case research design studies. *Journal of Autism and Developmental Disorders, 45*, 1513–1531.

White, P. J., O'Reilly, M., Streussand, W., Levine, A., Sigafoos, J., Lancioni, G., … Aguilar, J. (2011). Best practices for teaching joint attention: A systematic review of the intervention literature. *Research in Autism Spectrum Disorders, 5*, 1283–1295.

White, S. W., Keonig, K., & Scahill, L. (2007). Social Skills development in children with autism spectrum disorders: A review of the intervention research. *Journal of Autism and Developmental Disorders, 37*, 1858–1868.

Wing, L., Gould, J., Yeates, S. R., & Brierley, L. M. (1977). Symbolic play in severely mentally retarded and in autistic children. *Journal of Child Psychology and Psychiatry, 18*, 167–178.

Chapter 2
New Is Not Always Improved: Evidence-Based Practice in Play and Social Skills Intervention

In the past, children with intellectual and developmental disabilities were described in a number of ways that were later revealed to be inaccurate. For example, in the middle of the twentieth century, some children with severe disabilities (including some with autism spectrum disorder [ASD]) were classified as "untrainable" or "uneducable" by health-care professionals and school systems (Rothstein, 1982). Such descriptors reveal the prevailing paradigm of that time: there was little hope of successfully teaching some children any meaningful skills. For example, professional organizations devoted to special education described children labeled in this way as being nonresponsive to even "the most heroic efforts of today's most skilled therapists" (Rothstein, 1982). The special educators, psychologists, and other stakeholders were not any less devoted or compassionate than those working in the field today. They simply did not have a large body of existing information (i.e., an evidence base) derived from carefully controlled research to guide practice and inform policy (see Box 2.1).

Ill-informed assumptions that lead to labels such as "uneducable" existed until being sufficiently challenged by research. Pioneers in fields such as applied behavior analysis (ABA) and special education conducted studies directly aimed at testing the assumption that some children were beyond the reach of our "most heroic and skilled." Beginning with efforts to teach basic skills, early paradigm-shifting researchers began creating, testing, and refining interventions designed for children with severe developmental and intellectual disabilities, who in many cases were children with ASD (e.g., Dagoni-Weinberg, 1969; Ferinden & Cooper, 1973; Holman & Baer, 1979). The success of those early intervention studies—in tandem with increased awareness of the dismal educational outcomes and poor quality of life experienced by people with severe disabilities—drew more researchers to the field, and the pace of research quickened. As the body of research involving the education of the "uneducable" continued to grow, researchers carefully summarized and reviewed the research base every few years. In these early research reviews, progress toward more effective treatments and educational programs was

M.H. Charlop et al., *Play and Social Skills for Children with Autism Spectrum Disorder*, Evidence-Based Practices in Behavioral Health,
https://doi.org/10.1007/978-3-319-72500-0_2

acknowledged, missteps were identified, and new refinements were suggested for future research (e.g., Margolies, 1977; Oxman, Webster, Fruchter, & Konstantareas, 1980; Ward, 1970).

Over time, research involving people with ASD produced a rich evidence base that overcame the notion that children with ASD (and others) were in some way immune to the influence of treatment structure and environment (e.g., Volkmar, Hoder, & Cohen, 1985). Further, in some cases, intervention developers and researchers demonstrated that treatment could result in improved intellectual functioning and even placement in typical school classrooms (e.g., Loovas, 1987). The scientific process, which appropriately began by describing the disorder's seemingly insurmountable deficits, eventually led to the understanding that some forms of intervention can result in meaningful skill acquisition. The scientific process was undeniably indispensable in creating a field of study devoted to the education and treatment of children with ASD. Ultimately, it was research that dispelled the myth of the uneducable child.

Today, due to a much more robust research base, we suspect most educators and therapists are fully aware that children with ASD can be taught a large variety of skills, and the labels of "untrainable" and "uneducable" seem markedly ridiculous. In fact, it is so widely understood that teaching makes a difference for children with ASD; there is an abundance of new and purported "improved" treatment options available. Unfortunately, not all of those treatment options have been vetted by the very scientific process responsible for this enlightenment. Specifically, not all treatment options are derived from sound research, some have never been researched at all, and, most alarming, other interventions have been carefully researched but were found to be ineffective or dangerously counterproductive (Travers, Ayers, Simpson, & Crutchfield, 2016). In short, the evidence base comprising many decades' worth of data on the qualities of effective treatment is occasionally ignored, and it is not uncommon for ineffective and/or untested treatments to be disseminated directly to clinicians, in-service and preservice teachers, and families. Although the children receiving these fad, pseudoscientific, and invalidated treatments are certainly capable of making progress on their goals, failure to consider the evidence base when selecting treatment approaches all too often denies them that opportunity.

This chapter focuses on the importance of evidence-based practice and discusses issues in the context of interventions designed to teach play and social skills to children with ASD. The chapter aims to (a) provide a brief historical overview of the evidence-based practice movement beginning in the field of medicine and moving to psychology and education, (b) describe the common approaches to defining and identifying evidence-based practices, (c) identify specific evidence-based practices suitable for teaching play and social skills to children with ASD and note where each of those practices is presented in this text, and (d) discuss the reasons why practitioners and families may select practices that are not evidence-based. Ultimately, this chapter is intended to set the stage for subsequent chapters that focus on a variety evidence-based treatment options that have been repeatedly demonstrated to be capable of improving the play and social skills of children with ASD.

Brief History of the Evidence-Based Practice Movement

There was a time, not very long ago, when comparing potential risks and benefits across various medical treatments was much more difficult. In too many cases, doctors had to rely primarily on personal experience, anecdote, and intuition when treating some types of illnesses and injuries. There was more uncertainty when attempting to identify the best course of action, and even high-stakes medical decisions were sometimes made with limited or inaccurate information. The concept of evidence-based practice first arose in the field of medicine to address this challenging and dangerous context. The aim of the evidence-based medicine movement was to improve patient outcomes by offering doctors a systematic approach to identifying medical treatments based on the most rigorous supportive scientific research (Claridge & Fabian, 2005; Guyatt, Sackett, & Cook, 1993).

The evidence-based medicine movement has produced a large database of research reviews covering many areas of medicine (e.g., The Cochrane Collaboration, 2017). These reviews allow for different treatment options to be compared based on (a) the extent to which patients benefited from a specific treatment approach in research and (b) the relative rigor of the research supporting each approach (i.e., how carefully a study was conducted). By considering both the quality of the research (rigor) alongside participant (patient) outcomes, doctors are empowered to make more informed treatment choices (Higgins & Green, 2011). The evidence-based practice movement in medicine spread quickly. Evidence-based medicine is now emphasized in medical school training, and the concept drives medical decision-making in many places around the world (Vyse, 2005).

In part, the success of the evidence-based practice movement in medicine further highlighted the growing need for a similar systematic approach to making psychological treatment decisions (Wong et al., 2013). The American Psychological Association defined criteria for evaluating the relative efficacy and merit of various psychological treatment options (Chambless & Hollon, 1998). Specifically, Chambless and Hollon set criteria for identifying "empirically supported therapies" (p. 7). Their criteria emphasized a treatment's demonstrated efficacy, generalizability, feasibility, and cost-effectiveness. They also set specific requirements for how many studies are necessary for a therapy to be considered empirically supported and guidance for how to resolve discrepancies in results across studies. Chambless and Hollon's criteria are one option among several sets of criteria that can be used to identify evidence-based practices in psychology. Despite differences across options, each set of evidence-based practice criteria all share similar general areas of emphasis (e.g., efficacy, rigor, and feasibility).

Shortly after the evidence-based practice movement began in psychology, it spread to the field of education. In 2002, the What Works Clearinghouse was created by the US Department of Education's Institute for Education Sciences with the intent of being "a central and trusted source of scientific evidence for what works in education" (as cited by Wood, 2017). Other groups of stakeholders and practitioners released position statements supporting students' right to scientifically validated effective interventions (c.f., Van Houten et al., 1988). Despite these laudable value statements, the degree of emphasis placed on evidence-based practice during in-service training of teachers as well as the extent to which the evidence base drives educational decision-making has not yet reached the level seen in the field of medicine (Foxx & Mulick, 2015; Vyse, 2005). Further, although evidence-based practices are now mandated in several federal laws related to public education (e.g., Individuals with Disabilities Education Act), there is still considerable debate as to how those practices should be identified (Wood, 2017).

Unfortunately, perhaps due to the wider range of research methodologies and the variety of different underlying philosophies that characterize the fields of education and psychology compared to medicine, the progress of the evidence-based practice movement has been less efficient in these two fields. For example, some have presented a postmodernist argument suggesting that psychology, education, and other purported social sciences will never (or should never) attempt to achieve the level of certainty reached in the field of medicine (Gergen, 2001; Vyse, 2005). Whatever the reason, the evidence-based practice movement took longer to initiate in these fields and remains less ubiquitous than what is enjoyed in the field of medicine. There is currently no one agreed-upon way to define or identify evidence-based practice. Therefore, for this text, we have selected three different evidence-based practice reviews aimed specifically at identifying effective treatments for children with ASD. These three evidence-based practice reviews are described with a focus on social and play skill interventions in the next section.

Identifying Evidence-Based Practices for Children with ASD

Given the wide range of research designs and differences in the underlying philosophies that drive the various natural sciences (e.g., ABA and medicine) and social sciences (e.g., special education) involved in the education and treatment of children with ASD, it is understandable that there is no single agreed-upon approach to determining what practices are (or are not) "evidence-based" or for identifying a "best practice" for a given client's individualized treatment goals. Three reputable groups have suggested specific criteria that should be met for a practice to be classified as evidence-based: (a) the National Professional Development Center on Autism Spectrum Disorders, (b) the National Autism Center's National Standards Project (2009), and (c) the Autism Evidence-Based Practice Review Group (Wong et al., 2013). Using various procedures, all three of these groups have reviewed the research base. The sections of this chapter that follow will describe each of these groups' criteria for classifying a treatment as an evidence-based practice. Next, the evidence-based practices that could be used to teach social or play skills to children with ASD are listed in Tables 2.1, 2.2, and 2.3. These tables also highlight where each particular practice is discussed in this text. However, before we proceed, it is necessary to understand the terms "intervention," "treatment," "treatment component," and "treatment package" to interpret these tables properly. Box 2.1 provides definitions and a brief discussion of these terms (Box 2.2).

Box 2.1 What Is the Evidence Base?

What exactly does "evidence base" or "research base" refer to?

- The terms evidence base and research base can usually be used interchangeably.
- Both terms refer to collected or aggregate research findings across published studies. For example, in the writing of this text, we considered a large corpus of research studies involving treatments designed to improve the social and play skills of children with ASD.
- Any one study, regardless of the rigor of the research procedures and design, will have limitations. It is not possible to be reasonably certain that a treatment is effective based on the findings of a single study.
- Different studies have different strengths and weaknesses. For example, an experimental single-case design study has stronger internal validity (i.e., clear evidence of benefit for people who received treatment in the study) but weaker external validity (less certainty that those benefits will be achieved if the treatment is replicated with other people). However, group design studies have stronger external validity but weaker internal validity.
- Researchers conduct systematic reviews or meta-analyses (i.e., methods for studying findings across a group of studies) as a way to control for the limitations of any one study.
- The evidence base includes the entire body of research involving experimental single-case designs, group designs, and systematic or meta-analytic reviews.

Box 2.2 Clarification of the Terms *Intervention*, *Treatment*, *Package* and *Component*

What is the difference between an "intervention/treatment component" and a "intervention/treatment package"?

- The terms treatment and intervention are used interchangeably to refer to the specific actions taken in an effort to educate, treat, or in some other way ameliorate the symptoms or deficits associated with ASD.
- The term intervention component (or treatment component) refers to a single strategy or teaching procedure, for example, providing reinforcement for an appropriate behavior.
- The term treatment package (or intervention package) refers to a collection of intervention components that are used together as part of a combined approach.
- Differential reinforcement is an example of a treatment package because it involves reinforcing the desired behavior/skill and intentionally withholding reinforcement for a challenging behavior (extinction). The package

often includes prompting for the appropriate behavior and/or redirection for the challenging behavior. In this example, reinforcement, extinction, prompting, and redirection are all intervention components that make up the differential reinforcement treatment package.
- A single intervention component and a package can both be classified as evidence-based using some criteria (NPDC), but only treatment packages are considered evidence-based in other criteria (Wong et al., 2013).

In some cases, an evidence-based practice identified by an agency is a component of a larger intervention package covered in this text. In other cases, an intervention component covered in this text is part of one of the evidence-based practices identified by the group or agency. In both of those situations, the tables state "Component." For example, modeling and prompting are covered in Chap. 3, and, because these components are often used in functional communication training packages, "Component" is marked in Table 2.1 where the evidence-based practice identified by the agency intersects with the column indicating where in this text that practice is covered. Finally, when the exact treatment package or intervention component classified as an evidence-based practice by an agency is precisely the same as what is described in a corresponding chapter in this text, "Main Focus" is noted in the table. Tables 2.1, 2.2 and 2.3 are intended to (a) identify the evidence-based treatments and treatment components that have been used to improve social and play skills of children with ASD; (b) highlight the ubiquitous nature of some treatment components that are used within nearly all of the of the identified evidence-based practices (e.g., reinforcement); and (c) indicate where each one of these treatments (or components) is discussed in this book.

National Professional Development Center on Autism Spectrum Disorders

The National Professional Development Center on Autism Spectrum Disorders (NPDC) classifies a treatment as an evidence-based practice for people with ASD when the treatment's efficacy has been sufficiently evaluated in research published in peer-reviewed scientific journals. Further, individual studies as well as the body of research considered as a whole must be sufficiently rigorous and replicated. Specifically, effectiveness must be demonstrated in at least (a) two high-quality experimental or quasi-experimental group designs demonstrating effectiveness, (b) three different research teams which must have produced five single-case design studies demonstrating effectiveness, or (c) a comparable combination of group designs and single-case designs with results replicated by at least three different research teams. Using this set of criteria, it is not possible for a practice to be classified as evidence-based from only a single study nor is it possible for a single

Table 2.1 National professional development center on autism spectrum disorders evidence-based practices across chapters

		Treatment packages and components covered in this text					
	EBP identified by NPDC that can be used to teach social and play skills	Modeling and prompting (Chap. 3)	Video modeling (Chap. 4)	Visual and activity schedules (Chap. 5)	Naturalistic teaching strategies (Chap. 6)	Peer-mediated intervention (Chap. 7)	Parent-implemented intervention (Chap. 8)
National Professional Development Center on Autism Spectrum Disorders	Differential reinforcement	Component	–	–	Component	–	Component
	Extinction	–	–	–	Component	–	Component
	Functional communication training	Component	–	–	–	–	Component
	Naturalistic interventions	Component	–	–	*Main focus*	Component	Component
	Parent-implemented interventions	Component	–	–	Component	–	*Main focus*
	Pivotal response training	Component	–	–	Component	–	Component
	Peer-mediated intervention	Component	–	–	Component	*Main focus*	–
	Prompting	*Main focus*	Component	Component	Component	Component	Component
	Reinforcement	–	–	–	Component	Component	Component
	Response interruption and redirection	Component	–	–	–	–	Component
	Social narratives	Component	–	–	–	–	–
	Social skills training groups	Component	–	–	–	Component	–
	Stimulus control	Component	Component	Component	Component	Component	Component
	Task analysis	–	–	Component	–	–	–
	Time delay	Component	–	–	Component	–	Component
	Video modeling	Component	*Main focus*	–	–	–	–
	Visual supports	Component	Component	*Main focus*	–	–	–

Table 2.2 National autism center's national standards project evidence-based practices across chapters

		Treatment packages and components covered in this text					
	EBP identified by NSP that can be used to teach social and play skills	Modeling and prompting (Chap. 3)	Video modeling (Chap. 4)	Visual and activity schedules (Chap. 5)	Naturalistic teaching strategies (Chap. 6)	Peer-mediated intervention (Chap. 7)	Parent-implemented intervention (Chap. 8)
National Autism Center National Standards Project	Antecedent package	Component	Component	Component	Component	–	Component
	Behavioral package	Component	Component	Component	Component	Component	Component
	Joint attention intervention	Component	–	–	Component	–	Component
	Modeling	*Main focus*	*Main focus*	–	Component	Component	Component
	Naturalistic teaching strategies	Component	–	–	*Main focus*	Component	Component
	Peer training package	Component	–	–	–	*Main focus*	–
	Pivotal response treatment	Component	–	–	Component	–	–
	Schedules	–	–	*Main focus*	–	–	–
	Story-based intervention package	–	–	–	–	Component	–

Table 2.3 Autism evidence-based practice review group evidence-based practices across chapters

		Treatment packages and components covered in this text					
	EBP identified by Wong et al. (2013) that can be used to teach social and play skills	Modeling and prompting (Chap. 3)	Video modeling (Chap. 4)	Visual and activity schedules (Chap. 5)	Naturalistic teaching strategies (Chap. 6)	Peer-mediated intervention (Chap. 7)	Parent-implemented intervention (Chap. 8)
Autism Evidence-Based Practice Review Group	Antecedent-based intervention	Component	Component	Component	Component	–	Component
	Cognitive behavioral intervention	–	–	–	–	–	–
	Differential reinforcement	Component	–	–	Component	–	Component
	Discrete trial training	Component	–	–	–	–	–
	Functional communication training	Component	–	–	Component	–	Component
	Modeling	*Main focus*	Component	–	Component	Component	Component
	Naturalistic intervention	Component	–	–	*Main focus*	Component	Component
	Parent implemented	Component	–	–	Component	–	*Main focus*
	Peer-mediated instruction	Component	–	–	–	*Main focus*	–
	Picture exchange communication	Component	–	–	Component	–	Component
	Pivotal response training	Component	–	–	Component	–	Component
	Prompting	*Main focus*	Component	Component	Component	Component	Component
	Reinforcement	Component	–	–	Component	Component	Component
	Response interruption/redirection	Component	–	–	Component	–	Component
	Scripting	Component	–	*Main focus*	–	Component	–
	Social narratives	–	–	–	–	Component	–
	Social skills training	Component	–	–	–	Component	–
	Structured play groups	Component	–	–	Component	Component	–
	Task analysis	Component	–	Component	–	–	–
	Technology-aided instruction	–	Component	Component	–	–	–
	Time delay	Component	–	–	Component	–	Component
	Video modeling	Component	*Main focus*	–	–	–	–
	Visual supports	Component	–	*Main focus*	–	–	–

research team alone to make a practice evidence-based by conducting multiple studies. Put simply, to be considered an evidence-based practice, a treatment's beneficial outcomes must have been peer-reviewed, replicated across studies, and replicated across researchers.

Using these criteria, the NPDC examined hundreds of peer-reviewed studies and identified 24 specific intervention components and treatment packages (Table 2.1). Of these 24 practices that met the NPDC's definition of evidence-based, 16 have been used to improve the social and play skills of children with ASD in a sufficient number of studies. Table 2.1 lists those 16 evidence-based practices and identifies where they are covered in this book.

National Autism Center's National Standards Project

The National Autism Center's National Standards Project (NSP) solicited input from a select panel of nationally recognized clinicians, scholars, and scientists working in the field of ASD treatment to define criteria for classifying treatments as *established*, *emerging*, or *unestablished*. For the purpose of this text, the treatments classified as "established" by the NSP can be considered evidence-based practices. The NSP's criteria for a treatment to be considered an established evidence-based practice are similar to those used by the NPDC in that both require replication of research findings in multiple studies by more than one research team and those studies must be published in peer-reviewed scientific journals. However, for a treatment to be considered evidence-based by the NSP, there must be at least 2 group design or 4 single-subject design studies that include a minimum of 12 participants that all produce beneficial outcomes and no study that reports conflicting results. If a single study does suggest a treatment is ineffective or detrimental but other studies report beneficial outcomes (conflicting findings are found across studies), then there must be at least 3 group designs or 6 single-case designs with a minimum of 18 participants suggesting beneficial outcomes. If there is more than one study that reports negative findings (no improvement as a result of a treatment), then the treatment cannot be classified as evidence-based using the NSP criteria.

The NSP examined 775 peer-reviewed research studies and identified 11 specific intervention components and treatment packages as evidence-based (Table 2.2). Of these 11 practices that met the NPDC's criteria, 9 have a sufficient body of research demonstrating potential to improve the social and play skills of children with ASD. The two omitted were Comprehensive Behavioral Treatment for Young Children and Self-Management. These were omitted because the former is a broad description of intervention packages designed to address many areas of functioning simultaneously and are not designed to focus on any single skill domain (e.g., social or play). The latter is more commonly used with higher-functioning children and adults, and there is limited research evaluating self-management interventions on social and play skills specifically. Table 2.2 displays the nine remaining evidence-based practices and identifies where they are covered in this text as either a component of an intervention package or as the main focus of a chapter.

Autism Evidence-based Practice Review Group

The Autism Evidence-Based Practice Review Group included a core group of researchers from the University of North Carolina in Chapel Hill as well as a large team of experts that served as article reviewers (Wong et al., 2013). The team reviewed over 1000 peer-reviewed studies focused on the education and treatment of children with ASD. They initially grouped studies as either comprehensive treatment models (treatment packages intended to address a broad range of developmental goals and skills) or focused intervention practices (designed to address a single skill area or domain of functioning). For the same reason we omitted "Comprehensive Behavioral Treatment for Young Children" in the overview of the NSP's evidence-based practices, only Focused Intervention Practices on the NPDC's list were considered. The same criteria used by the NPDC (described earlier) were used to qualify a treatment as an evidence-based practice by this group.

Overall, the Autism Evidence-Based Practice Review Group identified 465 studies out of the 1000+ that were screened for inclusion in their review. Of those 465, 165 studies focused on social skills and 77 studies focused on play. A total of 27 treatments met the criteria for evidence-based practice of which 23 had been demonstrated to be effective in improving play and social skills. Those 23 treatments are presented in Table 2.3.

Summary of Three Evidence-Based Practice Reviews

We have now presented an overview of three different groups that have utilized various definitions and criteria for determining if a treatment can be classified as an evidence practice. Despite the different definitions, criteria, and review procedures used by the NPDC, the NSP, and the Autism Evidence-Based Practice Review Group, there is a great deal of consistency in what types of treatments were identified as evidence-based. Across Tables 2.1, 2.2, and 2.3, the treatments that consistently emerged as evidence-based included (a) modeling and video modeling, (b) systematic prompting and prompt fading, (c) visual supports and activity schedules, (d) naturalistic teaching strategies, and (e) peer-mediated strategies. Further, key intervention components such as reinforcement and extinction were identified either as stand-alone practices or as components within evidence-based treatment packages by all three groups.

We selected the treatment approaches covered in subsequent chapters of this text based on the findings of the three evidence-based practice reviews discussed in the chapter. Specifically, basic modeling and prompting procedures are covered in Chap. 3; naturalistic teaching strategies are detailed in Chap. 4; video modeling is presented in Chap. 5; and visual strategies including scripts and activity schedules are discussed in Chap. 6. The other intervention components identified across the three evidence-based practice reviews (e.g., reinforcement, extinction, and behavioral packages) are discussed as components within the intervention packages covered in other chapters. Chapters 7 and 8 discuss peer-mediated and parent-implemented interventions, respectively. Although peer-mediated strategies are identified as evidence-based practices in all three reviews and parent-implemented intervention is identified in two reviews, those strategies might best be considered intervention-delivery mechanisms as opposed to unique intervention packages in their own right. For example, parents are often trained to implement naturalistic teaching strategies, and research has demonstrated that peers can be trained to implement many of the treatments identified as evidence-based (e.g., peer modeling). However, in some cases, parents and peers are not taught effective evidence-based practices and training parents or peers to implement an ineffective treatment is not an evidence-based approach.

Factors that Influence Treatment Selection

Although essentially the same evidence-based practices were identified across agencies (Tables 2.1, 2.2, and 2.3), many children with ASD are still routinely exposed to nonevidence-based practices. For example, Hess, Morrier, Heflin, and Ivey (2008) examined what was being provided to children with ASD in schools and found that less than 10% could be considered evidence-based. Similarly, Hanson et al. (2007) surveyed parents and found that nearly 71% of treatments selected by parents lacked a supporting evidence base. This discrepancy between the scientific evidence base and what is actually done in practice is often referred to as the research-to-practice gap. The research-to-practice gap results in missed opportunities, wasted resources (e.g., time and money), and, in some cases, harm to the child receiving intervention.

Nonevidence-based practices are sometimes referred to as "pseudoscientific" or described as "fads," particularly when the treatment is described and marketed using scientific terms or concepts in unsubstantiated or misleading ways (Foxx & Mulick, 2015). There is a staggeringly large number of treatments and interventions that claim to improve the social and play skills for children with ASD that can be described as pseudoscientific fads. Although an intervention may be "new," that does not always mean it is "improved." For example, Green and colleagues (2006) surveyed 552 parents of children with ASD and identified 108 distinctly different treatment packages that were received by children with ASD. Over 50% of those treatments were never systematically investigated by researchers. In other cases, the treatment was researched but was found to be ineffective and/or unsafe (e.g., facilitated communication). Regrettably, there are many commonly provided interventions with almost no supporting evidence (e.g., Reichow, Barton, Sewell Neely, Good, & Wolery, 2010; Wallen, 2012).

In order to better understand the reasons why parents of children with ASD may select pseudoscientific treatments over evidence-based options, Green (2007) interviewed parents to identify (a) where parents obtained information about treatment options and (b) the factors they considered when selecting between treatment options. The three most common sources of information identified by parents included Internet sites, advice from other parents, and recommendations from practitioners specializing in the intervention approach being considered (e.g., occupational therapists recommending sensory integration therapy). When considering these sources of information, parents indicated that their decision was based on (a) perceived ease of implementation, (b) time commitment, and (c) anecdotal reports suggesting an approach might be effective. Similar results were also found when large diverse groups of parents were surveyed (e.g., Miller, Schreck, Mulick, & Butter, 2012).

Unfortunately, these sources of information (e.g., professional organization Internet sites) often provide little guidance in comparing treatment options and/or actually disseminate unsubstantiated claims regarding pseudoscientific interventions (e.g., Stephesnson, Carter, & Kemp, 2012). Further, factors such as ease of implementation—although clearly important—are not directly related to a treatment's actual effectiveness (Leong & Carter, 2008). Simply put, it does not matter how consistently and accurately one implements an ineffective treatment.

Consideration of nonscientific sources and treatment characteristics not directly related to treatment effectiveness is not limited to parents. Using an interview comparable to Green's (2007), another group of researchers examined special education teachers' and administrators' perspectives regarding evidence-based practices (Greenway, McCollow, Hudson, Peck, & Davis, 2013). Responses to the interview questions revealed a sincere desire to use effective practices and an understanding that evidence-based practices should be used. However, beliefs about what constitutes "evidence" and the criteria for classifying a practice as evidence-based varied considerably across teachers. Anecdotal testimonials, personal experiences, and the intuitive appeal of the intervention procedures were identified as primary considerations by many teachers. Overall, these variables are emphasized by both parents and teachers when considering treatment options for children with ASD (e.g., Borders, Bock, & Szymanski, 2015; Carson, 2014).

Research aimed at reducing the research-to-practice gap is being conducted with increasing frequency. For example, research aimed at improving the acceptability (intuitive appeal of interventions, sometimes referred to as social validity) of interventions has become more common. Callahan, Henson, and Cowan (2008) provided teachers, parents, and school administrators with a social validation survey and identified specific intervention characteristics valued by respondents (e.g., treatment involves active collaboration and focuses on long-term outcomes) and recommended these qualities be considered when evaluating existing ASD interventions and in the creation of improved intervention approaches. Further, efforts to educate teachers, parents, and other ASD stakeholders regarding the importance of evidence-based practice and/or on how to implement those practices have also become more common (e.g., Lang, Machalicek, Rispoli, & Regester, 2009; Lerman, Vorndran, Addison, & Kuhn, 2004; Machalicek, Lang, & Raulston, 2015; Rispoli, Neely, Lang, & Ganz, 2011). In keeping with this effort, this text focuses on interventions that have accumulated the most compelling and rigorous evidence base and should serve as a resource for those who seek to provide effective evidence-based interventions to improve the play and social skills of children with ASD.

Summary Points

- Before there was sufficient research evidence to indicate otherwise, children with the most severe intellectual and developmental disabilities (including many with ASD) were often considered to be uneducable.
- Researchers demonstrated that all children can learn and the evidence base involving the education and treatment of children with autism became more robust.
- Evidence-based practices are those that have been sufficiently demonstrated to be effective in multiple rigorous studies replicated by more than one research team.
- The evidence-based practice movement began in medicine and is now well underway in the fields of psychology and education.
- A number of specific evidence-based practices that can be used to improve the social and play skills of children with ASD have been identified by three separate review groups, and those practices are covered in subsequent chapters in this text.

References

Borders, C. M., Bock, S. J., & Szymanski, C. (2015). Teacher ratings of evidence-based practices from the field of autism. *Deaf Studies and Deaf Education*, *20*, 91–100.

Callahan, K., Henson, R. K., & Cowan, A. K. (2008). Social validation of evidence-based practices in autism by parents, teachers, and administrators. *Journal of Autism and Developmental Disorders, 38*, 678–692.

Carson, B. Y. (2014). *An evaluation of the attitudes teachers have towards adopting evidence-based practices for students with autism in preschool classrooms* (Doctoral dissertation). Retrieved from Dissertation abstracts international section A: Humanities and social sciences, 75, 3621868.

Claridge, J. A., & Fabian, T. C. (2005). History and development of evidence-based medicine. *World Journal of Surgery, 29*, 547–553.

Chambless, D. L., & Hollon, S. D. (1998). Defining empirically supported therapies. *Journal of Clinical and Consulting Psychology*, *66*, 7–18.

Dagoni-Weinberg, E. (1969). From total isolation to social communication: Treatment of a case of early infantile autism. *International Journal of Child and Adolescent Psychiatry*, *36*, 153–165.

Ferinden, W. E., & Cooper, J. M. (1973). Successful treatment of childhood autism. *Language, Speech, and Hearing Services in Schools*, *4*, 127–131.

Foxx, R. M., & Mulick, J. A. (Eds.). (2015). *Controversial therapies for autism and intellectual disabilities* (2nd ed.). Mahwah, NJ: Lawrence Erlbaum Associates Publishers.

Gergen, K. J. (2001). Psychological science in a postmodern context. *American Psychology*, *56*, 803–813.

Green, V. A. (2007). Parental experience with treatments for autism. *Journal of Developmental and Physical Disability*, *19*, 91–101.

Green, V. A., Pituch, K. A., Itchon, J., Choi, A., O'Reilly, M., & Sigafoos, J. (2006). Internet survey of treatments used by parents of children with autism. *Research in Developmental Disabilities*, *27*, 70–84.

Greenway, R., McCollow, M., Hudson, R. F., Peck, C., & Davis, C. A. (2013). Autonomy and accountability: Teacher perspectives on evidence-based practice and decision-making for students with intellectual and developmental disabilities. *Education and Training in Autism and Developmental Disabilities*, *48*, 456–468.

Guyatt, G. H., Sackett, D. L., & Cook, D. J. (1993). User guides to the medical literature II. How to use an article about therapy or prevention: Evidence-based medicine working group. *Journal of the American Medical Association*, *270*, 2598–2601.

Hanson, E., Kalish, L. A., Bunce, E., Curtis, C., McDaniel, S., Ware, J., et al. (2007). Complementary and alternative medicine among children diagnosed with autistic spectrum disorder. *Journal of Autism and Developmental Disorders*, *37*, 628–636.

Hess, K. L., Morrier, M. J., Heflin, L. J., & Ivey, M. L. (2008). Autism treatment survey: Services received by children with autism spectrum disorders in public school classrooms. *Journal of Autism and Developmental Disorders*, *38*, 961–971.

Higgins, J. P. T., & Green, S. (Eds.). (2011). *Cochrane handbook for systematic reviews of interventions version 5.1.0* [updated March 2011]. The Cochrane Collaboration. Available from www.cochrane-handbook.org

Holman, J., & Baer, D. M. (1979). Facilitating generalization of on-task behavior through self-monitoring of academic tasks. *Journal of Autism and Developmental Disorders*, *9*, 429–446.

Lang, R., Machalicek, W., Rispoli, M. J., & Regester, A. (2009). Training parents to implement communication interventions for children with autism spectrum disorders: A systematic review of training procedures. *Evidenced Based Communication Assessment and Intervention*, *3*, 174–190.

Leong, H. M., & Carter, M. (2008). Research on the efficacy of sensory integration therapy: Past, present and future. *Australasian Journal of Special Education*, *32*, 83–99.

Lerman, D. C., Vorndran, C. M., Addison, L., & Kuhn, S. (2004). Preparing teachers in evidence-based practices for young children with autism. *School Psychology Review*, *33*, 510–526.

Loovas, O. I. (1987). Behavioral treatment and normal educational and intellectual functioning in young autistic children. *Journal of Consulting and Clinical Psychology*, *55*, 3–9.

Machalicek, W., Lang, R., & Raulston, T. J. (2015). Training parents of children with intellectual disabilities: Trends, issues, and future directions. *Current Developmental Disorders Report*, *2*, 110–118.

Margolies, P. J. (1977). Behavioral approaches to the treatment of early infantile autism: A review. *Psychological Bulletin*, *84*, 249–264.

Miller, V. A., Schreck, K. A., Mulick, J. A., & Butter, E. (2012). Factors related to parents' choices of treatments for their children with autism spectrum disorder. *Research in Autism Spectrum Disorder*, *6*, 87–95.

National Autism Center. (2009). *National standards report*. Retrieved January 31, 2016, from http://www.nationalautismcenter.org/

Oxman, J., Webster, C. D., Fruchter, D., & Konstantareas, M. M. (1980). Autism: A review of the literature with particular emphasis on current approaches to treatment. *Child & Youth Services*, *3*, 3–14.

Reichow, B., Barton, E. E., Sewell Neely, J., Good, L., & Wolery, M. (2010). Effects of weighted vests on the engagement of children with developmental delays and autism. *Focus on Autism and Other Developmental Disabilities*, *25*, 3–11.

Rispoli, M., Neely, L., Lang, R., & Ganz, J. (2011). Training paraprofessionals to implement interventions for people autism spectrum disorders: A systematic review. *Developmental Neurorehabilitation*, *14*, 378–388.

Rothstein, L. F. (1982). Educational rights of severely and profoundly handicapped children, 61 Neb. L. Rev. Retrieved from http://digitalcommons.unl.edu/nlr/vol61/iss4/

Stephesnson, J., Carter, M., & Kemp, C. (2012). Quality of the information on educational and therapy interventions provided on the web sites of national autism associations. *Research in Autism Spectrum Disorders*, *6*, 11–18.

The Cochrane Collaboration. (2017). Our vision, mission, and principles. Retrieved from http://www.cochrane.org/about-us/our-vision-mission-and-principles

Travers, J. C., Ayers, K., Simpson, R. L., & Crutchfield, S. (2016). Fad, pseudoscientific, and controversial interventions. In R. Lang, T. Hancock, & N. N. Singh (Eds.), *Evidenced-based practice in early intervention for children with autism*. New York, NY: Springer.

Van Houten, R. V., Axelrod, S., Bailey, J. S., Favell, J. E., Foxx, R. M., Iwata, B. A., & Lovaas, O. I. (1988). The right to effective treatment. *Journal of Applied Behavior Analysis*, *21*, 381–384.

Volkmar, F. R., Hoder, L., & Cohen, D. J. (1985). Compliance, negativism, and the effects of treatment structure in autism: A naturalistic behavioral study. *Journal of Child Psychology and Psychiatry*, *26*, 865–877.

Vyse, S. (2005). Where do fads come from? In J. W. Jacobson, R. M. Foxx, & J. A. Mulick (Eds.), *Controversial therapies for developmental disabilities: Fad fashion and pseudoscience in professional practice*. Mahwah, NJ: Lawrence Erlbaum Associates.

Wallen, M. (2012). Weighted vests did not improve competing behaviours or joint attention of 2 years olds with autism spectrum disorder (ASD). *Australian Occupational Therapy Journal*, *59*, 468–470.

Ward, A. (1970). Early infantile autism: Diagnosis, etiology, and treatment. *Psychological Bulletin*, *73*, 350–362.

Wong, C., Odom, S. L., Hume, K., Cox, A. W., Fettig, A., Kucharczyk, S., ... Schultz, T. R. (2013). *Evidence-based practices for young children, youth, and young adults with Autism Spectrum Disorder*. Chapel Hill, NC: The University of North Carolina, Frank Porter Graham Child Development Institute, Autism Evidence-Based Practice Review Group.

Wood, T. W. (2017). *Does the what works clearinghouse really work? Investigations into issues of policy, practice, and transparency*. A National Institute for Direct Instruction White Paper, Office of Research and Evaluation.

Chapter 3
All Children Can Play: Prompting and Modeling Procedures to Teach Play to Children with Autism Spectrum Disorder

Why Teach Play?

Teaching play to children with ASD is extremely important for several reasons. First, play is one of the earliest behaviors that typically developing children display. These play behaviors are exploratory and functional play (described below) and enable the children to learn about the world. As the children do so, they develop cognitively (Bijou & Baer, 1965). Teaching exploratory and functional play to children with ASD may also facilitate their cognitive development. Second, it has been shown that play is a precursor behavior to language development in typically developing children (Warreyn, Van der Paelt, & Roeyers, 2014). As we know, children with ASD also show marked deficiencies in speech and language behaviors. Teaching play has been shown to facilitate language (Kasari, Freemans, Paparella, & Jahromi, 2008). Third, joint attention, an important social behavior and another precursor behavior to language, has been taught through play (White et al., 2011). Fourth, many forms of play are socially based behaviors such as cooperative play, sociodramatic play, and group play. Finally, and importantly, research has shown that the presence of play in children with ASD's repertoires has been associated with better prognosis in treatment outcome (Sherer & Schreibman, 2005) and long-term follow-up (Charlop-Christy & Kuriakose, 2007).

The importance of teaching play in terms of facilitating cognitive development, language, joint attention, and treatment responsiveness is clear. Moreover, play is the milieu in which the majority of social interactions between children take place. As the setting for acquisition of social skills, there is none better. There are even additional benefits to teaching play to children with ASD. Play promotes better relationships within families and communities (Bijou, 1977; Gewirtz & Peláez-Nogueras, 1992; Rosales-Ruiz & Baer, 1997). The children with ASD can learn to play with their brothers and sisters and neighborhood members (see peer-mediated chapter). It has been noted that within families, older siblings who are more skilled

M.H. Charlop et al., *Play and Social Skills for Children with Autism Spectrum Disorder*, Evidence-Based Practices in Behavioral Health,
https://doi.org/10.1007/978-3-319-72500-0_3

at fantasy play often have a positive effect on sociodramatic play of young children. For example, children's play becomes more advanced with older siblings than during play with mothers (Farver & Wimbarti, 1995). This may suggest that it is important to include siblings in play interventions for children with ASD as well.

Not only does play allow for important social interaction with siblings and peers, but it also provides opportunities to practice and acquire important activities necessary for cultural participation later in life (Goncu, 1999; Jordan, 2003). Certain cultures value different forms of play more than other cultures. For example, the Japanese culture values pretend play more than other cultures, and therefore the pretend play of Japanese children on both continents is much more complex than that of American children (Tamis-LeMonda, Bornstein, Cyphers, Toda, & Ogino, 1992). It is important to consider these cultural differences when designing play interventions for children with ASD as culture and community are important social validity indicators.

A Behavioral Approach to Play

The first step in a behavioral approach to play consists of viewing the individual parts of play as a collection of separate skills and then identifying the component skills necessary for increasing play. The second step is analyzing the sequences of these play skills, such that prerequisites, antecedents, reinforcers, and ultimately behavior chains are identified. Ultimately, the behavioral approach focuses on establishing, analyzing, and continually refining the optimal teaching strategies for promoting play skills.

Bijou (1975) described three main antecedents in children's development that relates to play: (1) the anatomy and physiology of the child's body, (2) relationship of the body to physical objects in the environment, and (3) relations with people in the social environment. Thus, play can be initially defined as a child interacting with toys or objects in an explorative, functional, and appropriate manner. Next, children begin to use their imagination in play by using toys, other objects, and eventually other people in creative ways. Finally, and importantly, many play activities are done socially with a partner or in a group.

Creating Play Programs for Children with ASD

Some general goals of a play program for children with ASD include increasing functional toy play and decreasing stereotyped object manipulation. It is also important to increase social forms of play and decrease isolate or solitary play, especially when social opportunities are available (Warreyn et al., 2014; Wolfberg & Schuler, 1993). Immediate outcomes may include positive social interactions, language gains, and cognitive gains. Many aspects of play programs are also geared toward promoting long-term and far-reaching developmental consequences for children in that many play behaviors can lead to further play or social tasks requiring more complex behaviors (Bijou, 1977). Toward this end, play activities can promote skills for learning from others and developing friendships across the life span (Lifter, Foster-Sanda, Arzamarski, Briesch, & McClure, 2011; Rosales-Ruiz & Baer, 1997).

Types of Play with Toys

Exploratory and Functional Play with Toys

In infancy, children begin to learn that their actions result in corresponding effects on the environment and act to reproduce these effects (Ginsburg & Opper, 1988). Bijou and Baer (1965) described this as "exploratory behavior" and suggest that stimuli in the child's environment have many inherent properties that are natural or "ecological" reinforcers (e.g., textures, sounds, smells, colors, etc.). Functional play is an extension of exploratory play and involves manipulating objects in the manner in which they are intended (Isenberg & Jalongo, 2005). For example, attempting to place puzzle pieces in an inset box or assembly of Lego blocks would be examples of functional play.

Children with ASD, however, generally do not display appropriate exploratory or functional toy play. Instead, they tend to manipulate a toy in a stereotypical way (Kang et al., 2013). This type of behavior is not considered play, even though at times the child may be using toys in a manner that is explorative, or considered partly functional. For example, gazing at the repetitive spinning of wheels on a toy car rather than rolling the car on the floor is considered stereotypy, despite the fact that the wheels were designed to spin.

Also, many children with ASD engage in low levels of play with toys and show preference for non-toy items (e.g., sticks, pencils, plastic game pieces) or for engaging in stereotyped behavior with their body (e.g., finger flapping, body rocking). In these situations, even attending to and engaging in exploratory behavior with toys must be encouraged with prompting and reinforcement. For those with ASD, learning appropriate play with toys can be associated with reductions in repetitive behavior and stereotyped interactions with play-related items (Koegel, Firestone, Kramme, & Dunlap, 1974; Nuzzolo-Gomez, Leonard, Rivera, & Greer, 2002; Stahmer & Schreibman, 1992). Older children with ASD who engage in stereotypy, in lieu of age appropriate functional play, should then be taught to play with toys of their preference.

Imaginative and Pretend Play with Toys

Pretend play involves the use of the imagination during play. Generally, the toy is used appropriately, but an element is missing. For example, children place empty spoons in their mouths in imitation of eating, or give dolls and animals a "drink" with empty cups. Children also begin to respond to the pretend actions of others through imitation. For example, if a peer pretends to sleep, the child may close her eyes and lay her head down.

A more advanced aspect of pretend play is constructive play, in which children use toys and objects to create something new. For example, using Play-Doh to make animals and pretend food or crayons to draw a picture (as opposed to coloring in a coloring book) is an example of constructive play (Wilson, 2015). When using objects to represent other objects, this is called symbolic play (Walker-Andrews & Kahana-Kalman, 1999). During symbolic play, children may substitute a block for a car and push the block across the floor treating it as if it were actually a rolling car.

In sociodramatic play, children take on imaginary personalities and play roles in an imaginary situation (Trawick-Smith & Dziurgot, 2011). This type of play is more elaborate than symbolic play with toys, because it might involve some aspects of social perspective-taking. The types of roles and characters typically revolve around familiar adults or involve characters from screen media such as super heroes (Rogoff, 2003).

Children with ASD often show deficits in symbolic and sociodramatic play (Lee et al., 2016; Wolfberg, DeWitt, Young, & Nguyen, 2015). For example, children with ASD's pretend play often involves repetitive actions and fewer novel actions (Desha, Ziviani, & Rodger, 2003; Jarrold, Boucher, & Smith, 1993). Often, direct intervention and prompting is necessary to evoke pretend play behavior (Charman & Baron-Cohen, 1997). Similarly, the complexity doesn't venture far from the functional use of objects and toys (Thiemann-Bourque, Brady, & Fleming, 2012). With respect to sociodramatic play, emerging research using drama groups suggests that perspective-taking and social imagination are also impaired in these contexts (Neufeld, 2013).

Categories of Pretend Play

Solitary and Pretend Play

When children are playing alone with blocks, puzzles, or rolling cars, for example, they are said to be engaging in solitary play. This is a developmental phase for all children, but children with ASD tend to prefer to play by themselves long after the age of mere exploratory play is over. Much older, school-aged children with ASD will demonstrate a preference to be by themselves and not interact with others. While typically developing toddlers will develop to parallel play and maintain close proximity to other children, children with ASD will generally leave the immediate area or turn their back on others. Thus, even in the early stages of play, children with ASD stand out from typically developing children in their play behaviors. Not only do they lack the exploratory and functional toy play, as described above, but the deficits in the social aspects of play are early indicators of the children's special needs.

Associative and Cooperative Play

In associative play, children share a common space and toys, but do not necessarily have much interaction with one another. Instead, children are more engaged in their own tasks, but do exchange materials and periodically make comments on one another's activities. For example, two children may be individually working on building with blocks or separate coloring pages, and both will draw the blocks or crayons from a common pile. Social exchanges are limited, but may involve comments including "Wow, a dog!" or simple requests to share such as "I want blue." Accordingly, skills of sharing and waiting for a turn begin to emerge within associative play.

Cooperative play involves two or more children engaged in a common activity and interacting together in the play process toward a common goal or theme. Therefore, children are required to acknowledge one other's participation in the joint activity. An example of cooperative play is two children constructing a block tower together. Each participant must wait for his turn and be attentive while the other child takes his turn.

Group Play and Games with Rules

Group play includes any activity where there are two or more participants and predetermined rules for participating correctly (Wolfberg & Schuler, 1993). With group play, cooperation and coordination is required, and imaginative play can also be involved. Group sports such as kickball, basketball, and soccer are types of group play with rules. Other examples include games of tag and capture the flag. Group play can also involve acting out themes in sociodramatic play. For example, cops and robbers require participants to take on roles and act in a specified way, and cooperation with rules is expressed in the hiding, capturing, and jailing of participants. There are also board and card games that are designed for two or more players; however cooperation toward a common goal is not always involved. In this way, games such as BINGO can be more of an associative play type group game because it involves individual players winning rather than working together as a team.

How to Teach Play

What to Choose

As discussed above, incorporating play into the treatment programs of children with ASD is very important in that it not only facilitates the acquisition of other important skills such as language, social interaction, and perspective-taking, but it is a socially valid behavior in and of itself. Play takes on many forms over the life span, starting with exploratory and functional play through leisure skills. Steps for selecting activities the children will enjoy, as well as prompting strategies to use for teaching solitary play, cooperative play, symbolic play, and group play, are described below.

Child-Preferred Toys, Activities, and Play Partners

Children with ASD frequently show strong preferences for particular activities or toys and may engage in such activities to the exclusion of most others (DiCarlo, Reid, & Stricklin, 2003). Children's preference for particular activities can be used to teach and increase appropriate play, as well as facilitate the social aspects of play. There are several studies that suggest this. For example, Hoch, McComas, Johnson, Faranda, and Guenther (2002) showed that social interactions by children with ASD could be increased when their preferred toys were simply placed in close proximity to peers. Similarly, Koegel, Dyer, and Bell (1987) found that children with ASD were much more social with play partners when they engaged in activities that they had chosen, compared with toys selected by adults. Baker (2000) found positive increases in joint attention during sibling training when the child with ASD's ritualistic interests (i.e., preferred toys) were included in the play training. Thus, family and peer socialization can potentially increase if activities are available that the child with ASD find interesting or motivating.

Preference Assessments

There are many ways to find out which toys and activities are most preferred by the children. Often, simple observation and asking people who spend a lot of time with the children will yield fruitful information. Asking verbal children can also be helpful to an extent; however, some research suggests children may not always accurately report their preferences or tend to choose other activities when the time comes to play with their choices (Northup, George, Jones, Broussard, & Vollmer, 1996). For other children and particularly those who are nonverbal, a systematic approach to assessing their preferences may be most effective.

Fortunately, researchers have explored a variety of observational measures to assess the preferences of children with ASD. Assessing preference is a common method for identifying items and activities that may be enjoyable for children with

ASD who are not able to clearly communicate this information to others (Ivancic et al., 1997). Knowing preference for items can help teachers and clinicians promote the effectiveness of positive behavior interventions and increase happiness in their students and clients. For example, using preferred items as contingent reinforcement following positive behavior is one of the most effective means of increasing positive behavior, as well as decreasing problem behavior within positive behavior interventions (Pace, Ivancic, Edwards, Iwata, & Page, 1985). Accordingly, preferred items in general are more likely to function as reinforcers compared to non-preferred items (Green & Striefel, 1988). During preference assessments, various items and activities are physically presented in front of a child in an array. When the child approaches (e.g., moves toward or touches item) or interacts with some items more often than others, this suggests likely enjoyment or preference for the approached items (DeLeon & Iwata, 1996) and indicates the items' potential utility as reinforcers during play interventions.

Types of Preference Assessments

There are several approaches to assessing preference, and these are outlined below. Often, preference assessment procedures are repeated a few times within a session to gauge for consistency in preference, as well as monitor for real-time changes in preference and motivation across a session. The simple observational approach is the free-operant method of assessing preference. This procedure first involves arranging all of the toys that a child is reported to enjoy on the floor or a table. Next, the child is instructed to play with the toys, and the teacher or therapist uses a stopwatch to record how much time the child spends engaging with each available toy. Items with greater durations of engagement suggest possible preferred items. For children who have difficulty selecting from an array, or have motor limitations that make reaching and grabbing challenging, the single-stimulus presentation assessment can be used (e.g., Pace, Ivancic, Edwards, Iwata, & Page, 1985). The single-stimulus method involves presenting toys to a child, one at a time, and recording whether or not the child takes and plays with the toy (i.e., approaches), or chooses not to play with the toy (i.e., avoidance). Items with greater numbers of approach behavior are considered as more preferred than those that the child did not play with very often.

To increase accuracy of preference and potential for reinforcing effectiveness relative to other toys, the paired-stimulus or "forced-choice" method can be used (Fisher, Piazza, Bowman, Hagopian, Owens, & Slevin, 1992). The paired-stimulus method takes the same selection of toys that would be presented in a single-stimulus presentation but instead presents them two at a time, until all possible combinations of toys are presented together. Although somewhat time consuming, this approach can provide insight into what toys children like more than other toys. This approach can also be useful with children who have a tendency to grab or explore any toy given to them. Finally, DeLeon and Iwata's (1996) multiple-stimulus method (without replacement; MSWO) offers similar rank ordering of toy preference as the paired-stimulus, yet can take considerably less time to administer because more toys are presented at a given time. In the MSWO approach, the child is first given

Table 3.1 Types of preference assessments and steps

Preference assessment	Steps
Free-operant (observation)	1. Arrange all toys (5–10) the child is reported to enjoy on a table or on the floor 2. Instruct the child to play with the toys 3. Record the total duration of engagement with each toy the child plays with, until 5-min elapses 4. Toys with more time spent for engagement suggest higher preference
Single choice (approach vs. avoidance) (Pace, Ivancic, Edwards, Iwata, & Page, 1985)	1. Gather five to ten toys the child is reported to enjoy 2. Present each toy, one at a time, and allow up to 30 s of play 3. Record a "+" if the child played with the toy and "- "if s/he did not play with the toy 4. Repeat this _# of times
Paired choice (forced choice) (Fisher, Piazza, Bowman, Hagopian, Owens, & Slevin 1992)	1. Gather ten toys the child is reported to enjoy 2. Present two at a time 3. Record which toy the child selects 4. Present each toy paired with each other so you have every combination 5. The most preferred toys are the ones which the child choses the most often out of a set of predetermined trials
Multiple-stimulus without replacement (rank order) (DeLeon & Iwata, 1996)	1. Gather ten toys the child is reported to enjoy 2. Present each toy, one at a time, so the child may interact for 30s with each toy 3. Place all ten toys in front of the child and record which one the child selects 4. Allow the child to play for 30 s with the first toy (this is said to be the first choice). Remove this item from the group and allow the child to pick from the remaining nine toys 5. The child then may choice the next toy (second choice) and play for 30 s, and then this toy is removed from the group and the remaining eight toys are available for choice 6. This is repeated until the first five rank ordered toys are selected

30 s to play with each toy. Next, all the toys are arranged on a table (or floor), and the child is instructed to pick one toy to play with from the array. After the child makes a selection, he plays with it again for 30 seconds. Next the teacher or therapist removes that item from view and then rearranges the positions of the remaining toys. For example, if ten toys were originally presented, then the second test will involve only nine toys. The child is asked to make another selection from the toys that remain, and this process is repeated until five selections are made. In this manner, the item selected first can be considered the most preferred, and so on, down through the selections Table 3.1.

Considerations and Trouble-Shooting

There are some considerations when systematically assessing preferences. For example, Mangum, Fredrick, Pabico, and Roane (2012) found that items may function as reinforcers, and children may enjoy playing with them, even though they weren't identified as highly preferred in a preference assessment. In their study, the availability of other choices seemed to make a big difference for children's preference. That is, children were motivated for *any* preferred toy when it was the only choice available, but they usually chose their favorite when a couple of toys were offered simultaneously. This isn't always a terrible problem to have when teaching children to play appropriately. In fact, having a variety of reinforcing toys can help combat satiation and keep the play fresh and exciting! The key finding of Raone et al. though suggests implications for organizing the teaching context. In other words, when teaching a child how to roll a favorite toy truck, for example, he may become distracted and interact with other toys he likes in the play area, and this can reduce instructional opportunities. This might occur at times when the therapist has the toy truck and is modeling how to use it, or when other types of prompts are used to interrupt stereotyped behavior or promote playing with a toy correctly. In these situations, it may be advisable to limit the number of toys in the play setting to maintain motivation for the toy targeted in the play intervention.

Other children may not indicate strong preferences during observation or formal assessment. The children might readily interact with any toy offered to them, or they may not interact with any toys offered to them. When children tend to interact with many toys, adding a duration measure may help clarify which toys he likes more, which might have been overlooked when observing. For example, if he plays with all five toys at least once, but plays with the truck for 30 s, and the ball for 10 s, it is likely the truck is the favored toy. Measuring facial expressions of smiling and laughing can also be used as indicators of preference (Green & Striefel, 1988; Green, Reid, Canipe, & Gardner, 1991; Ivancic & Bailey, 1996; Realon, Favell, & Phillips, 1989). Including happiness behaviors can increase indication of preference when many toys are selected, or be used as an alternative behavior to playing when selections are not readily made.

Preference for Inappropriate Behavior and Nonplay Items

Unfortunately, it may be the case that some children with ASD have preference for specific play items or activities, but do not use them correctly or do so inappropriately (e.g., mouthing items, dropping handfuls of blocks on the floor). Other children may find entertainment with items that are not considered conventional toys (e.g., waving towels in the air, placing marker caps on fingers, and tapping on table). Often, these types of behavior are considered stereotyped behavior rather than play and commonplace among children with ASD (Kang et al., 2013). In these situations, we want to increase preference for conventional toys.

The first approach can involve finding out what sensory consequences the children get out of inappropriate activities with toys, so we can encourage them to engage with toys that might provide similar sensory consequences and how to do so appropriately. Conducting a free-operant preference assessment might yield hypotheses about the reinforcing properties of certain items or consequences produced by the manner in which they are manipulated. Several research studies have examined matching the sensory consequences of behavior maintained by automatic reinforcement (e.g., stereotyped behavior, hand mouthing, and pica), but none have explicitly done so with the goal of increasing the development of play skills (e.g.,

Lanovaz, Sladeczek, & Rapp, 2011; Piazza et al., 1998). For example, Piazza, Adelinis, Hanley, Goh, and Delia (2000) found the reductive effects of providing items that matched hypothesized sensory consequences of problem behaviors, such as dangerous jumping, hand mouthing, and saliva manipulation, were greater than providing access to highly preferred items that did not match the sensory consequences of problem behavior in three children with intellectual disabilities.

In another approach aimed toward increasing interest in specific toys, Leaf et al. (2012, 2015) used modeling to help expand toy preferences in several children with ASD and varied intellectual functioning. In their studies, they used a pairing procedure that involved the children's preferred adults manipulating toys that the children did not originally have an affinity for, in new and exciting ways. For example, the adults pretended that non-preferred toys were another toy or activity that the children enjoyed such as a train. The researchers also used the non-preferred toys in creative ways such as taking a toy dinosaur and making it fly or giving it baths in the sink. Their results indicated that all children selected the toys that the adults had played with in novel ways, more often than the toys they typically had a preference for.

In sum, there are several approaches to discovering toys and play activities that might be preferred by children with ASD. Using preferred items in play training may therefore increase the probability of approach and subsequent engagement with toys and play partners. For children who do not show interest in toys and play items, observation, matching, and modeling may serve as methods to promote exploratory and more complex forms of play.

General Prompting Procedures

This section will focus on how to teach play to children with autism spectrum disorder. Since basic prompting and modeling procedures have been presented in many applied behavior analysis texts, this chapter will focus on the types of play and how to adapt basic prompting and modeling to these types of play. As always, whenever using prompting procedures, there is always the concern that the children with ASD will become "prompt dependent." This means that the prompt becomes a necessary component and thus needs to be faded out of play instruction. This is often quite difficult to do and frequently requires many fading steps. For this reason, the reader is encouraged to consider other procedures presented in this book such as naturalistic teaching strategies, picture activity schedules and other visual strategies, and video modeling which often do not use the traditional prompting techniques and therefore do not require prompt fading. Traditional prompting techniques are described in Table 3.2.

Table 3.2 Types of prompting procedures

Prompt type	Prompt procedure	Definition and example
Physical prompts	Modeling	This is a demonstration of the desired behavior. There are many types of modeling, but in general, for a modeled behavior in this category of physical prompts, it usually entails the change agent merely engaging in the play behavior (either all or part of it)
	Physical guidance	This is when a therapist uses his or her hand to guide a child's hands or body to play correctly. For example, if the expectation is for the child to stack building blocks, a physical prompt would involve the therapist placing his/her hand over the child's hand to guide reaching, grasping, placing, and releasing a block onto another block. Physical prompts can be used across a continuum of intrusiveness from full assistance, to a light touch, to no assistance at all. For example, fading physical prompts might involve physically moving the child in the right direction but not completing the task for them. For example, if the demand is "roll car," a faded prompt would be moving the child's hand toward the car and then allowing the child to roll it on his own
	Proximity	Children often need corresponding items to complete a play activity. For example, puzzles involve several pieces. Similarly, pretend baby play might require a bottle, a bib, and a blanket. Therefore, locating and choosing the correct items can be paramount for play participation. Children with ASD often need prompts to locate the correct items
	Gestures	A gestural prompt is when the instructor gestures toward the correct response. For example, if a play partner requests a car or a puzzle piece, the therapist may point to the location of the toy as a prompt for the child to find it
Verbal prompts	Verbal modeling	A verbal model prompt is when a therapist says the correct verbalization for the child. For example, if the expectation is for the child to make motor sounds while rolling a car, the therapist might provide a model of the full verbalization by saying "Vrooom!" and have the child repeat the statement. Gradually, the therapist will want the child to make the play statement with more independence. A therapist can fade assistance by modeling less of the phrase to only the beginning part of the word or phrase and allowing the child to finish it. For example, if the child is expected to say "ready, set, go!" to initiate a car race down a ramp, a faded verbal prompt would be saying "Rrr" to cue the student to say the remainder of the phrase

Play Interventions

Imitation to Teach Functional Play

Many children with ASD do not play with toys appropriately and instead are either disinterested in them or use toys in a stereotypic way. Since toy play is a socially and age-referenced behavior, it is important to be taught. Also, as stated above, as toy play increases, stereotypy decreases. Box 3.1 lists the steps to teach simple imitation of functional use of toys. Basically, the therapist models an appropriate action with a toy, and the child imitates the action and receives reinforcement.

Box 3.1 Teaching Imitation of Functional Toy Play
Teaching imitation of functional toy play

1. Make eye contact with the child. You then say the appropriate play action such as "Roll car."
2. Model (demonstrates) the appropriate play action with the toy. For example, roll a car across the table, make a toy dog run, or spin a top. Then hand the toy to the child and say, "Your turn."
3. If the child does not imitate the action within about 5–10 s, make sure he/she is attending to you, repeat the phrase, and model the action again.
4. Provide praise and reinforcement for imitation, e.g., "Good playing!"
5. If the child is not imitating the action, prompt appropriate play using the following steps:

   (a) Manually guide the child to do the action. For example, take the child's hand, place it on top of the car, and guide him through rolling the car back and forth.
   (b) Provide praise and reinforcement for "Good playing."
   (c) Begin a new trial saying, "Roll car," and model appropriate play. This time do not provide the physical prompt. If the child imitates play, provide praise and reinforcement.
   (d) If the child does not imitate, continue prompting using gradually less directive prompts, as outlined below.

      – Place the child's hand on the toy (e.g., on top of the car, on the handle of the top). Guide the child through the play action.
      – Place the child's hand on the toy. Initiate his play action with the toy, then remove your prompt. For example, help him push the car, but only for a few inches, or lift his hand up while holding the top handle, then remove your prompt.
      – Simply place the child's hand on the toy.
      – Remove all prompts.

Independent Activities

Independent play is a difficult behavior to teach because often children with ASD have difficulty staying engaged with toys when there is no supervision. Toy choice is important so make sure you have highly preferred toys that have been selected from a preference assessment. Also, you will want to select toys that the child will likely require time to play with. For example, coloring in a coloring book is a good activity for independent play. Here the child can color several pages that may take time, as opposed to several cars that the child may not linger on. A puzzle with many pieces, or several puzzles, is another good example. A building toy, such as blocks, Legos, or Play-Doh, which may keep the child's interest is also a good example.

You will also have to work up to increase the amount of time that the child can play alone. Keep this in mind so you don't have unrealistic expectations. This is a gradual process. Immediate removal of an adult's presence might result in the child using the toy in a stereotypic manner or in a lack of play altogether. Box 3.2 lists the steps to teach simple imitation of functional use of toys.

Box 3.2 Teaching Independent Activities

Teaching independent activities

1. Present a toy(s) to the child and give an instruction such as "Time to play by yourself."
2. Gradually remove your presence from the play environment by implementing the following fading procedure:

   (a) After instructing the child to play, scoot your chair back a foot or so.
   (b) After instructing the child to play, stand up next to your chair.
   (c) After instructing the child to play, stand by the door.
   (d) After instructing the child to play, open the door and stand in the doorway.
   (e) After instructing the child to play, open the door and leave the room. Leave the door open so that you can observe the child and he can see you.
   (f) After instructing the child to play, leave the room, closing the door behind you. Observe the child through the one-way mirror.

3. Gradually increase the amount of time the child plays independently. Initially, trials may be 30 seconds long. Gradually increase trials to 45 s, then a minute, a minute and a half, and so on until the child is playing appropriately without your assistance for up to 5 min.

"Rules of thumb": Advice for teaching independent play

- Because you are teaching *independent* play, it is vital that you gradually remove yourself from the play situation as soon as possible. Otherwise the child would not really be playing independently, but rather would be playing with guidance and attention from you! Remember that prompts should be faded as soon as possible, and you must then gradually fade your presence from the play environment.
- Always provide praise and reinforcement for good playing. Eventually the play activity will become reinforcing to the child, particularly if he is interacting with a preferred toy. However, initially the child needs encouragement and reinforcement to let him know he is doing a good job and to keep him motivated.
- Provide opportunities to play with a variety of toys. This will help prevent the child from becoming bored with the activity, keep him motivated, and aid in generalization of play skills.

Cooperative Play

Essentially, any play activity that requires that the child take turns constitutes cooperative play. Thus, there are numerous activities you can use to teach cooperative play, using the following turn-taking procedure such as playing catch, doing a puzzle, or playing a board game. Box 3.3 lists the steps to teach simple imitation of functional use of toys.

Box 3.3 Teaching Cooperative Play and Turn-Taking
Teaching cooperative play and turn-taking

1. Sit facing the child, with the play activity placed between you. If you are playing catch/roll, stand or sit at a close distance, no more than four feet initially.
2. Provide a cue that it's time to play by saying something like, "O.K. Sally, let's play!" When a child is first learning to take turns, you can initiate play by saying, "Your turn" or "My turn." An alternative initiation phrase is "Go" or "Go Johnny." This phrase is good to use when first teaching turn-taking to a child who does not know pronouns yet.
3. If it is your turn, take your turn, and then say, "Your turn," or "Go," to the child. The child should take his turn, and then look at you and say, "Your turn" or "Go." The game should continue on in this manner until the end, or the puzzle is completed.
4. If the child does not take his turn, prompt his response using the following prompt fading procedure:

   (a) Place the child's hand on a puzzle piece, spinner, playing piece, etc., and guide his hand through the appropriate play motion.
   (b) Place the child's hand on the game piece. Initiate the motion and let him finish it unassisted.
   (c) Place the child's hand on the game piece.
   (d) Lift the child's hand. If necessary, point to the game piece. As with all prompt fading procedures, start at the point where the child requires assistance. For example, if the child can spin the spinner unassisted, or knows how to put the puzzle piece in, skip steps a. and b. and start at step c.

5. If the child takes his turn, but does not indicate to you that it is your turn, prompt his response using the following prompt fading procedure:

   (a) Model the phrase. For example, say, "Go Jose."
   (b) Provide a partial model of the phrase (e.g., "Go" or "Gah").
   (c) Say, "Whose turn is it?"
   (d) Provide a time delay prompt after the child has completed his turn

6. If you are playing a board game where one of you "wins," have the child indicate who won. For example, if the child wins, he should say, "I win!," whereas if you win, he should say, "You win!" with equal enthusiasm. It is important not only to teach play skills, but to teach good sportsmanship as well!
7. Always provide reinforcement for good playing

Group Play

Group games play an important role in the daily social interactions of children. Children participate in group games during P.E. and class and at recess. Most group games, such as baseball, soccer, and basketball, require the child to use multiple complex skills, including social interaction skills, attention to the environment, and knowledge of the rules of the game. These types of games might initially appear to be overwhelming for a child with ASD. However, children with ASD can and do learn to play in group settings and enjoy group games. Recommended games to teach include baseball or tee-ball (depending on age and ability), soccer/kickball, and basketball. Games can be easily modified to match the child's level and motor-coordination skills. Box 3.4 lists skills for each of the group games. These are the skills to model, prompt, and reinforce during play. The bottom half of Box 3.4 also provides some simple rules of thumb for teaching group game play.

Box 3.4 Suggested Target Behaviors for Group Games

Game	Target behaviors (steps)
Baseball/tee-ball	Hold bat correctly
	Stand at plate
	Watch pitcher/ball
	Swing bat
	Drop bat
	Run to base
	Wait at base
	Watch next batter
	Run bases after ball is hit
	Run to home plate
	High five at home plate
Soccer/kick	Use only feet to maneuver ball
	Kick ball to another player
	Chase missed balls
	Stop ball from another player
	Maneuver ball past other players
	Kick ball toward goal

Game	Target behaviors (steps)
Basketball	Dribble ball
	Aim ball at basket
	Retrieve missed balls
	Pass ball to another player
	Catch ball tossed by another player
	High fives for baskets

"Rules of thumb": Advice for teaching group play

- Each child receives individual attention during play. That is, one therapist is assigned to assist the child and reinforce specific skills. Thus, one therapist is usually assigned to teach each separate set of behaviors. A therapist might be assigned to batting behaviors, where he/she would model, prompt, and reinforce the behaviors listed above. Therapists standing on the first, second, and third base would assist the child through base running behaviors, while another therapist, standing at the home plate, would assist the child in the scoring behaviors.
- At first, outside reinforcers may be necessary for the children to help them go through and learn the steps of the games and to reinforce their patience while waiting their turn.
- Make sure directions and instruction are as clear and understandable as possible.

Prompts for group game play may be physical (manual) or verbal. For example, a manual prompt to support playing tee-ball might include holding the child's hands over the bat and guiding him through hitting a ball off a tee. Spoken reminders for specific behaviors (e.g., "Look at the ball") are forms of verbal prompts that are used with nearly all children as they learn organized sports and may be particularly necessary with children with ASD.

Middle School-Aged and High School-Aged Children

For these children, independent play is typically referred to as leisure skills, although cooperative play, group play, and so on are still considered play. Adults play, but we tend to call it a hobby or leisure activity. So for the older children, we will likely teach them how to play video games, drawing and painting, looking or reading books and magazines, and other activities that can be done independently. We would like to avoid, as much as possible, providing lengthy amounts of time of watching TV/movies, sitting and eating snacks, or being idle. These are not productive. Many older children with ASD do not have any leisure skills because they have not been taught any. In addition, many children do know that some of these leisure activities, once learned, may be quite enjoyable. So, like any other task or lesson, we need to teach them the leisure activity as a skill. Once learned, they then can choose what they want to do. Some leisure activities initially may be more difficult to learn than the leisure activities they already know how to do. For example, it is much more difficult to learn how to draw or trace their favorite superheroes than it is to watch a video of the superhero. So, we must be patient and view the teaching of an appropriate leisure skill such as drawing pictures or tracing pictures or even coloring superheroes as something that the child might find less preferable than just kicking back and watching TV. However, once the child learns to draw (if drawing is for them), he/she might find it an entertaining hobby, and it may reveal a talent that no one knew about.

It is also important to teach the children a variety of leisure skills. For example, for the child who wants to spend most of his free time with his object of obsession, Batman, it will be important to teach him various ways to do so instead of just watching a video. In addition to drawing Batman, there may be Batman cards that the child can use to play a version of "Solitaire" involving matching up the numbers on the cards. Or, they can look at Batman comic books. Even if they are not actually reading the comic books, they may enjoy looking at the pictures. There also may be a Batman pencil that the child can use to do homework. Perhaps the child would be more likely to shoot baskets or bounce a ball if it was a Batman ball. These are all ways to initially use Batman to teach new leisure skills. Then, we would want to promote generalization to other stimuli so we may want to have the child use other stimuli (another superhero or just a plain ball, etc.).

Conclusion

Basic modeling and prompting procedures are generally used to teach functional, cooperative, and independent play. These procedures are used to teach the more basic building blocks or foundation of play. Instructions for teaching more sophisticated forms of play such as pretend play or sociodramatic play procedures are discussed in later chapters such as Chap. 5 on Video Modeling and Chap. 6 on Visual Strategies.

References

Baker, M. J. (2000). Incorporating the thematic ritualistic behaviors of children with autism into games. *Journal of Positive Behavior Interventions, 2*, 64–84. https://doi.org/10.1177/109830070000200201

Bijou, S. W. (1975). Development in the preschool years: A functional analysis. *American Psychologist, 30*, 829–837.

Bijou, S. W. (1977). Practical implications of an interactional model of child development. *Exceptional Children, 44*, 6–14.

Bijou, S. W., & Baer, D. M. (1965). *Child development: Vol. 2. Universal stage of infancy*. New York, NY: Appleton-Century-Crofts.

Charlop-Christy, M. H., & Kuriakose, S. (2007). The importance of play in the treatment of children with autism. *Autism News, 4*, 13–15.

Charman, T., & Baron-Cohen, S. (1997). Brief report: Prompted pretend play in autism. *Journal of Autism and Developmental Disorders, 27*, 325–332.

DeLeon, I. G., & Iwata, B. A. (1996). Evaluation of a multiple-stimulus presentation format for assessing reinforcer preferences. *Journal of Applied Behavior Analysis, 29*(4), 519–533.

Desha, L., Ziviani, J., & Rodger, S. (2003). Play preferences and behavior of preschool children with autistic spectrum disorder in the clinical environment. *Physical & Occupational Therapy in Pediatrics, 23*, 21–42. https://doi.org/10.1080/J006v23n01_03

DiCarlo, C. F., Reid, D. H., & Stricklin, S. B. (2003). Increasing toy play among toddlers with multiple disabilities in an inclusive classroom: A more-to-less, child-directed intervention continuum. *Research in Developmental Disabilities, 24*, 195–209.

Farver, J. M., & Wimbarti, S. (1995). Indonesian children's play with their mothers and older siblings. *Child Development, 66*, 1493–1503.

Fisher, W., Piazza, C. C., Bowman, L. G., Hagopian, L. P., Owens, J. C., & Slevin, I. (1992). A comparison of two approaches for identifying reinforcers for persons with severe and profound disabilities. *Journal of Applied Behavior Analysis, 25*(2), 491–498.

Gewirtz, J. L., & Peláez-Nogueras, M. (1992). BF Skinner's legacy in human infant behavior and development. *American Psychologist, 47*, 1411.

Ginsburg, H. P., & Opper, S. (1988). *Piaget's theory of intellectual development*. Englewood Cliffs, NJ: Prentice-Hall.

Goncu, A. E. (1999). *Children's engagement in the world: Sociocultural perspectives*. New York, NY: Cambridge University Press.

Green, G., & Striefel, S. (1988). Response restriction and substitution with autistic children. *Journal of the Experimental Analysis of Behavior, 50*(1), 21–32.

Green, C. W., Reid, D. H., Canipe, V. S., & Gardner, S. M. (1991). A comprehensive evaluation of reinforcer identification processes for persons with profound multiple handicaps. *Journal of Applied Behavior Analysis, 24*(3), 537–552.

Hoch, H., McComas, J. J., Johnson, L., Faranda, N., & Guenther, S. L. (2002). The effects of magnitude and quality of reinforcement on choice responding during play activities. *Journal of Applied Behavior Analysis, 35*, 171–181. https://doi.org/10.1901/jaba.2002.35-171

Isenberg, J. P., & Jalongo, M. R. (2005). *Creative thinking and arts-based learning: Preschool through fourth grade* (4th ed.). New York, NY: Prentice Hall.

Ivancic, M. T., & Bailey, J. S. (1996). Current limits to reinforcer identification for some persons with profound multiple disabilities. *Research in Developmental Disabilities, 17*(1), 77–92.

Ivancic, M. T., Barrett, G. T., Simonow, A., & Kimberly, A. (1997). A replication to increase happiness indices among some people with profound multiple disabilities. *Research in Developmental Disabilities, 18*(1), 79–89.

Jarrold, C., Boucher, J., & Smith, P. (1993). Symbolic play in autism: A review. *Journal of Autism and Developmental Disorder, 23*, 281–307.

Jordan, R. (2003). Social play and autistic spectrum disorders: A perspective on theory, implications and educational approaches. *Autism, 7*, 347–360. https://doi.org/10.1177/1362361303007004002

Kang, S., O'Reilly, M., Rojeski, L., Blenden, K., Xu, Z., Davis, T., … Lancioni, G. (2013). Effects of tangible and social reinforcers on skill acquisition, stereotyped behavior, and task engagement in three children with autism spectrum disorders. *Research in Developmental Disabilities, 34*, 739–744. https://doi.org/10.1016/j.ridd.2012.10.007

Kasari, C., Freemans, S., Paparella, T., & Jahromi, L. B. (2008). Language outcome in autism: Randomized comparison of joint attention and play interventions. *Journal of Child Psychology and Psychiatry, 76*, 125–137.

Koegel, R. L., Dyer, K., & Bell, L. K. (1987). The influence of child-preferred activities on autistic children's social behavior. *Journal of Applied Behavior Analysis, 20*(3), 243–252.

Koegel, R. L., Firestone, P. B., Kramme, K. W., & Dunlap, G. (1974). Increasing spontaneous play by suppressing self-stimulation in autistic children. *Journal of Applied Behavior Analysis, 7*, 521–528. https://doi.org/10.1901/jaba.1974.7-521

Lanovaz, M. J., Sladeczek, I. E., & Rapp, J. T. (2011). Effects of music on vocal stereotypy in children with autism. *Journal of Applied Behavior Analysis, 44*, 647–651.

Leaf, J. B., Kassardjian, A., Oppenheim-Leaf, M. L., Tsuji, K. H., Dale, S., Alcalay, A., … McEachin, J. (2015). Observational effects on preference selection for four children on the autism spectrum: A replication. *Behavioral Interventions, 30*, 256–269. https://doi.org/10.1002/bin.1411

Leaf, J. B., Oppenheim-Leaf, M. L., Leaf, R., Courtemanche, A. B., Taubman, M., McEachin, J., … Sherman, J. A. (2012). Observational effects on the preferences of children with autism. *Journal of Applied Behavior Analysis, 45*, 473–483. https://doi.org/10.1901/jaba.2012.45-473.

Lee, Y., Chan, P., Lin, S., Chen, C., Huang, C., & Chen, K. (2016). Correlation patterns between pretend play and playfulness in children with autism spectrum disorder, developmental delay, and typical development. *Research in Autism Spectrum Disorders, 24*, 29–38. https://doi.org/10.1016/j.rasd.2016.01.006

Lifter, K., Foster-Sanda, S., Arzamarski, C., Briesch, J., & McClure, E. (2011). Overview of play: Its uses and importance in early intervention/early childhood special education. *Infants & Young Children, 24*, 225–245. https://doi.org/10.1097/IYC.0b013e31821e995c

Mangum, A., Fredrick, L., Pabico, R., & Roane, H. (2012). The role of context in the evaluation of reinforcer efficacy: Implications for the preference assessment outcomes. *Research in Autism Spectrum Disorders, 6*,(1) 158–167. https://doi.org/10.1016/j.rasd.2011.04.001

Neufeld, D. J. (2013). Integrated drama groups: Promoting symbolic play, empathy, and social engagement with peers in children with autism. *Dissertation Abstracts International Section A, 74*.

Northup, J., George, T., Jones, K., Broussard, C., & Vollmer, T. R. (1996). A comparison of reinforcer assessment methods: The utility of verbal and pictorial choice procedures. *Journal of Applied Behavior Analysis, 29*, 201–212.

Nuzzolo-Gomez, R., Leonard, M. A., Rivera, C. M., & Greer, R. D. (2002). Teaching children with autism to prefer books or toys over stereotypy or passivity. *Journal of Positive Behavior Interventions, 4*, 80–87. https://doi.org/10.1177/109830070200400203

Pace, G. M., Ivancic, M. T., Edwards, G. L., Iwata, B. A., & Page, T. J. (1985). Assessment of stimulus preference and reinforcer value with profoundly retarded individuals. *Journal of Applied Behavior Analysis, 18*(3), 249–255.

Piazza, C. C., Adelinis, J. D., Hanley, G. P., Goh, H. L., & Delia, M. D. (2000). An evaluation of the effects of matched stimuli on behaviors maintained by automatic reinforcement. *Journal of Applied Behavior Analysis, 33*, 13–27.

Piazza, C. C., Fisher, W. W., Hanley, G. P., LeBlanc, L. A., Worsdell, A. S., Lindauer, S. E., & Keeney, K. M. (1998). Treatment of pica through multiple analyses of its reinforcing functions. *Journal of Applied Behavior Analysis, 31*, 165–189.

Realon, R. E., Favell, J. E., & Phillips, J. F. (1989). Adapted leisure materials vs. standard leisure materials: Evaluating several aspects of programming for persons who are profoundly handicapped. *Education and Training in Mental Retardation, 24*, 168–177.

Rogoff, B. (2003). *The cultural nature of human development*. New York, NY: Oxford University Press.

Rosales-Ruiz, J., & Baer, D. M. (1997). Behavioral cusps: A developmental and pragmatic concept for behavior analysis. *Journal of Applied Behavior Analysis, 30*, 533–544. https://doi.org/10.1901/jaba.1997.30-533

Sherer, M. R., & Schreibman, L. (2005). Individual behavioral profiles and predictors of treatment effectiveness for children with autism. *Journal of Consulting and Clinical Psychology, 73*, 525.

Stahmer, A. C., & Schreibman, L. (1992). Teaching children with autism appropriate play in unsupervised environments using a self-management treatment package. *Journal of Applied Behavior Analysis, 25*, 447–459. https://doi.org/10.1901/jaba.1992.25-447

Tamis-LeMonda, C. S., Bornstein, M. H., Cyphers, L., Toda, S., & Ogino, M. (1992). Language and play at one year: A comparison of toddlers and mothers in the United States and Japan. *International Journal of Behavioral Development, 15*(1), 19–42.

Thiemann-Bourque, K. S., Brady, N. C., & Fleming, K. K. (2012). Symbolic play of preschoolers with severe communication impairments with autism and other developmental delays: More similarities than differences. *Journal of Autism and Developmental Disorders, 42*, 863–873. https://doi.org/10.1007/s10803-011-1317-7

Trawick-Smith, J., & Dziurgot, T. (2011). 'Good-fit' teacher–child play interactions and the subsequent autonomous play of preschool children. *Early Childhood Research Quarterly, 26*(1), 110–123.

Walker-Andrews, A. S., & Kahana-Kalman, R. (1999). The understanding of pretence across the second year of life. *British Journal of Developmental Psychology, 17*(4), 523–536.

Warreyn, P., Van der Paelt, S., & Roeyers, H. (2014). Social-communicative abilities as treatment goals for preschool children with autism: The importance of imitation, joint attention, and play. *Developmental Medicine & Child Neurology, 56*, 712–716. https://doi.org/10.1111/dmcn.12455

White, P. J., O'Reilly, M., Streusand, W., Levine, A., Sigafoos, J., Lancioni, G., … Aguilar, J. (2011). Best practices for teaching joint attention: A systematic review of the intervention literature. *Research in Autism Spectrum Disorders, 5*, 1283–1295.

Wilson, H. E. (2015). Patterns of play behaviors and learning center choices between high ability and typical children. *Journal of Advanced Academics, 26*, 143–164.

Wolfberg, P., DeWitt, M., Young, G. S., & Nguyen, T. (2015). Integrated play groups: Promoting symbolic play and social engagement with typical peers in children with ASD across settings. *Journal of Autism and Developmental Disorders, 45*, 830–845. https://doi.org/10.1007/s10803-014-2245-0

Wolfberg, P. J., & Schuler, A. L. (1993). Integrated play groups: A model for promoting the social and cognitive dimensions of play in children with autism. *Journal of Autism and Developmental Disorders, 23*, 467–489.

Chapter 4
Keeping It Real: Naturalistic Teaching Strategies (NaTS) for Play and Social Skills with Children with Autism Spectrum Disorder

Naturalistic teaching strategies (NaTS) is an umbrella term for those treatment procedures that have a similar philosophical approach, similar treatment components, and also similar treatment outcomes. NaTS are carried out in loosely structured environments such as play settings, home settings, or community settings that are typical of the natural environment. NaTS are considered "naturalistic" not only because of the setting, but because of the manner in which the treatment is delivered. Treatment providers are also typically persons from the natural environment, such as parents or teachers, or can even be peers and siblings. Since play and social skills are behaviors that occur in the natural environment, it makes sense that these procedures have typically been used and that there is a substantial body of scientific literature addressing the use of NaTS for play and social skills acquisition. Naturalistic teaching procedures are an excellent choice to use with children with autism spectrum disorder (ASD).

Naturalistic teaching strategies are tailor-made to teach play and social skills not only because of the less structured treatment environment but also because they promote generalization of treatment gains. NaTS incorporate facilitators of generalization clearly outlined by Stokes and Baer (1977) and Stokes and Osnes (1986). NaTS tend to use direct reinforcers, common stimuli, behaviors that mediate generalization, procedures that train loosely, and looser stimulus control, while employing thinner schedules of reinforcement (all to be discussed below). A specific description of naturalistic teaching strategies is provided below. Several treatment protocols ranging from more structured (natural language paradigm) to less structured (multiple incidental teaching procedures) will be discussed.

M.H. Charlop et al., *Play and Social Skills for Children with Autism Spectrum Disorder*, Evidence-Based Practices in Behavioral Health,
https://doi.org/10.1007/978-3-319-72500-0_4

Three Basic Components of NaTS

There are three basic components to naturalistic teaching strategies: (1) motivation-enhancing techniques, (2) functional relationships, and (3) facilitators of generalization. First, motivation-enhancing techniques include strategies that may focus on reinforcers such as the use of varied reinforcers and the continued and repeated use of preference assessments for both preferred stimuli and novel stimuli to determine items of current interest (DeLeon & Iwata, 1996; Egel, 1981). Also included is the incorporation of child choice, both in terms of reinforcers and type of task. As well, task interspersal techniques keep the child responding and motivation levels high, while boredom and escape behaviors are kept at low levels. Using treatment environments that are less structured and associated with play increases motivation. When motivating techniques are included during treatment, positive attitudes have been reported by parents (Schreibman, Kaneko, & Koegel, 1991).

Second, in order to create a functional relationship, there must be a genuine relationship between the behavior and the consequence. In other words, a child with ASD who requests "train" should be given the train to play with as the consequence, not candy or a high five or praise ("good talking"). Behaviors that are functional to the child should be taught. That is, behaviors (such as mands) that are likely to get this kind of response from the environment should be selected. Play and social skills are functional skills for children. As a child develops, one can see that a toddler will explore toys to play with. As the child grows, the preschooler, though most interested in play with toys, has an emerging interest in other children as playmates. During the elementary years, the peer group then becomes of paramount importance to the child, as the child participates in athletic and group games. These play activities, and the concomitant social interactions, need to be targeted for children with ASD and are of prime functional importance. However, they are often left off of IEPs and other therapeutic curricula. Play and social behaviors are functional for a child with ASD.

What the literature has shown us about functional behaviors is that they often are associated with other behaviors as well. The scientific literature has shown us that play is associated with better long-term outcomes (Kasari, Gulsrud, Freemans, Paparella, & Hellemann, 2012), increases in joint attention (Basso, Charlop, & Gumaer, 2017; Kasari, Freemans, & Paparella, 2006), and communication (Kasari et al., 2012; Siller & Sigman, 2002). So, play not only has immediate relevance and function for the child with ASD, but it has concomitant gains in other areas of importance for the child. It is no wonder, then, that the majority of NaTS programs have focused on teaching communication and social behaviors (Charlop-Christy, LeBlanc, & Carpenter, 1999).

Third, naturalistic teaching strategies include those variables that are facilitators of generalization. These include employing natural environments (home) to treat in; using parents, peers, and siblings to be change agents; and using reinforcers that can be found in the natural environment (cf. Stokes & Baer, 1977). As defined earlier, generalization is the occurrence of newly learned behaviors in non-trained settings and/or with untrained persons. Generalization is quite difficult to achieve, but it is probably the most important aspect of treatment. What good is treatment if the child only learns a behavior in the therapy setting? So, we must think about generalization from the very moment we start to interact with the child.

The three basic components of naturalistic teaching strategies are detailed below. Step-by-step guides are provided to add motivation enhancers, functional relationships, and facilitators of generalization into your treatment of play and social skills.

Motivation

Motivation is a term that has been defined in a variety of different ways. Many view motivation as something intrinsic, something that comes from within, part of a person's innate personality. However, from a behavioral framework, motivation is considered from an extrinsic point of view, something we can observe and measure. When dealing with motivation in terms of NaTS, it is also implied that motivation would have a positive connotation. So, while we can view motivation as a way to behave in a certain way due to a need to avoid or escape a noxious stimulus, with NaTS we are defining it as a positive phenomenon. For our purposes here, we define motivation as "using stimuli and procedures that encourage or impel the child to learn or perform a particular behavior." Thus, when we refer to NaTS as including motivating procedures, we are saying that task stimuli, environmental arrangements, and consequences are all conducive to making learning as enjoyable. Providing an enjoyable learning experience will then lead to better outcomes. Motivation with a NaTS paradigm means making learning enjoyable, which leads to better outcomes.

Below are specific ways to increase motivation used in NaTS. These all have a strong evidence base, facilitate the child to reach learning outcomes, and make the process of learning easier and more pleasant for both the child and change agent.

Task Variation One way to motivate children with ASD during a NaTS is to *vary* the tasks that are presented. Some common teaching procedures call for a "massed trial" approach where the same task is presented several times consecutively, often ten discrete times (Lovaas, 1977). There is a rationale for using this rehearsal format. Repetition and rehearsal can aid memory and retention and, purportedly, this facilitates learning. Also, when plotting data, it is much easier to deal with blocks of ten trials when calculating percentages. However, such redundancy in teaching can cause some negative side effects that do not promote learning and can decrease motivation. First, there may be a boredom effect when the same task is presented over and over. Second, if the task is a new task, referred to as an *acquisition task*, this may take some time for the child to learn. If reinforcement occurs after each correct response, it may be a while before a child earns a reinforcer, and therefore this may induce frustration and lead to escape-motivated behaviors. Third, being presented with a task that may be too difficult, with a low probability of earning reinforcement, may cause behavior problems such as tantrums, aggression, SIB, and so on. Finally, this type of instruction has been criticized for leading to "rote" learning and memorization, which does not generalize well. Task variation can remediate these issues.

Task variation is the interspersing of the new tasks (acquisition tasks) with old, previously learned tasks (referred to as maintenance tasks). It is that simple; and you have solved the problems mentioned above and increased motivation. Thus, while learning a new skill, which is potentially difficult, the response-reinforcer ratio is higher than if reinforcers were provided for only acquisition tasks. This is true even if non-tangible (attention only) reinforcers are provided for maintenance tasks (Charlop, Kurtz, & Milstein, 1993). Guidance on varying tasks is offered in Box 4.1.

Box 4.1 How to Do Task Variation

How to do task variation

1. Do a preference assessment to determine items of high interest to the child. Gather your items (toys, task stimuli) for both acquisition task (new task to be taught) and maintenance task (previously learned task).
2. Present two to three trials or episodes of the acquisition task, and then present a maintenance task and then two or three more of the acquisition task. For reinforcers, use the preferred items, praise, or, depending on the task, a desired treat.
3. Keep in mind that maintenance consists of *any* previously learned task, even basic tasks like gaining eye contact, a quick play imitation task (press a button on a cause-effect toy), and so on. The variation should be for every two to three trials of the acquisition task, at the most, in which you should request a maintenance task and provide a reinforcer for it. This mix-up will make sure the child is very likely to get a reinforcer while learning new (acquisition) tasks by getting these maintenance tasks correct.
4. Always provide a reinforcer upon correct response of the acquisition task. That which is reinforced will increase. The maintenance tasks are put into the mix to insure that reinforcers will be earned for the acquisition task soon because motivation will be optimized.
5. You may use several maintenance tasks too, so that the task variation intersperses with maintenance tasks that are not always the same. This makes treatment even more interesting.

Reinforcers Motivation relies heavily upon reinforcer selection, schedule, and manner of delivery. Reinforcers are specific to the child, and desirability often changes. Preference assessments need to be done frequently, at the minimum daily, and possibly within session. That is, what is initially reinforcing at the start of a treatment session may not be in the middle or at the later stages of the session. The literature is filled with studies on preference assessments for reinforcer selection (Cooper, Heron, & Heward, 2007; Parsons & Reid, 1990). It may initially seem contradictory to do preference assessments when using naturalistic teaching strategies because the emphasis is on the use of reinforcers that are related to the behavior, not unrelated reinforcers. For example, with NaTS, when teaching a child to comment about a play item, the child is provided with the play item *as* the reinforcer. One might ask: "What if he has difficulty learning the commenting behavior and a food reinforcer is the more reinforcing item for the child?" This is often the case with children with ASD, and indeed it has been cautioned that during preference assessments *not* to use both food and toys together because food is usually chosen (Bojak & Carr, 1999).

This situation could be a conundrum. However, there are several motivation-enhancing procedures at use, and they may not all be able to be employed at the same time. In this situation, it is advised to keep the integrity of the NaTS and provide the play item upon completion of the commenting behavior. However, here would be a good time to mix it up a bit by inserting a maintenance task in with a highly preferred food item as the reinforcer. Also note that reinforcer variation is just as important as task variation. To keep motivation high, use a variety of highly salient reinforcers. In fact, research shows that variation in reinforcers, even if they are *not* the most preferred, do just as well as the most highly preferred reinforcers (Bowman, Piazza, Fisher, Hagopian, & Kogan, 1997). Satiation can occur with the most highly preferred reinforcers, so varying reinforcers is a more important concept than reinforcer saliency.

Child Choice and Shared Control Demand characteristics of a setting can decrease motivation quite quickly. When the child feels like a litany of demands or requests are made, the treatment setting can become unpleasant. When this happens, escape-motivated behavior is increased, and the child may not necessarily actually leave the scene, but may engage in interfering behaviors. Research has shown that if the child can make some choices and exert some control over what is going on, motivation to participate in learning increases (Koegel et al., 1989). Being a participator and invested partner, and not merely a recipient of treatment, seems to increase motivation. Guidance for providing child choice opportunities are provided in Box 4.2.

Box 4.2 How to Include Child Choice
How to include child choice

1. Put out a few different items for activities/tasks for the child such as a puzzle, a car wash toy, and the "Don't Break the Ice" game. Instruct the child to "pick one." If the child doesn't respond, repeat, but this time, push one of the items out in front a bit closer to the child (as a prompt) and then say: "pick one." The child will usually pick the toy pushed out in front. Proceed with number 3 below.
2. Vary the toy you have placed out front, and as soon as possible, fade this prompt out by backing up all items so that when you instruct the child to "pick one," all three play items are in a row.
3. If the child complains indicating that he/she wants the other item, redo the choice assessment, place his hand on the item he "complained for," and remove the other items.
4. If the child is choosing between an acquisition task stimulus and two maintenance task items, the child has chosen the stimuli that he wants to do first. Present this activity regardless of whether it is an acquisition or maintenance task. However, you will need to present acquisition task eventually, regardless of whether it has been chosen.
5. Remember that *child choice* is one of several motivation techniques that you will be using (including interspersal of maintenance tasks, reinforcer preference assessments, and so on). A child will need to learn behaviors that he may not choose to or indicate a desire to learn. The child can exert choice and control over the treatment setting, but they cannot exert final decision over what is on their curriculum or IEP. Professionals and parents decide on this. But the children can lend their voices on what is happening, at present, and this will increase their motivation. We determine what they need to learn, but they can determine some of the specifics.

Enhancing Generalization

Previously, the importance of generalization and maintenance was discussed, and it was emphasized that it is imperative that generalization of treatment gains occur. All too often, generalization is not thought about until after acquisition of the behavior. Then the arduous task of attempting to promote generalization is begun. Sequential modification is a procedure in which generalization is programmed in every condition (e.g., across persons, settings, stimuli) where generalization has not occurred (Stokes & Baer, 1977). This can often be a tedious process, especially in situations where generalization must occur across many stimuli. For example, if you are teaching a child to play a card game, you might have to teach him how to play multiple card games with different people in different settings. Stokes and Baer (1977) categorized several ways to promote generalization, and NaTS incorporates many of these discussed below.

A better method than sequential modification is to train sufficient exemplars. With this approach, you would use multiple sets of cards, multiple playmates, and multiple settings from the start of treatment. None of the work required after treatment would be necessary, and it is thought that if you trained sufficient exemplars, only a few would be needed (Stokes, Baer, & Jackson, 1974). The motivation-enhancing techniques seem to overlap here because varying the tasks and task stimuli is not only increasing motivation but also increasing the number of exemplars and thereby improving the chances of generalization.

Making the treatment setting more similar to the natural environment (Stokes & Baer, 1977) is a core component of NaTS. A play setting is one that is more likely to be in the child's natural environment. Playing a real card game, one you would find in the child's environment, (buy one at the local toy store where peers are likely to get similar games), further enhances the similarity between treatment setting and the natural environment.

Stokes and Baer (1977) pointed out the importance of using naturally maintaining contingencies (natural reinforcers) during treatment. This will also make the treatment setting more like the natural environment. Reinforcers should be similar to those that could be encountered in natural settings. Additionally, specific behaviors that are more likely to acquire such reinforcers should be taught (Carr, 1979). A social phrase is a good example because the social phrase, such as a greeting, is a functional behavior that is likely to obtain a natural reinforcer—a greeting will be returned. See Box 4.4 for additional tips of reinforcing generalization.

Using common stimuli is one of the easiest provisions for promoting generalization as delineated by Stokes and Baer (1977). When teaching play behaviors to children with ASD, use toys and task stimuli that can be purchased at any chain toy store or any typical online store. This increases the likelihood of the treatment activities and items being available in the natural environment. There are two important points here. At many conferences and on certain websites, "special" toys and educational stimuli are sold indicating that these items are "better" for children with ASD. There is no scientific evidence that these special toys are better. However, (1) they often cost more than a similar item at a regular toy store and may or may not last longer, and (2) they are less likely to be in the natural environment and thus do *not* serve as common stimuli that facilitate generalization. Allow the child with ASD that you are working with the benefits of having toys similar to the ones other children have.

Finally, mediated generalization is when the children are taught behaviors that they can take from one setting to another. Essentially, this behavior is "portable" and can go from the treatment setting to the natural environment. The most common mediator is language (Charlop, 1983). Play and social skills are also common mediators because these behaviors are often occasioned in a variety of environments; peers, siblings, and families call upon these skills. Additional guidance for supporting generalization is provided in Box 4.3.

Box 4.3 Promoting Generalization

Promoting generalization across stimuli, people, and settings	
Generalization context	Strategy
Across stimuli	1. Use multiple items from the natural environment. Use several examples to teach one concept and replace with different examples. 2. For example, if you are teaching "cup," use different colored cups, different textured cups, different sizes, and so on. 3. Use real objects (not obscure "educational stimuli") that are meaningful to the child. Get a cup from the child's home, school, etc. Put water or juice in the cup and have the reinforcer a natural part of learning "cup."
Across people	1. Use multiple change agents—don't just have one or two therapists. 2. Do parent training and have parents deliver the treatment at home (both mom and dad). 3. Have siblings participate in treatment and/or deliver treatment. 4. Other natural persons in the child's life should participate in the treatment, such as grandparents and peers. 5. In school, have all personnel knowledgeable and trained on the child's treatment and have aides, teachers, speech therapists, and other personnel coordinated.
Across settings	1. Make treatment setting as similar to the natural setting as possible; use a play setting instead of an artificial treatment setting. 2. Treat in multiple settings including home and community settings such as outside, park settings, group settings, and social settings with other children. 3. Make treatment settings more like natural setting by loosening up structure, thinning reinforcement schedule, and using natural reinforcers.

"Rules of thumb": Generalization and reinforcement

- Use reinforcers found in the natural environment. The natural environment does not have persons standing around saying "Good talking" with handfuls of M&M's! If the child is expecting this, and these contingencies aren't available, the newly learned behavior will extinguish.
- Use intermittent schedules of reinforcement so that the child does not receive a reinforcer each time she engages in a behavior. In the real world, a child does not receive a "high five" or really any type of reinforcer every time a behavior is performed. This does not happen in the natural environment. The child should expect that sometimes a reinforcer is available, but not every time, and if this is the expectation, the newly learned behavior will not extinguish.
- Teach the child to learn how to accept delayed contingencies in that a reinforcer will be provided, but just not right away. This is what happens in the natural environment!

Specific Naturalistic Strategies that Work Well for Teaching Play

Natural Language Paradigm (NLP)

The natural language paradigm (NLP) was designed to combine aspects of discrete trial language-based programs (i.e., Lovaas, Koegel, Simmons, & Long, 1973) with naturalistic programs, such as the mand-model procedure (Rogers-Warren & Warren, 1980). While NLP was designed to teach language, it has a large play component so will be discussed here. NLP was originally designed by Koegel, O'Dell, and Koegel (1987) and expanded upon by Laski, Charlop, and Schreibman (1988) as a motivation-oriented procedure that is fun for both the child and the therapist (parent). There are four basic components of NLP (i.e., direct reinforcement, turn-taking, task variation with multiple exemplars, and shared control), each of which is discussed in more detail.

Direct Reinforcement Direct reinforcement of verbal attempts such as "cah" as an approximation of "car" as the teacher rolls the toy car. The reinforcement consists of access to the object used in the demonstration (functionally related item). Eventually more is required of the child to access reinforcement. Shaping or the direct reinforcement of successive approximations increases motivation by maximizing the likelihood of the child's success, while the use of natural reinforcers enhances functional relationships and generalization.

Turn-Taking The second component is turn-taking with the toys. Both the teacher and the child take turns talking about and playing with the toy. The teacher models a verbalization (says "car") about the toy while engaging in a play activity with the toy (i.e., rolling the car). When the child either imitates or attempts to imitate the verbalization, the teacher gives the child the toy for a few seconds for "his turn." The teacher then says "my turn" and takes the toy and models another phrase about the toy. This turn-taking process facilitates generalization by increasing the similarity between the NLP sessions and play. Turn-taking adds a more game-like or play atmosphere to the work session, which may facilitate motivation. Overall NLP increases turn-taking, and turn-taking is a developmentally appropriate social skill.

Task Variation and the Use of Multiple Exemplars NLP uses a variety of toys to illustrate a particular phrase and uses a variety of phrases to describe a particular toy. For example, the teacher can model "car rolls" but then would also model "truck rolls" while demonstrating the rolling movement with the toys. Additionally, the teacher may say "car goes vroom" for the toy car but will also vary the phrase and say "car stops" or "truck goes vroom." This variation makes the speech training session more fun and also promotes generalization.

Shared Control At the start of each NLP trial, the teacher presents three toys that were previously selected from a preference assessment at the beginning of the session. These three toys are now presented in a mini preference assessment, as the child is instructed to "pick one." The child now shares in the control of what is going to be played with/spoken about in the NLP session. Also, if the child changes a verbalization or indicates that he would like to play with another object, the teacher should "follow the child's lead" and change the toys. Thus, NLP makes use of the concept of shared control to maximize the effects of momentary changes in motivating operations that may work to increase reinforcer effectiveness.

Box 4.4 summarizes guidelines for implementing NLP.

Box 4.4 How to Do NLP
How to do natural language paradigm

1. The therapist will sit facing the child with ASD. The child with ASD's preferred items will be available after a preference assessment.
2. The therapist will place three items in front of the child with ASD and will tell him to "pick one." The child with ASD will signify his choice either with a verbal or gestural indication.
3. The item(s) the child selected will be kept and the other items will be removed.
4. The therapist will verbally model an appropriate phrase two times and then model an appropriate play action while saying the phrase (e.g., if the child with ASD chooses a ball, the therapist may say "bounce ball" while bouncing the ball).
5. The therapist will wait 5–10 s for the child to respond (by either repeating the phrase or uttering an approximation).
6. While the child with ASD plays with the acquired item, the therapist should repeat the phrase. For example, if the child is bouncing the ball, "bounce ball, bounce ball" should be spoken several times.
7. After about 5 s of play, the therapist will say "my turn" to have the child return the item back. The same item can be used but with a different phrase (e.g., "roll ball") or a new choice may be made.
8. Many changes of items and phrases should occur to maintain the child with ASD's interest.

Pivotal Response Training

Pivotal response training (PRT) was derived from the natural language paradigm (NLP) and applied to other behaviors in addition to language. PRT was first described by Koegel et al. (1989) to address behaviors that, when changed, would promote collateral improvement on other behaviors and therefore were "pivotal" to the child's progress. Such pivotal behaviors are (1) responding to multiple cues, (2) motivation, (3) self-management, and (4) initiations. The manner in which these pivotal behaviors are taught is through the use of the components of naturalistic teaching. As such, PRT incorporates child choice of tasks and stimuli, naturalistic settings, direct response-reinforcer relationships, and opportunities for turn-taking. As well, PRT also reinforces attempts at a correct response as part of shaping the acquisition task. This will lead to improved motivation and a higher ratio of reinforcement to responding. Since the reinforcers are the task items, the preference assessment is essentially done at the beginning of every teaching episode. Response to multiple cues is taught by way of presentation of varying task stimuli. That is, a ball can be a big red ball, a small yellow ball, and so on. These multiple cues are presented so that the child must pay attention to all the cues presented for "ball" (i.e., color, size, as well as shape). Box 4.5 includes guidelines for implementing PRT.

Box 4.5 How to Do PRT
How to do pivotal response training

1. Clear away distractions and make sure the child is attentive.
2. Present the child with a clear and direct instruction, question, or other contextual opportunity for a response.
3. If the child attends to a different stimulus other than the instruction, remove this distraction and direct their attention back to the appropriate stimulus.
4. Reinforce behavior as follows:
   (a) If a verbal response, praise the child for good speaking and provide a reinforcer directly related to the response.
   (b) If the child attempts to respond and responds incorrectly, praise the child for trying and present the instruction again.
   (c) All responses, including attempts at responses, should be reinforced with praise and related reinforcer. If it is known that the child can respond more fully than a present attempt, do not reinforce but provide instruction again.
5. Use task variation and intersperse new acquisition tasks with maintenance tasks.
6. Present tasks that require response to multiple cues (big red ball instead of red ball). This requires the child to respond to both size and color cues instead of just color cues.
7. Use opportunities in everyday life for educational moments.
8. In order to increase child motivation, be aware of what motivates the child and what frustrates him/her.

Differences Between NLP and PRT While NLP and PRT share many common elements and some basic intervention components (e.g., natural reinforcement contingencies), there are also a number of important differences between the two intervention packages. NLP is a specific intervention expressly designed for speech, coupled with a play action, focusing on verbal imitation, whereas PRT is more of a general approach, like other naturalistic programs, that seeks out more widespread, collateral gains by focusing on key areas that are "pivotal" in affecting significant change in the child's repertoire. Additionally, NLP shapes verbalizations to match the verbal referent and accepts approximations in the early stages. However, once a "closer" approximation is made, a lesser one is not accepted as a correct response. In PRT approximations are allowable at any stage to maintain motivation. Finally, NLP has specific steps and can be viewed as a trial-based procedure. PRT's more general approach has guidelines for target behaviors and goals aimed at changes in pivotal areas to facilitate collateral changes in others.

Self-management

Self-management procedures have been used to teach a wide variety of social skills to children with ASD. First, the children are trained to monitor their own behavior (Deitchman, Reeve, Reeve, & Progar, 2010; Southall & Gast, 2011). The teacher then identifies a specific behavior that the child should increase or decrease and sets a goal for how many times this behavior should occur in a specific time period or during a certain activity (e.g., five initiations in 30 min or taking five turns during a board game). The child with ASD is also taught to record the occurrence or nonoccurrence of the target behavior and self-evaluate the frequency of the behavior recorded. When a child achieves the predetermined goal, the child provides the preselected reinforcer to himself or reports to the teacher to be awarded the reinforcer.

There are a number of studies showing the efficacy of self-monitoring upon the social skills of children with ASD (Lee, Simpson, & Shogren, 2007; Southall & Gast, 2011). In one study, four children were taught how to use a wrist counter to monitor providing answers to questions (Koegel, Koegel, Hurley, & Frea, 1992). Generalization of appropriate responses occurred at home and in community settings. Disruptive behaviors were also decreased.

Variation in verbal responses and play behaviors were also increased via self-monitoring (i.e., pretend play and drawing) (Newman, Reinecke, & Meinberg, 2000). During baseline, three children with ASD demonstrated high frequencies of restricted and repetitive behaviors (e.g., repeating the same verbal answer or play sequence). During treatment, the children were initially taught to correctly self-monitor these behaviors with the therapist and then independently. The children did not self-monitor their behavior with a high degree of accuracy, but they still demonstrated significantly more variation in the target behaviors.

Stahmer and Schreibman (1992) implemented a treatment package that included a component of self-management to increase appropriate play. Three children with ASD were first trained to discriminate between appropriate and inappropriate play behaviors and then to monitor their own play behaviors during intervals gradually increasing in length. As in the previously discussed study, the children were not always accurate in their self-management, but still increased their demonstration of appropriate play and continued to do so during independent play.

These studies indicate that self-management is a procedure that increases social and play behaviors of children with ASD. Although self-management has not shown to be something that children with ASD can master, it is still associated with treatment gains. As well, self-management programs maintain several advantages that other treatment approaches do not. First, increasing of one's own behavior can often result in change of that behavior (Cooper et al., 2007). Self-management programs are designed to enable the child to run his or her own program, eventually in any setting. Thus, it promotes generalization because it essentially teaches the child "to generalize" the behaviors not only in the natural environments but also across their lives (Stokes & Baer, 1977). Self-management also minimizes the involvement of treatment providers once the child is adroit at self-managing (Lee et al., 2007). This is especially useful in classroom settings where teachers supervise numerous students at the same time.

Milieu Teaching Strategies

Milieu teaching has been defined as "teaching a child a particular skill in the context of its use" (Pierce & Schreibman, 1997, p. 208). Milieu strategies include the use of motivating materials, following the child's lead and joining in the activities the child has initiated, offering choices to the child, and the use of incidental teaching techniques (e.g., placing a preferred item out of the child's immediate reach so that the child must make a communicative request for it). In short, milieu teaching takes advantage of "teachable moments" that occur naturally during the child's daily schedule and/or sets up the natural environment to embed possible "learning episodes" to happen. The evidence base for milieu teaching has ranged from teaching play skills to preschoolers (Garfinkle & Schwartz, 2002) through school-aged children with ASD (Kohler, Greteman, Raschke, & Highnam, 2007; Stahmer, 1995). Research has also demonstrated social interactions between children with ASD and children with other disabilities (Alpert & Kaiser, 1992; Hemmeter & Kaiser, 1994; Kohler, Anthony, Steighner, & Hoyson, 2001; McGee, Morrier, & Daly, 1999). Importantly, milieu teaching occurs throughout the day-to-day activities of the child in the natural environments, so interactions with typically developing peers are a key component (Diamond & Carpenter, 2000).

Mand-Model

Rogers-Warren and Warren (1980) developed this naturalistic teaching program that, while still occurring in the natural environment, similar to other NaTS procedures, differs in that it uses adults to initiate interactions and other identified target responses by "manding" (i.e., requesting) the child's attention and target behavior (Rogers-Warren & Warren, 1980). First, the adult arranges the environment with a toy or item that is of interest to the child but is out of the child's immediate reach. This is establishing a "temptation" for the child. Then the adult makes eye contact with the child and waits for the child to request the item and, if the child does not, provides a prompt (says, "what do you want?) or models the request (e.g., the adult says "I want car") for the child to imitate in order to obtain the item. Ultimately, the natural reinforcer is provided for the child (i.e., the toy car).

Multiple Incidental Teaching Sessions (MITS)

A hybrid of incidental teaching (IT) and discrete trial training (DTT) is multiple incidental teaching sessions (MITS) (Charlop-Christy & Carpenter, 2000). Teaching is done within the natural environment while simultaneously incorporating the use of multiple trial instruction (Charlop-Christy & Carpenter, 2000). It is similar to incidental teaching in that teaching occurs at the appropriate time and setting during the typical day of the child. However, unlike incidental teaching in which one learning "episode" or trial per day generally occurs, MITS provides that one learning trial but also adds on two additional rehearsal trials "in the moment" to provide more practice during the natural context. While these extra practice trials are seemingly "not naturalistic," they are designed to increase the rate of learning while maintaining all other naturalistic elements of NaTS procedures. In the MITS procedure, a child initiates a naturalistic setting interaction, as with incidental teaching. However, the parents/teachers maintain control over the number of interactions that follow. Accordingly, MITS incorporates the benefits of incidental teaching, however, with two extra rehearsal learning trials to maximize and speed learning (Charlop-Christy & Carpenter, 2000). The number of sessions in a day can also vary. On average, parents conduct two blocks of three trials each. For example, if the child initiates twice per day to play with the legos, then there would be two sessions with three trials each (one learning trial plus two rehearsal trials in each session). This increases the number of total trials for that day to six, but they are spread out through two sessions, which happen during the natural course of the day (Charlop-Christy & LeBlanc, 2001). Charlop-Christy and Carpenter (2000) compared the effects of MITS, incidental teaching, and traditional discrete trial training on children with ASD to acquire and generalize social speech. Parents were taught how to use these procedures in their homes. The results showed that while all three procedures did work, MITS was associated with rapid learning of the social speech and superior generalization of these social verbal skills within the natural environments (Charlop-Christy & Carpenter, 2000; Charlop-Christy et al., 1999).

Recall that MITS includes two rehearsal trials embedded with each incidental teaching trial to increase the overall number of trials in order to optimize learning. For example, there is only one opportunity per day to teach a child to say "Goodbye" to his/her mother when getting on the school bus. So, it might take several weeks or months for the child to learn to spontaneously state this greeting to his mom (e.g., Charlop, Schreibman, & Thibodeau, 1985). However, with MITS, a learning episode would look like the following:

Aiden puts on his backpack in the morning and walks to the corner with his mother. This is the usual daily event. The school bus arrives and opens its door for Aiden to get in. Mom stands in front of Aiden and waits until he gives her eye contact. She then models (says), "Have a good day," and Aidan imitates "good day." Aidan's mom says, "Have a good day to you, Aidan. Let's do it again." Aidan's mom repositions herself, waiting for her eye contact from Aidan. When he does, she says, "Have a good day." Aidan says "Have a good day," and his mom then says, "Have a good day. Again, that was so good. Let's practice one more time." When Aidan looks at his mom, she says, "Have a good day," and waits for him to respond with "Have a good day." At this point Aidan's mom says, "Have a good day. You did a great job! Enjoy school!"

For this behavior, the "Have a good day" send-off to school, treatment is over for the day. But Aidan's mother provided three learning trials within a time frame that would have ordinarily taken 3 days if she were using an incidental teaching procedure (one trial per day as per a naturally occurring daily event). These trials took place at the naturally occurring time and place, and although the trials were repeated a couple of times, they are naturalistic and occurred by the school bus, during the morning, with mother, and when the child was at send-off to school. Box 4.6 provides a summary of MITS considerations.

Box 4.6 How to Do MITS

How to do multiple incidental teaching sessions

1. Identify the behavior you want to teach and the naturally occurring setting during the day when it would likely occur.
2. Decide on the specific way you are going to teach the behavior (i.e., use modeling prompt, mand-model, milieu training, etc.).
3. When the child initiates the learning episode, his behavior should be reinforced. Remember that there are three trials; the first one should receive praise.
   (a) Say, "Let's practice this," and praise but do not provide access to the natural reinforcer.
   (b) Repeat the trial two more times and provide the desired item as the reinforcer.

Conclusion

Naturalistic teaching strategies are designed for all who can provide treatment procedures in the child with ASD. This would include not only therapists and teachers, but parents, siblings, and peers. NaTS have been shown in the literature to be effective not only for acquisition of social and play behaviors but tend to have superior outcomes when it comes to generalization and maintenance over time. These procedures have been noteworthy because they have been reported to be not only more pleasant for the children but for the change agents as well. NaTS can turn the everyday natural environment of children with ASD into an easily accessible setting of continued improvement.

References

Alpert, C. L., & Kaiser, A. P. (1992). Training parents as milieu language teachers. *Journal of Early Intervention, 16*, 31–52.

Basso, T., Charlop, M. H., & Gumaer, C. (2017). *Increasing joint attention through teaching functional play*. Unpublished manuscript. Claremont, CA: Claremont McKenna College.

Bojak, S. L., & Carr, J. E. (1999). On the displacement of leisure items by food during multiple-stimulus preference assessments. *Journal of Applied Behavior Analysis, 32*, 515–518.

Bowman, L. G., Piazza, C. C., Fisher, W. W., Hagopian, L. P., & Kogan, J. S. (1997). Assessment of preference for varied versus constant reinforcers. *Journal of Applied Behavior Analysis, 30*, 451–458.

Carr, E. G. (1979). Teaching autistic children to use sign language: Some research issues. *Journal of Autism and Developmental Disorders, 9*, 345–359.

Charlop, M. H. (1983). The effects of echolalia on acquisition and generalization of receptive labeling in autistic children. *Journal of Applied Behavior Analysis, 16*, 111–126.

Charlop, M. H., Kurtz, P. F., & Milstein, J. P. (1993). Too much reinforcement, too little behavior: Assessing different reinforcement schedules in conjunction with task variation with autistic children. *Journal of Applied Behavior Analysis, 26*, 225–239.

Charlop, M. H., Schreibman, L., & Thibodeau, M. G. (1985). Time delay: A generalization technique designed to increase appropriate verbal responding in autistic children. *Journal of Applied Behavior Analysis, 18*, 155–166.

Charlop-Christy, M. H., & Carpenter, M. H. (2000). Modified incidental teaching sessions (MITS): A procedure for parents to increase spontaneous speech in their children with autism. *Journal of Positive Behavior Interventions, 2*, 98–112.

Charlop-Christy, M. H., & LeBlanc, L. A. (2001). Naturalistic teaching strategies for acquisition, generalization, and maintenance of speech in children with autism. In P. Ghezzi, L. Williams, & J. Carr (Eds.), *Autism: Behavior analytic perspectives* (pp. 169–186). Reno, NV: Content Press.

Charlop-Christy, M. H., LeBlanc, L. A., & Carpenter, H. M. (1999). Naturalistic Teaching Strategies (NaTS) to teach speech to children with autism: Historical perspective, development, and current practice. *The California School Psychologist, 4*, 30–46.

Cooper, J. O., Heron, T. E., & Heward, W. L. (2007). *Applied behavior analysis*. Upper Saddle River, NJ: Pearson.

Deitchman, C., Reeve, S. A., Reeve, K. F., & Progar, P. R. (2010). Incorporating video feedback into self-management training to promote generalization of social initiations by children with autism. *Education and Treatment of Children, 33*, 475–488.

DeLeon, I. G., & Iwata, B. A. (1996). Evaluation of a multiple-stimulus presentation format for assessing reinforcer preferences. *Journal of Applied Behavior Analysis, 29*, 519–533.

Diamond, K. E., & Carpenter, E. S. (2000). Participation in inclusive preschool programs and sensitivity to the needs of others. *Journal of Early Intervention, 23*, 81–91.

Egel, A. L. (1981). Reinforcer variation: Implications for motivating developmentally disabled children. *Journal of Applied Behavior Analysis, 14*, 345–350.

Garfinkle, A. N., & Schwartz, I. S. (2002). Peer imitation increasing social interactions in children with autism and other developmental disabilities in inclusive preschool classrooms. *Topics in Early Childhood Special Education, 22*, 26–38.

Hemmeter, M. L., & Kaiser, A. P. (1994). Enhanced milieu teaching: Effects of parent-implemented language intervention. *Journal of Early Intervention, 18*, 269–289.
Kasari, C., Freemans, S., & Paparella, T. (2006). Joint attention and symbolic play in young children with autism: A randomized controlled intervention study. *Journal of Child Psychology and Psychiatry, 47*, 611–620.
Kasari, C., Gulsrud, A., Freemans, S., Paparella, T., & Hellemann, G. (2012). Longitudinal follow-up of children with autism receiving targeted interventions on joint attention and play. *Journal of the American Academy of Child & Adolescent Psychiatry, 51*, 487–495.
Koegel, L. K., Koegel, R. L., Hurley, C., & Frea, W. D. (1992). Improving social skills and disruptive behavior in children with autism through self-management. *Journal of Applied Behavior Analysis, 25*, 341–353.
Koegel, R. L., O'Dell, M. C., & Koegel, L. K. (1987). A natural language teaching paradigm for nonverbal autistic children. *Journal of Autism and Developmental Disorders, 17*, 187–200.
Koegel, R. L., Schreibman, L., Good, A., Cerniglia, L., Murphy, C., & Koegel, L. C. (1989). *How to teach pivotal responses to children with autism: A training manual*. Santa Barbara, CA: University of California.
Kohler, F. W., Anthony, L. J., Steighner, S. A., & Hoyson, M. (2001). Teaching social interaction skills in the integrated preschool: An examination of naturalistic tactics. *Topics in Early Childhood Special Education, 21*, 93–103.
Kohler, F. W., Greteman, C., Raschke, D., & Highnam, C. (2007). Using a buddy skills package to increase the social interactions between a preschooler with autism and her peers. *Topics in Early Childhood Special Education, 27*, 155–163.
Laski, K. E., Charlop, M. H., & Schreibman, L. (1988). Training parents to use the natural language paradigm to increase their autistic children's speech. *Journal of Applied Behavior Analysis, 21*, 391–400.
Lee, S. H., Simpson, R. L., & Shogren, K. A. (2007). Effects and implications of self-management for students with autism: A meta-analysis. *Focus on Autism and Other Developmental Disabilities, 22*, 2–13.
Lovaas, O. I. (1977). *The autistic child*. New York, NY: Irvington.
Lovaas, O. I., Koegel, R. L., Simmons, J. Q., & Long, J. S. (1973). Some generalization and follow-up measures on autistic children in behavior therapy. *Journal of Applied Behavior Analysis, 6*, 131–166.
McGee, G. G., Morrier, M. J., & Daly, T. (1999). An incidental teaching approach to early intervention for toddlers with autism. *Journal of the Association for Persons with Severe Handicaps, 24*, 133–146.
Newman, B., Reinecke, D. R., & Meinberg, D. L. (2000). Self-management of varied responding in three students with autism. *Behavioral Interventions, 15*, 145–151.
Parsons, M. B., & Reid, D. H. (1990). Assessing food preferences among persons with profound mental retardation: Providing opportunities to make choices. *Journal of Applied Behavior Analysis, 23*, 183–195.
Pierce, K., & Schreibman, L. (1997). Multiple peer use of pivotal response training to increase social behaviors of classmates with autism: Results from trained and untrained peers. *Journal of Applied Behavior Analysis, 30*, 157–160.
Rogers-Warren, A., & Warren, S. F. (1980). Mands for verbalization. Facilitating the display of newly trained language in children. *Behavior Modification, 4*, 361–382.
Schreibman, L., Kaneko, W. M., & Koegel, R. L. (1991). Positive affect of parents of autistic children: A comparison across two teaching techniques. *Behavior Therapy, 22*, 479–490.
Siller, M., & Sigman, M. (2002). The behaviors of parents of children with autism predict the subsequent development of their children's communication. *Journal of Autism and Developmental Disorders, 32*, 77–89.
Southall, C. M., & Gast, D. L. (2011). Self-management procedures: A comparison across the autism spectrum. *Education and training in Autism and Developmental Disabilities, 46*, 155–171.
Stahmer, A. C. (1995). Teaching symbolic play skills to children with autism using pivotal response training. *Journal of Autism and Developmental Disorders, 25*, 123–141.

Stahmer, A. C., & Schreibman, L. (1992). Teaching children with autism appropriate play in unsupervised environments using a self-management treatment package. *Journal of Applied Behavior Analysis*, *25*, 447–459.

Stokes, T. F., & Baer, D. M. (1977). An implicit technology of generalization. *Journal of Applied Behavior Analysis*, *10*, 349–367.

Stokes, T. F., Baer, D. M., & Jackson, R. L. (1974). Programming the generalization of a greeting response in four retarded children. *Journal of Applied Behavior Analysis*, *7*, 599–610.

Stokes, T. F., & Osnes, P. G. (1986). Programming the generalization of children's social behavior. *Children's Social Behavior: Development, Assessment, and Modification*, *4*, 407–443.

Chapter 5
Lights, Camera, Action! Teaching Play and Social Skills to Children with Autism Spectrum Disorder Through Video Modeling

Background Rationale for Video Modeling

The rationale for video modeling dates all the way back to Albert Bandura's early work on social learning theory: observational learning (Bandura, 1991; Bandura & Huston, 1961). The premise is relatively simple for neurotypical children; with observational learning, children learn behaviors by observing others (Gaskins & Paradise, 2010). A child can learn a new behavior by watching another engage in it and increase the occurrence or performance of a behavior already in his/her behavioral repertoire. For neurotypical children, observational learning comes naturally to them, and it has been shown that they can learn through observation as early as 21 days old. How do we know that observational learning has taken place? The child observes and subsequently imitates the behavior.

In their seminal article on observational learning, Bandura and Huston (1961) showed that modeled play behaviors observed by 3–5-year-old preschool children affected their subsequent behavior. Children, who viewed a model playing aggressively with a punching "Bobo" doll, demonstrated significantly more aggressive play than the children who observed someone playing without aggression. Additional research has found that neurotypical children can learn a range of skills through observational learning (Bandura, 1977), including motor behaviors (Kampiotis & Theodorakou, 2007), facial expressions (Meltzoff & Moore, 1977), and moral judgments (Brody & Henderson, 1977). In fact, neurotypical children engage in observational learning throughout their daily routines, and this is a core mechanism that facilitates child development (Fenstermacher & Saudino, 2006).

However, children with ASD do not learn in the ways that neurotypical children do, or they would not need specific techniques to teach them. We know this is the case not only in play and social skills, but with speech and communication as well as with many other skills. Indeed, the first studies attempting to teach children with ASD through observational learning had initially failed (e.g., Varni, Lovaas, Koegel,

M.H. Charlop et al., *Play and Social Skills for Children with Autism Spectrum Disorder*, Evidence-Based Practices in Behavioral Health,
https://doi.org/10.1007/978-3-319-72500-0_5

& Everett, 1979). This made sense because if children with ASD could learn from observation, they would be learning from their interactions with the environment like neurotypical children. It was also suggested that children with ASD, due to their stimulus overselectivity, could not learn from observing modeled behavior. However, it was suggested that observational learning paradigms needed to be set up in a way that would be more likely to facilitate learning for the child with ASD and additional research took root.

Subsequent research then started to be more fruitful and demonstrated that children with ASD did in fact learn through observation if the manner in which the behaviors/tasks were modeled were more consistent with the ways children with ASD learned. Egel, Richman, and Koegel (1981) found that observing peer models effectively increased the ability of children with ASD to learn shapes and colors, and Charlop, Schreibman, and Tryon (1983) also demonstrated that children with ASD could learn receptive labeling tasks by observing peer models. These findings have been replicated across skills (e.g., Ledford, Gast, Luscre, & Ayres, 2008; Tryon & Keane, 1986).

Visual Learning and ASD

It is clear from our earlier chapter that structured modeling procedures have been a basic technique of direct instruction for children with ASD. We model specific play and social behaviors for the children to imitate and then reinforce the imitative behaviors. Indeed, imitation is at the core of learning for children with ASD. But we have come far in our understanding of how to present material for children with ASD to learn, and over the years, we have learned a lot about ASD children and how they learn. We have learned that many of the children with ASD are much better visual learners and that when we present information, of any kind, the children learn "better" if the material is presented visually. What do we mean by "better?" We mean many things. For example, children with ASD sometimes learn material that they did not learn through traditional means, using visual strategies (among which video modeling is just one) (Quill, 1997). It's interesting to note that Hodgdon (1995) described visual strategies as tools used to compensate for inadequate auditory processing, sequencing, and organization.

If we consider what we know about children with ASD, in general, then we will be able to view these children as visual learners. Speaking in generalities, children with ASD tend to be good at visually based skills and not good at verbally based skills. That is, children with ASD, in general, are good with puzzles, mechanical toys, and visual recognition of items such as alphabet letters and numbers. They may also learn sight words or be hyperlexic yet lack reading comprehension. Their obsessions or insistence upon sameness is based on visual dimensions. For instance, a child may have a preference for any sticklike attributes, organize according to color or shape, or need a certain route to the supermarket. These are all visual dimensions. To the contrary, skills that are learned via the auditory domain, most notably speech and language, are a pervasive deficit for children with ASD. In fact, children with ASD may vocalize, as in echolalia (or "scripting") but do know the meaning of what they are saying. One of the most well-known quotes, spoken by one of Leo Kanner's first diagnosed child with infantile autism was, "Don't throw the dog off the balcony" which depicts the non-communicative verbal utterance of a child's delayed echolalia in Leo Kanner's office. What was known about this vocalization was that this child's parent had scolded him prior to the appointment with Kanner about dropping his stuffed animal off the balcony of their hotel room the day before.

We also know that children with ASD have higher nonverbal IQ scores than verbal IQ scores. Lincoln, Courchesne, Kilman, Elmasian, and Allen (1988) studied persons with ASD aged 8–29 years on the WISC and WAIS and found that these participants did best on the visual subtests of block design and object assembly and did worst on verbal comprehension subtests. Rumsey and Hamburger (1988) studied men with ASD, as compared with neurotypical controls on a neuropsychological test battery and found that men with ASD did worse on verbal tasks than the neurotypical controls but that there were no differences on the visual tasks. Ozonoff, Pennington, and Rogers (1991) studied persons with ASD aged 8–20 years and compared them with neurotypical controls on a battery of visual and verbal tasks. The outcome was that the persons with ASD did worse on verbal tasks, and like the Rumsey and Hamburger (1988) study, there were no differences on visual tasks. Finally, Minshew, Goldstein, and Siegel (1997) administered neuropsychological battery of tests and compared teens and adults with ASD with neurotypical controls. Similarly, the participants with ASD did worse on verbal tasks, with no difference on spatial tasks between the two groups. These studies all point to superior visual processing in persons with ASD and poorer verbal understanding.

There are many visual strategies that of recent have shown to be efficacious with children with ASD. Included in these evidence-based visual strategies are picture activity schedules and the Picture Exchange Communication System (PECS) (Frost & Bondy, 1994). These visually based systems have been pivotal in teaching children with ASD. Video modeling, discussed in this chapter, remains quite applicable to social skills and play behaviors.

Visual Strategies and Video Modeling

Video modeling is a visual strategy, based on Bandura's in vivo modeling paradigm. Video modeling is a commonly utilized intervention in which the child watches short, filmed clips of a model completing the targeted behavior or behaviors and is then given the opportunity to demonstrate the complete behavior (Bellini & Akullian, 2007). In traditional video modeling programs, the child watches the video on a television screen or computer monitor until he or she consistently exhibits the targeted behaviors. It carries certain advantages for children with ASD due to its format. It has also been hypothesized that visual formats help lessen some of the tendency of response to irrelevant information in the learning setting by simply presenting just the relevant information. This relates to issues of stimulus overselectivity, which refers to the tendency to respond to a subset of simultaneously presented environmental cues (Lovaas, Schreibman, Koegel, & Rehm, 1971; Ploog, 2010). Instead of combining incoming stimuli to understand the overall meaning, children with autism tend to focus on certain features or components of a scenario (Happé & Frith, 2006). Responding only to a subset of relevant stimuli negatively affects children's acquisition of modeled behaviors. Visual strategies may help the child with ASD focus into and respond to only the parts of the learning situation that are relevant for learning. For example, when teaching a child to play with a pilot to fly a toy plane, a teacher needs to use many verbal commands and finger pointing prompts to show the child how to put the pilot into the plane and make the plane fly. The child can "overselect" to the teacher's verbal instructions or more likely the finger prompts, but sometimes the child may respond to an irrelevant cue in the setting such as an inadvertent hand gesture made by the teacher. There are so many possible factors that can go wrong. But, if you make a video of the play activity, a short film clip of, for example, closeup hands placing the pilot in cockpit of the plane and the plane then flying through the air, the child can imitate the play activity with few distractions.

The visual presentation of material is often not only an easier mechanism through which children with ASD learn, but it is often also the more preferred medium. *Motivation*, which has been defined in many ways (e.g., Charlop-Christy, LeBlanc, & Carpenter, 1999; Cooper, Heron, & Heward, 2007), has been said to be associated with visual strategies, especially video modeling. Children with ASD seem to prefer to learn via watching a short "show" on a screen than learning through traditional methods. It has also been hypothesized that for some children with ASD, omitting some of the difficult social cues, which may cause confusion in the teaching situation, may initially at least be of help and benefit to the children. For example, when learning a conversational question, children with ASD often get confused between times when they are supposed to *ask* questions versus *answer* questions. Needless to say, learning pronouns is typically a time of much confusion as the child must reverse the pronoun just used in a question to him (e.g., "How are *you*?" "*I* am fine, how are *you*?") Finally, Charlop-Christy, Le, and Freeman (2000) calculated a cost-benefit analysis and found a video modeling program to be much more cost-efficient and personnel conserving than in vivo modeling.

Video Modeling

Video modeling (VM) is defined as the occurrence of a behavior by an observer that is similar to the behavior shown by a model on a videotape. There are many reasons why VM is an appealing and effective treatment approach to use with children with autism. First, VM minimizes attentional and language requirements, requiring the child only to look at a small spatial area (i.e., a television monitor) and to hear only the minimum necessary language. Second, many children with ASD frequently and spontaneously imitate what they see on television or in videos (Charlop-Christy & Daneshvar, 2003; Shane & Albert, 2008), and video modeling interventions capitalize on this tendency to imitate. Third, it is relatively easy and fast to create footage of models. For instance, Alberto, Cihak, and Gama (2005) found that developing video materials is less time-consuming than developing many photographic learning tools. Also, use of a VM intervention is relatively economical in terms of resources and materials, especially when compared to interventions that use in vivo instruction (Gena, Couloura, & Kymissis, 2005; Shipley-Benamou, Lutzker, & Taubman, 2002). Finally, video footage can be used repeatedly with the same child or other children who have similar deficits, although it is cautioned that proper protocol suggests that video modeling is designed individually for each child.

Numerous studies to date have demonstrated that VM is an effective intervention in teaching conversational skills such as social initiations and play-related statements (Charlop & Milstein, 1989; Nikopoulos & Keenan, 2003; Taylor, Levin, & Jasper, 1999), imaginative play (D'Ateno, Mangiapanello, & Taylor, 2003), and perspective-taking skills (Charlop-Christy & Daneshvar, 2003; LeBlanc et al., 2003) to children with ASD. Only one published study conducted by Charlop-Christy et al. (2000) has compared video modeling to in vivo (live) modeling. The results from this study found that video modeling led to faster acquisition of play, language, and self-help skills than the in vivo condition. Additionally, greater generalization of the skills acquired was observed in the video modeling condition. While further studies are needed to support these findings, it is clear that at least in this study, video modeling was more effective than a live model at providing consistent learning trials and a wide range of exemplars. Some possible explanations for why this is the case are because video modeling procedures are more motivating to children with autism than in vivo procedures and compensate for their characteristic stimulus overselectivity (Charlop-Christy et al., 2000). In addition, video modeling may increase attention because stimulus novelty increases attention and enhances observational learning (Bandura, 1965; Dowrick, 1986).

The first video modeling study to teach conversational speech to children with autism was conducted by Charlop and Milstein (1989). In this study, three boys with autism were taught using video modeling to participate in a conversation about preferred toys. Results demonstrated that all three participants successfully learned conversations through the video modeling intervention, as well as generalized this skill to other toys, people, and settings. The participants also maintained their conversational speech skills over a 15-month period. Charlop, Gilmore, and Chang (2008) built upon Charlop and Milstein's study (1989) to teach variation in conversational speech to two boys with autism using video modeling. Six sets of toys (i.e., robot and typewriter, Big Bird and Bert, car and a jet transformer) served as the basis for seven conversation scripts used during video modeling. For example, for Conversation A, about a robot and a typewriter, the child was presented with five versions of the conversation, A1, A2, A3, A4, and A5. Each of these versions consisted of different lines of the script, in order for the child to learn how to generate varied responses. In addition, the toys that served as the basis of the conversation were changed regularly. This was done so that the child had to learn how to talk about the toys present, as opposed to responding based on memorized lines from the scripted conversations modeled for them. Not only did results replicate the previous rapid effects of video modeling of Charlop and Milstein (1989), but this study also demonstrated the efficacy of multiple conversation presentation formats to increase variation in conversation for children with ASD. Generalization probes also suggested generalization for both stimuli and responses. In addition, this research bypassed the limitations of previous interventions by teaching variation in conversation speech under naturalistic conditions and with a variety of conversational partners (i.e., another peer with ASD, a typically developing peer, and a sibling at home).

Video Modeling Procedures and Perceived Advantages Video modeling was developed to address the negative effects of stimulus overselectivity and increase the efficiency of teaching children with autism via observation. Although videos vary in their procedures, many are filmed to focus on the relevant stimuli and present the different components separately so that only one action or verbalization is shown at a time. The videos also allow service providers to repeatedly present a standardized clip of the targeted behavior (Charlop-Christy et al., 2000; McCoy & Hermansen, 2007). In addition, video modeling allows the treatment provider to have complete control over the modeled scenario as the treatment provider can film and edit the scenario until satisfied. Practically, video modeling is less expensive and time-consuming than live modeling (Charlop-Christy et al., 2000; McCoy & Hermansen, 2007; Thelen, Fry, Fehrenbach, & Frautschi, 1979).

Empirical Support

Existing research indicates that video modeling is a more effective means of intervention than in vivo (or live) modeling. Using a multiple baseline, within-subject comparison design, Charlop-Christy et al. (2000) compared the effectiveness of in vivo and video modeling. Two behaviors of similar difficulty were selected for each participant and randomly assigned to be targeted via in vivo or video modeling. In both conditions, the child observed the targeted behavior (either by watching a live model or a televised clip) and was then instructed to demonstrate that behavior. Four of the five children acquired the behaviors targeted by video modeling faster than those targeted by in vivo modeling. For the fifth child, rate of acquisition was the same for both treatment conditions. Further, video modeling was found to lead to better generalization across persons, setting, and stimuli. This increased utilization of acquired skills in untrained environments indicates that video modeling interventions are more likely to affect the children's functioning during their daily routines, which is the ultimate goal of treatments. These findings support the efficiency of video modeling interventions.

Additionally, a large body of literature supports the efficacy of using traditional video modeling interventions presented on television screens or computer monitors to increase a range of skills across behavioral domains (Bellini & Akullian, 2007; McCoy & Hermansen, 2007). The following reviews the literature on using video modeling to increase the social-communicative and adaptive skills of children with autism.

There is now a robust literature on the use of video modeling in teaching social behaviors to children with autism. Video modeling has been successful in teaching conversational speech (Charlop & Milstein, 1989; Sherer et al., 2001), play-related statements (Taylor et al., 1999), perception of emotion (Corbett & Abdullah, 2005), spontaneous requesting (Wert & Neisworth, 2003), imaginative play (D'Ateno et al., 2003), and perspective-taking skills (Charlop-Christy & Daneshvar, 2003; LeBlanc et al., 2003). However, only four video modeling studies to date have taught basic social initiation skills to children with autism, and none have taught persistence in social initiations.

Charlop and Milstein (1989) reported on the successful use of video modeling to teach conversational skills, including social initiations, to three high-functioning children with autism. All children rapidly acquired reciprocal conversational speech through a video modeling intervention, and improvements generalized to other people and topics. These effects were maintained over a 15-month follow-up period. More recently, Charlop, Dennis, Carpenter, and Greenberg (2010) replicated and expanded upon this finding.

In addition, Nikopoulos and Keenan (2003, 2004) demonstrated decreased latency in socially initiating to researchers and increased appropriate play in children with autism using this approach. Nikopoulos and Keenan (2007) also found that video modeling was effective in building sequential social skills that included social initiations. While it is important to recognize that none of these studies taught child participants what to do if their peer was unresponsive, it seems promising to use video modeling to teach persistence in initiations of play bids to children with autism.

These studies suggest that video modeling has been associated with rapid acquisition rates and strong generalization results to teach social initiation behaviors to children with autism. Additionally, with current-day technological advances, it seems that there are now means that are even more advantageous than traditional video modeling using TV or computer monitors. That is, with portable technology, video modeling can be done more easily and be presented in a variety of environments. In other words, we can bring the video modeling technology to the children as opposed to bringing the children to the technology. Also, in this way, children with autism can practice persistence in social initiations in typical play settings around their peers without fear of social stigma.

The present study incorporated the use of an iTouch portable appliance to provide video modeling to four children with autism and teach them persistence in social initiations of bids to play with neurotypical peers. Persistence in making social initiations of bids to play was recorded as well as generalization and follow-up of bid making across children and setting. The social validity of the children's behavior was evaluated to assess the clinical significance of the children's behavioral gains.

Social-communicative skills Video modeling has been used to address a variety of social-communicative skills. One study used video modeling to increase the conversational speech of three children with autism (Charlop & Milstein, 1989). During baseline, the children only spoke in short phrases. Following intervention, the children were able to engage in conversations with phrases of up to eight words. Further, the children increased their conversational speech when discussing new topics and interacting with different conversational partners in novel settings, maintaining their gains 15 months after intervention was completed. Sherer et al. (2001) also used video modeling procedures to increase the conversational speech of children with autism.

In addition to increasing conversational speech, video modeling has been used to effectively promote variation in conversational speech (Charlop et al., 2008). After watching video clips consisting of multiple conversational topics, the children with autism demonstrated more variation in their own conversation.

Video modeling has also increased other communicative behaviors. Nikopoulos and Keenan (2007) used video modeling to target verbal and gestural play initiations. After watching the videos, all three participants increased their social initiations. Gains were maintained as long as 3 months following intervention. Video modeling procedures also effectively increased the spontaneous verbal requests of young children with autism (Wert & Neisworth, 2003). Another study found that video modeling increased the functional mands (i.e., verbal behavior that specifies a desired outcome) demonstrated by children with autism and that children generalized observed gains (Plavnick & Ferren, 2011). Buggey (2005) used video modeling to target a number of social behaviors, including language and social initiations. The intervention effectively increased the children's demonstration of the targeted behaviors, and gains were maintained several months following intervention. Cardon and Wilcox (2011) utilized video modeling to effectively increase the imitations skills of three boys with autism. Gains continued to be observed up to 3 weeks following intervention and with untrained stimuli.

Video modeling has also been used to facilitate children with autism's mastery of PECS (Cihak, Smith, Cornett, & Coleman, 2012). Although the children with autism demonstrated progress when exposed to traditional PECS procedures alone, they acquired the skills more rapidly when a modeling video was shown before the traditional intervention.

Several studies used video modeling to target different types of play in children with autism. D'Ateno et al. (2003) showed video modeling clips to increase the solitary pretend play of a child with autism. After watching the videos, the child increased both his play actions and verbalizations. These findings were later replicated with a larger sample of preschool children with autism (MacDonald, Clark, Garrigan, & Vangala, 2005). Additionally, these children also exhibited unscripted play actions and verbalizations. Lydon, Healy, and Leader (2011) found that video modeling increased the scripted play actions and verbalizations of five children with autism and the children also exhibited increases in untrained settings.

Another study used video modeling to teach children with autism reciprocal pretend play with a neurotypical peer (MacDonald, Sacramone, Mansfield, Wiltz, &

Ahearn, 2009). All three participants acquired the targeted actions and verbalizations. The children also expanded on the modeled scenarios and demonstrated new actions and verbalizations. Similarly, Taylor et al. (1999) used video modeling to effectively increase the number of comments demonstrated by children during play activities. Another study successfully increased the verbal responses demonstrated by children with autism during play activities (Buggey, Toombs, Gardener, & Cervetti, 1999).

Video modeling has also been used to simultaneously target multiple verbal and nonverbal social-communicative behaviors (Charlop et al., 2010). During intervention, the three participating children watched a video of an adult actor demonstrating appropriate verbalizations, intonations, gestures, and facial expressions. After watching the video three or four times, all of the children increased their demonstration of at least three of the four behaviors.

Video modeling has also successfully increased more abstract social-communicative behaviors, like perspective taking (i.e., the ability to determine another person's mental state to predict behavior) (Shipley-Benamou et al., 2002). The intervention increased three participating children's performance on the targeted perspective-taking task. The children also demonstrated gains when exposed to new stimuli.

Additional research has used video modeling in conjunction with other treatment strategies to increase the social-communicative skills of children with autism. For example, video modeling and prompting procedures have been found to increase the social initiations and perspective-taking abilities of children with autism (Apple, Billingsley, Schwartz, & Carr, 2005; LeBlanc et al., 2003). When used along with instructional computer programs, video modeling has also been found to increase a number of prosocial behaviors (Simpson, Langone, & Ayres, 2004).

In Grosberg and Charlop (2014), a portable video modeling intervention (PVMI) was used to teach persistence in social initiations to children with autism. Persistence was defined as making verbal initiations to play to up to three peers in spite of experiencing peers declining to play. Three different video clips were created and downloaded onto the iTouch in which an undergraduate actor's social initiation attempt to ask peers to play was accepted on her first, second, and third attempt across the three clips. The child watched the clips on the iTouch and was then told to pick a toy and find a friend to play with. If a child with autism asked a peer to play, the neurotypical peer was prompted by a student therapist to either accept or reject the social initiation request. Results indicated that all four children successfully learned persistence in social initiations through the PVMI, maintained the target behavior at 1- and 2-month follow-ups, and generalized the target behavior to at least one untrained setting. This intervention was effective because it incorporated basic video modeling principles and a technology that was highly motivating to watch and learn from for the participants in the study. For example, participants in the study often requested to "watch their videos" when they came to their behavioral treatment program.

Together, these studies indicate that video modeling interventions effectively facilitate the skill acquisition of many children with autism. Further, the consistently rapid rate of acquisition suggests that video modeling interventions may be an especially efficient means of promoting child progress. However, the reviewed research examines the effectiveness of video modeling interventions implemented on televisions or occasionally computer screens. Recent technological innovations have changed the implementation of video modeling interventions, with the treatment now being delivered on portable handheld technology (e.g., Cihak, Fahrenkrog, Ayres, & Smith, 2010; Kellems, 2010).

For example, children could watch videos targeting academic skills at their school desks or clips promoting social initiations on the playground with peers. If video modeling implemented on portable handheld devices in these settings is effective, this would increase children with autism's functioning in their natural environments. This is especially important because children with autism who make gains in one setting often fail to apply these skills when in different settings (Stokes & Baer, 1977). Further, the portability of the devices would allow the treatment to be administered in a range of different settings, which promotes generalization to untrained settings (Stokes & Baer, 1977).

Increased child motivation It has been suggested that children with autism find portable handheld devices reinforcing and that using them in treatment may increase the children's motivation to participate in and respond to the intervention (Goldsmith & LeBlanc, 2004; Harrell, 2010). More specifically, children often use these technological devices to engage in highly preferred activities like watching movies or playing video games. The child may come to associate these positive experiences with the device itself, thus making interventions that use the device more enjoyable and interesting (Goldsmith & LeBlanc, 2004). Further, children with autism may prefer to engage in interventions using these devices because research demonstrates that these individuals are especially adept at mechanical tasks like working electronic devices (e.g., Goldstein, Beers, Siegel, & Minshew, 2001; Kanner, 1943). While many report that children with autism like portable handheld devices and think that they are "cool" (Harrell, 2010; Kagohara et al., 2011; Kellems, 2010), research has not systematically examined children with autism's perceptions of these devices or whether they prefer them over the traditionally used television. Assuming that children with autism do view handheld devices favorably, there is no research supporting the view that this improves their response to treatments delivered on these devices.

Increased social validity of intervention Social validity of intervention refers to the extent to which the intervention (e.g., goals, procedures, and outcomes) is relevant to and acceptable in the children's environments (Kazdin, 2005). Many have speculated that implementing interventions on common and popular portable handheld technology will increase the social validity and decrease the stigma of intervention procedures (Ayres, Mechling, & Sansosti, 2013; Goldsmith & LeBlanc, 2004; Shane et al., 2012). More specifically, it is believed that these devices will allow interventions to be acceptable to those implementing the intervention and to the targeted children's peers.

Preliminary evidence indicates that those implementing interventions do find handheld portable devices acceptable. Teachers who have used these devices to implement video modeling interventions in the classroom have said that the portable video modeling interventions are appropriate and that they would implement them again in the future (Cihak et al., 2010). However, there is a need for more research in this area.

While it is generally accepted that neurotypical children and adolescents view portable handheld devices favorably, there is mixed research on how this affects their perceptions of the interventions or the participating children. However, related research indicates that individuals with autism who use socially desirable items when interacting may be more appealing to peers. For example, one study found that adolescents with autism received more social initiations from peers when they had items their peers preferred (e.g., a video game) during school recesses (Gaylord-Ross, Haring, Breen, & Pitts-Conway, 1984). More research is needed to extend this finding to the use of portable handheld devices.

How to Do Video Modeling

Video Modeling Readiness

In order for video modeling to be effective, the child watching the video model must already be familiar with watching screens of any sort. The child must have a history of liking and/or viewing television, videos, computer monitors, iPads, or even movies or games on smartphones. The child should have attention skills that include eye contact toward the screen for several minutes at a time as well as the ability to stay seated for the duration of a very short video clip. In video modeling, we will be presenting a model engaging in a behavior for the child to observe and subsequently imitate. So, if the child cannot observe this model on the screen, then he/she is not a candidate for video modeling. Also, since the child will be imitating the behavior of the model, the child must have basic nonverbal or verbal imitation skills, depending upon what behaviors are to be modeled.

Thus, the prerequisite skills for video modeling are (1) prior history of viewing screens, (2) ability to focus attention and sustain attention to the screen for a short period of time, and (3) imitation skills. It is important to note that the assumption about prior viewing of screens is that the child enjoys viewing! Video modeling should be a fun alternative to traditional treatment paradigms. Also, while a child may have all the prerequisites, the bottom line is that we won't know if VM is right for a child until we try it. Remember that the evidence base shows us that the preponderance of research studies has included participants ranging from moderate to high functioning. Only a few studies have included children with ASD who were described as being on the lower end of the spectrum. So while it is possible for children with

ASD who are considered lower functioning to learn via VM, this should be kept in mind. As well, prerequisite skills are needed depending upon the target behavior in mind. For example, if a child is nonverbal, don't expect her to be able to learn conversational speech from VM. However, it is possible that a nonverbal child may learn beginning sounds from VM. Or, if a child is just at the level of functional toy play, then he is not likely to learn complex cooperative play skills with other children such as board games. Remember that VM is not a magic bullet (there are no magic bullets in autism treatment). However, video modeling may be successful, whereas other treatments have failed for the reasons discussed above. This brings us to the next section of choosing target behaviors.

Choose a Target Behavior

The target behavior you choose is the play or social skill to be acquired by the child. Determining the target behavior will depend on many variables such as the child's functioning level, verbal ability, skills already in his/her repertoire, tasks on the IEP or other program curricula, parent interviews, teachers and therapists' interviews, and other various guidelines. There may be prerequisite skills necessary for the child in addition to the attention skills. Also, the behaviors should have social validity and be useful to the child in his/her life. For example, the social skill of "manners" may be a request of the child's parents, but may not be of utmost importance to a child who does not know basic peer interaction skills. Knowing how to prioritize social skills and play is important when choosing target behaviors. A card game may be an appropriate goal for a 10-year-old child with ASD, but a particular child may not have the precursor matching skills to play cards yet. Thus, a good VM target behavior would be a matching game before teaching a matching card game. Guidelines for selecting a target behavior are offered in Box 5.1.

Box 5.1 Considerations When Selecting Target Behaviors

Considerations when selecting target behaviors

1. What do neurotypical children the same age play?
2. How long would a neurotypical child stay with that activity?
3. What do children with a mental age similar to the child play?
4. How long do you think the child will focus on a video of the play?

For example, you may have a child who is 10 years old but is nonverbal and does not have many social or play skills. So, when thinking about what a neurotypical child of 10 years plays with, this might not be helpful because these children use a lot of language in their play or play games (e.g., board games, card games, athletic games) with a lot of rules. A neurotypical child of 10 years could sustain a play activity and be involved for a long time, whereas your child may only be able to be involved for short bursts of play activities. Plus, your child may be more interested in more basic forms of play as opposed to sophisticated forms of play. That is, a matching card game where the child categorizes color cards for a few minutes may be more appropriate than a 20-min game of rummy. These are all important factors to be considered.

Operationally Define Target Behavior

After you have your target behavior chosen, you will need to operationally define it so you can do two things: (1) figure out how to come up with a script to put it on the video, and (2) tell that the child has learned through VM. Operationally defining a target behavior puts it into terms that are observable, measurable, and individually specific. You break it down into small pieces so you can easily model it. Not only that, but it is easy for others to replicate it. Finally, and importantly, you make every aspect of the behavior easily observed by the child for subsequent imitation.

One of the important aspects of the operational definition is that it is individually specific. That means that the behavior is defined with the specific child in mind. The ramifications of this one sentence are actually quite large. What this means is that a video is made to order for each child, so that a particular video may or may not work with other children. For example, what is "independent play" for one child may not be independent play for another. For one child, independent play may be pushing the buttons of a cause-effect toy so that an operational definition might be "pushing down the buttons on the toy, in any manner." For another child, independent play may be operationally defined as "pushing down the buttons on the cause-effect toy, alternating between the various buttons so that each of the five different buttons is pushed and that after each button is pushed, the child also closes back the pop-up mechanism." Finally, for a completely different look at an operational definition of independent play, for another child it might be "playing a video game as per the rules of the game for 3 min consecutively" or "playing with pretend food in a functional manner so that the child uses the food items as they were designed to be used: (a) preparing a food item such as making a sandwich; (b) pretend eating of a food item; (c) feeding a food item to an appropriate recipient such as a doll, puppet, or stuffed animal; or (d) packing up the food items in a bag." Clearly, operational definitions are individual child specific and can be easily observed so that they are easily measured. In the section above, a "matching card game" for one child is matching two cards of like color from five pairs of cards, while for another child it is playing a rummy game with half a deck.

The operational definition is also measurable and observable. This means that we break down the target behavior into terms that we can count in some way (measure) and clearly see (observe). We can easily determine if the behavior is occurring by watching the child. Now that we have a target behavior that is clearly operational, we can easily move on with making the video for VM. Also, should someone want to replicate this VM program, the target behavior needs to be clear enough so others will be able to do it. One can also see how two children with the same goal may differ in the videos they may need. Finally, it will be easy to tell whether or not the video clearly depicts the target behavior and whether the child is imitating the desired behavior. So, operational behaviors may be seen as the foundation of treatment for children with ASD. We need to focus first and foremost on the behavior and know exactly what it is, what it looks like, and how we define and measure it.

Task Analysis

One quick step before we make our script for the video is to break down the operational definition into a task analysis. This is merely writing out the steps of the target behavior as defined. The task analysis further breaks down the behavior into its component parts and teaching steps, so that we would be able to model each step.

Now consider the above example of using a cause-effect toy and pushing its buttons. The operational definition of independent play used in the example above is that the child is to push down the buttons that are on the toy. So, our task analysis must be a step-by-step breakdown of how to use this toy. A sample task analysis is offered in Box 5.2.

Box 5.2 Task Analysis of Play with a Cause-Effect Toy Example 1

Sequential steps to playing with cause-effect toy

Preparation: Toy is placed on the table.

Step 1: Push down first button on the left.
Step 2: Push down second button to the left.
Step 3: Push down middle button.
Step 4: Push down second button to the right.
Step 5: Push down last button on the right.

Notice that the task analysis consists of the correct way to play with the toy, but the operational definition for the child is that the child only needs to press the buttons. What we accept as independent play may be different from the task analysis.

Let's take the case of the second example of the operational definition for the child who must push back down the pop-up mechanism. That would need to be added into this task analysis (Box 5.3).

Box 5.3 Task Analysis of Play with a Cause-Effect Toy Example 2

Sequential steps to playing with cause-effect toy

Preparation: Toy is placed on the table.

Step 1: Push down first button on the left.
Step 2: Push down to close pop-up flap.
Step 3: Push down second button to the left.
Step 4: Push down to close pop-up flap.
Step 5: Push down middle button.
Step 6: Push down to close pop-up flap.
Step 7: Push down second button to the right.
Step 8: Push down to close pop-up flap.
Step 9: Push down last button on the right.
Step 10: Push down to close pop-up flap.

Your operational definition for this child, as you recall, was pushing the buttons down and closing the pop-up flap and then going on to another button. However, you may also want to require that the child not repeat buttons, move from side to side, and so on. You may make your operational definitions of independent play any way you want. For example, you might find that the child will perseverate on one button only, so you do not want to have a "loose" operational definition.

Here is another task analysis that you might find interesting. Suppose the operational definition is that while playing independently with this toy, the child must also repeat the animal sound the pop-up creature makes. So, for this toy, each of the five buttons triggers the pop-up mechanism of an animal with its corresponding sound (i.e., the cow pop-up makes a "moo" sound, the dog pop-up makes a "woof" sound, etc.). Since the task analysis is just a breakdown of what is going to be modeled, not what the child does (i.e., the operational definition), the child's behavior does not appear in the task analysis. So, the task analysis will look the same. Incorporating time for the child to imitate the animal comes in during the making of the script, which will be based on the task analysis, but includes pauses, breaks, and so on, for child responses (see below).

One way to get good at creating task analyses is for you to complete a task, while observing and recording every little step you take and everything you do in the order you do it and write it down. Below is another example of a task analysis (Box 5.4).

Box 5.4 Task Analysis of a Car Wash Toy Play

Task analysis of car wash toy play

Preparation: Place car wash set on the table. Actor or participant says, "Let's play carwash."

Step 1: Car is placed at the beginning of the driveway.
Step 2: Car goes up driveway.

Step 3: Car is placed on car wash tracks.
Car goes through "the wash."

1. Red button is pushed and car is squirted with water.
2. Car moves to nozzle dryer.
3. Nozzle is picked up and "dries" car.
4. Car drives down ramp.

Step 4: Car is put into a parking spot.

Script

Here is where the task analysis becomes very helpful. Your script will be a detailed combination of your task analysis, directions for the actors, and directions for the camera. Additionally, notes regarding scene display will also be in the script. Below is an example of a script for the car wash task analysis; note the differences (Box 5.5).

Box 5.5 Script for Car Wash Toy Play
Script: car wash

Car wash toy set is placed on the table for filming. Camera zooms in on the toy.

Actor: Places hand on car (without obscuring the car) and while looking into camera says in a slow, clear voice, "Let's play car wash."
Camera: Zooms in on actor's hands and car and subsequently follows the car.
Actor: Moves car slowly to starting point of game set.
Actor: With left hand, guides car through game set. First goes up ramp, then turns right onto tracks, slides car through wash, pushes blue button with the right hand to wet car, takes car to drying section of game set, picks up nozzle, pretend dries car, places car on track, manually drives car out of game set.
Camera: Stop filming once car is off of game set.

Models

Adults such as teachers, parents, therapists, college students, etc. are highly suggested as models in your video modeling tape. Adults are easier to train and are able to remember scripts better than most children. They require less rehearsing and make filming the video more time-efficient. Since research has been inconclusive in terms of suggesting that any specific type of model is really superior, we recommend that models are selected based on the ease necessary to train the models. However, it is also important to take into account the specific child you are creating the video for, the specific behavior, and the context it is desired to occur. For example, if the target behavior is a greeting to peers, then it may be more appropriate and advantageous to have the peer as the model. Actors should have the script memorized prior to filming.

Video modeling tapes can be made where the child is used as his/her own model. Again, it depends upon a number of factors to use the self as a model, but there is a strong point to make in favor and a strong point to be made against. The benefit of using this method is that many children love to watch themselves in the monitor, so often you get good attention. Good attention is the precursor to imitation. The big problem with using this method is that the child must have this behavior in his/her own repertoire already for it to be caught, put on video, and used for modeling. It is unlikely that the child has or displays frequently the target behavior.

Another type of modeling that can be done is "model-less" modeling. This has been called point-of-view modeling. It demonstrates the target behavior as if the child is engaging in it and is self-observing. For example, the camera is placed to simulate eye level of the child, and the modeling is filmed from that angle.

Scene Setup

Filming should take place in a very plain open space, with as few distractions as possible. The target behavior should be made very clear. Ideally, only those objects necessary in displaying the completion of the target behavior should be present. Familiar or well-liked toys can be used in the film (if appropriate) to increase the attention of the participant. Keep it simple! The fewer distractions, the better.

If the target behavior is one that needs to happen while embedded in a group (circle time within a classroom, line up to enter classroom, play on the playground, etc.), the scene in the video should be void of these distractions. That is, the behavior should be displayed with as few other persons as possible or with other persons in the video but with noise edited out. The video scene should be set up to show only the target behavior, with the background scene just that, in the background. True, the child needs to learn the behavior in context, and the context may naturally include distractions, noise, many other children, and so on. But, the purpose of video modeling is NOT to make the scene as similar to the exact environment, but to provide an easy-to-imitate behavior to later be acted out in the appropriate environment. Remember that as briefly presented above, there is a huge body of scientific literature demonstrating that video modeling works very well for a wide variety of behaviors, including play and social behaviors, and that when taught this way, with the scenes highlighting the behavior not the context, the children do generalize to the appropriate contexts.

So, the scene setup is done to provide minimal distractions and accentuate the behavior. If you are concerned about generalization of the target behavior to the appropriate contexts, there are many things you can do to facilitate generalization in addition to using some of the components discussed in the Naturalistic Teaching Strategies chapter. First, you can use multiple exemplar training during video modeling. This means that you may make several examples or several versions of your video (usually three is sufficient) to increase the likelihood of generalization to appropriate contexts. So, for example, if you are concerned that the target behavior of "allowing enough personal space" while waiting in-line transfers to appropriate contexts, you can tape three slightly different versions of the model waiting in-line in three different settings with different children in front and behind. In addition to providing multiple exemplars, you may actually do the video modeling intervention in the context in which you want the behavior to occur. For example, we taught children with ASD to complement each other ("That was a big kick!") and provide corresponding gestures (e.g., thumbs up) by videotaping multiple exemplars (three different compliments and three different gestures) on an iPad and presenting video modeling teaching sessions right on the kickball field (Macpherson, Charlop, & Miltenberger, 2015). In general, however, video modeling does not have to be done in context for the behavior to later be done in context.

In summary, set up the scene for your videotaping so that distractions are at a minimum and the target behavior can be shot and emphasized.

Filming

Gather your materials, models, script, and props (usually toys), and lights, camera, action! Do you need a professional video camera? No. Do you need professional actors? No. Do you need professional lighting equipment, props, and scenery? No! The minimum requirements for video modeling filming are really quite practical. You may use any video camera, even an iPad or your smartphone, but you will want to be able to have some control over how zoomed in the shot is. Who is going to work the camera? You can. Who is going to be your model? Anyone can. Where can you do this: in a studio? No, you can do this at home, at school, in the park, and just about anywhere. You just need to take a few things into account such as ambient noise (if you film outside, you will be surprised how loud a slight breeze will be on a video or even quiet children in a classroom). You want to avoid as many unforeseeable distractions as possible.

Take a look at your models. Can you see their eyes or do they have long hair in their faces? What are your models wearing? In the first video modeling research we did (Charlop & Milstein, 1989), we taught three children with ASD to engage in conversational speech. Two of the children learned exceptionally quickly, varied their speech, and generalized their speech, while one of the children was still stuck on learning the first conversation. We went back and did a careful study of his video and noticed that his two models were both wearing bright orange shirts. We thought that maybe the child was not identifying with the models speaking the conversational phrases and therefore not learning. So we reshot the video making sure that the models were wearing plain clothes but of different colors. The child quickly reached learning criterion!

Sometimes mistakes like these aren't realized until the final run-through of the video. For example, during one video modeling study, we noticed that a video had been made to teach geometric shapes but that two shapes were the same size and one was a different size. These small differences can become big obstacles to learning. These are mistakes you want to try and catch during filming. Also, before filming, you will want to have a few rehearsals to make sure everything goes smoothly.

When filming commences, it is a good idea to start big and frame the setting. Give the child the big picture and what and who is in the video. Then you want to zoom in so that the behavior is isolated. While this isn't done in everyone's video modeling research, it is what is recommended here. Zooming can be awkward, take time, and be a pain, but it can take off sessions of learning time so I strongly recommend it. When teaching social behaviors, it is important to highlight eye contact, even if it is not the target behavior. For example, if you are teaching a greeting, as mentioned earlier, you may want to teach by the door. You would start out presenting the entire setting, zoom in and out when necessary, but include eye contact in addition to "Hi". Below is a sample script (Box 5.6).

Box 5.6: Script for Car Wash Toy Play
Script of greeting "Hi" upon arrival

Model 1: Model of teacher standing by open door.
Camera: Filming starts of teacher by the door.
Model 2: Model of child walks up to teacher.
Camera: Camera zooms in on teacher's face.
Model 1: Model of teacher is looking at child and smiling.
Camera: Camera zooms over to model of child looking at teacher.
Model 2: Child's model says, "Hi!" in a loud, enthusiastic voice.
Camera: Camera pulls back to focus on both of the models heads and stops.
Model 1: Teacher model says "Hi! Welcome to school today!"

Intervention

Watch the finished video with the child in a room with minimal distractions. Ideally, this would be an uninteresting room (no toys) with only a monitor (TV, computer monitor, iPad) and no other people (siblings, other classmates). The monitor should be placed at the eye level of the participant. There is conflicting research in the literature as to whether or not to use an iPad (Miltenberger & Charlop, 2015). That is, it may be too distracting to use an iPad as the method of video modeling delivery or it may be fine; it depends on the child. We have found that in some cases it can be successful (Macpherson et al., 2015), but we have also had to limit the iPad's use because some children tend to want to hold it and try to find their favorite movies and games on it, which defeats the point of video modeling. We find using a computer screen or laptop interesting enough for the children, and many of our participants in our more recent video modeling research can use the mouse to click on the videos and then sit still and enjoy watching the videos of the target behaviors.

Prior to showing the video, you should say, "We are going to watch a movie. Please pay attention to the screen." Praise him/her for paying attention. When not paying attention, you should remind the child to pay attention and can lightly tap the screen to show where the child needs to look. After completely viewing the film twice (Charlop & Milstein, 1989), take the child to the setting/context where the target behavior needs to be demonstrated, give the child access to the materials present in the film, and say, "Do what you saw in the video, or now it is your turn." The child then has the opportunity to engage in the modeled behavior. If the child does the behavior, give him/her an opportunity to do it again, in other settings, and do it for follow-up probes and generalization probes. This doesn't have to be right away; but it is good for the child to be able to engage in the learned behavior soon after.

If the child does not reach your criterion of learning the behavior you have set, present the video again at a later time (next day, week) only once (Charlop & Milstein, 1989) and assess for learning by having the child do what he/she saw in the video. We recommend showing the video twice in a row, and then upon subsequent viewings, just play the video once. Continue this cycle of viewing the video once and test for learning until the child has learned the behavior. We decided to do this so the child would have some initial repetition, but not become bored by continually repeated presentations. We have been doing it this way since our first study (Charlop & Milstein, 1989), and the majority of our research seems to be effective, so we continue to use this approach. However, it is important to note that other researchers do not follow this rhythm and show success.

Conclusion

You should now know how to create and do your own video modeling intervention with positive effects! Remember that video modeling generally works fairly quickly if your designated child has met the pre-assessment criteria. If the child is having difficulty learning, go back over this chapter and make sure you have been following the suggestions as stated. Throughout the years of doing video modeling research, I have found that children with ASD not only learn relatively quickly from video modeling, but seem to enjoy the process. This has been indicated by requests to view the videos after completion of the research. Once, a child ased to view the videos used in video modeling as his selected reinforcer!

References

Alberto, P. A., Cihak, D. F., & Gama, R. I. (2005). Use of static picture prompts versus video modeling during simulation instruction. *Research in Developmental Disabilities, 26*, 327–339.

Apple, A. L., Billingsley, F., Schwartz, I. S., & Carr, E. G. (2005). Effects of video modeling alone and with self-management on compliment-giving behaviors of children with high-functioning ASD. *Journal of Positive Behavior Interventions, 7*, 33–46.

Ayres, K. M., Mechling, L., & Sansosti, F. J. (2013). The use of mobile technologies to assist with life skills/independence of students with moderate/severe intellectual disability and/or autism spectrum disorders: Considerations for the future of school psychology. *Psychology in the Schools, 50*, 259–271.

Bandura, A. (1965). Influence of models' reinforcement contingencies on the acquisition of imitative responses. *Journal of Personality and Social Psychology, 1*, 589.

Bandura, A. (1977). *Social learning theory*. Englewood Cliffs, NJ: Prentice Hall.

Bandura, A. (1991). Social cognitive theory of self-regulation. *Organizational Behavior and Human Decision Processes, 50*, 248–287.

Bandura, A., & Huston, A. C. (1961). Identification as a process of incidental learning. *The Journal of Abnormal and Social Psychology, 63*, 311.

Bellini, S., & Akullian, J. (2007). A meta-analysis of video modeling and video self-modeling interventions for children and adolescents with autism spectrum disorders. *Exceptional Children, 73*, 264–287.

Brody, G. H., & Henderson, R. W. (1977). Effects of multiple model variations and rationale provision on the moral judgments and explanations of young children. *Child Development, 62*, 1117–1120.

Buggey, T. (2005). Video self-modeling applications with students with autism spectrum disorder in a small private school setting. *Focus on Autism and Other Developmental Disabilities, 20*, 52–63.

Buggey, T., Toombs, K., Gardener, P., & Cervetti, M. (1999). Training responding behaviors in students with autism: Using videotaped self-modeling. *Journal of Positive Behavior Interventions, 1*, 205–214.

Cardon, T. A., & Wilcox, M. J. (2011). Promoting imitation in young children with autism: A comparison of reciprocal imitation training and video modeling. *Journal of Autism and Developmental Disorders, 41*, 654–666.

Charlop, M. H., Dennis, B., Carpenter, M. H., & Greenberg, A. L. (2010). Teaching socially expressive behaviors to children with autism through video modeling. *Education and Treatment of Children, 33*, 371–393.

Charlop, M. H., Gilmore, L., & Chang, G. T. (2008). Using video modeling to increase variation in the conversation of children with autism. *Journal of Special Education Technology, 23*, 47–66.

Charlop, M. H., & Milstein, J. P. (1989). Teaching autistic children conversational speech using video modeling. *Journal of Applied Behavior Analysis, 22*, 275–285.

Charlop, M. H., Schreibman, L., & Tryon, A. S. (1983). Learning through observation: The effects of peer modeling on acquisition and generalization in autistic children. *Journal of Abnormal Child Psychology, 11*, 355–366.

Charlop-Christy, M. H., & Daneshvar, S. (2003). Using video modeling to teach perspective taking to children with autism. *Journal of Positive Behavior Interventions, 5*, 12–21.

Charlop-Christy, M. H., Le, L., & Freeman, K. A. (2000). A comparison of video modeling with in vivo modeling for teaching children with autism. *Journal of Autism and Developmental Disorders, 30*, 537–552.

Charlop-Christy, M. H., LeBlanc, L. A., & Carpenter, M. H. (1999). Naturalistic Teaching Strategies (NaTS) to teach speech to children with autism: Historical perspective, development, and current practice. *California School Psychologist, 4*, 30–46.

Cihak, D., Fahrenkrog, C., Ayres, K. M., & Smith, C. (2010). The use of video modeling via a video iPod and a system of least prompts to improve transitional behaviors for students with autism spectrum disorders in the general education classroom. *Journal of Positive Behavior Interventions, 12*, 103–115.

Cihak, D. F., Smith, C. C., Cornett, A., & Coleman, M. B. (2012). The use of video modeling with the picture exchange communication system to increase independent communicative initiations in preschoolers with autism and developmental delays. *Focus on Autism and Other Developmental Disabilities, 27*, 3–11.

Cooper, J. O., Heron, T. E., & Heward, W. L. (2007). *Applied behavior analysis*. Upper Saddle River, NJ: Pearson.

Corbett, B. A., & Abdullah, M. (2005). Video modeling: Why does it work for children with autism? *Journal of Early and Intensive Behavior Intervention*, 2, 2.

D'Ateno, P., Mangiapanello, K., & Taylor, B. A. (2003). Using video modeling to teach complex play sequences to a preschooler with autism. *Journal of Positive Behavior Interventions, 5*, 5–11.

Dowrick, P. W. (1986). *Social survival for children: A trainer's resource book*. New York, NY: Brunner/Mazel.

Egel, A. L., Richman, G. S., & Koegel, R. L. (1981). Normal peer models and autistic children's learning. *Journal of Applied Behavior Analysis, 14*, 3–12.

Fenstermacher, S. K., & Saudino, K. J. (2006). Understanding individual differences in young children's imitative behavior. *Developmental Review, 26*, 346–364.

Frost, L. A., & Bondy, A. S. (1994). The picture exchange communication system. *Focus on Autistic Behavior, 9*, 1–19.

Gaskins, S., & Paradise, R. (2010). Chapter five: Learning through observation in daily life. *The Anthropology of Learning in Childhood, 85*, 85–110.

Gaylord-Ross, R. J., Haring, T. G., Breen, C., & Pitts-Conway, V. (1984). The training and generalization of social interaction skills with autistic youth. *Journal of Applied Behavior Analysis, 17*, 229–247.

Gena, A., Couloura, S., & Kymissis, E. (2005). Modifying the affective behavior of preschoolers with autism using in-vivo or video modeling and reinforcement contingencies. *Journal of Autism and Developmental Disorders, 35*, 545–556.

Goldsmith, T. R., & LeBlanc, L. A. (2004). Use of technology in interventions for children with autism. *Journal of Early and Intensive Behavior Intervention, 1*, 166.

Goldstein, G., Beers, S. R., Siegel, D. J., & Minshew, N. J. (2001). A comparison of WAIS-R profiles in adults with high-functioning autism or differing subtypes of learning disability. *Applied Neuropsychology, 8*, 148–154.

Grosberg, D., & Charlop, M. (2014). Teaching persistence in social initiation bids to children with autism through a portable video modeling intervention (PVMI). *Journal of Developmental and Physical Disabilities, 26*, 527–541.

Happé, F., & Frith, U. (2006). The weak coherence account: Detail-focused cognitive style in autism spectrum disorders. *Journal of Autism and Developmental Disorders, 36*, 5–25.

Harrell, A. (2010). iHelp for Autism. Online news retrieved December 30, 2010 from http://www.sfweekly.com/2010-08-11/news/ihelp-forautism/

Hodgdon, L. A. (1995). *Visual strategies for improving communication: Practical supports for school and home* (Vol. 1). Troy, MI: QuirkRoberts Pub.

Kagohara, D. M., Sigafoos, J., Achmadi, D., van der Meer, L., O'Reilly, M. F., & Lancioni, G. E. (2011). Teaching students with developmental disabilities to operate an iPod Touch® to listen to music. *Research in Developmental Disabilities, 32*, 2987–2992.

Kampiotis, S., & Theodorakou, K. (2007). The influence of five different types of observation based teaching on the cognitive level of learning. *Kineziologija, 38*, 116–125.

Kanner, L. (1943). Autistic disturbances of affective contact. *The Nervous Child*, 2, 217–250.

Kazdin, A. E. (2005). Treatment outcomes, common factors, and continued neglect of mechanisms of change. *Clinical Psychology: Science and Practice, 12*, 184–188.

Kellems, R. O. (2010). *Using video modeling delivered through iPods to teach vocational tasks to young adults with autism spectrum disorders (ASD)* (Doctoral dissertation). Available from KU ScholarWorks at http://kuscholarworks.ku.edu/dspace/handle/ 1808/8270

LeBlanc, L. A., Coates, A. M., Daneshvar, S., Charlop-Christy, M. H., Morris, C., & Lancaster, B. M. (2003). Using video modeling and reinforcement to teach perspective-taking skills to children with autism. *Journal of Applied Behavior Analysis, 36*, 253–257.

Ledford, J. R., Gast, D. L., Luscre, D., & Ayres, K. M. (2008). Observational and incidental learning by children with autism during small group instruction. *Journal of Autism and Developmental Disorders, 38*, 86–103.

Lincoln, A. J., Courchesne, E., Kilman, B. A., Elmasian, R., & Allen, M. (1988). A study of intellectual abilities in high-functioning people with autism. *Journal of Autism and Developmental Disorders, 18*, 505–524.

Lovaas, O. I., Schreibman, L., Koegel, R., & Rehm, R. (1971). Selective responding by autistic children to multiple sensory input. *Journal of Abnormal Psychology, 77*, 211.

Lydon, H., Healy, O., & Leader, G. (2011). A comparison of video modeling and pivotal response training to teach pretend play skills to children with autism spectrum disorder. *Research in Autism Spectrum Disorders, 5*, 872–884.

MacDonald, R., Clark, M., Garrigan, E., & Vangala, M. (2005). Using video modeling to teach pretend play to children with autism. *Behavioral Interventions, 20*, 225–238.

MacDonald, R., Sacramone, S., Mansfield, R., Wiltz, K., & Ahearn, W. H. (2009). Using video modeling to teach reciprocal pretend play to children with autism. *Journal of Applied Behavior Analysis, 42*, 43–55.

Macpherson, K., Charlop, M. H., & Miltenberger, C. A. (2015). Using portable video modeling technology to increase the compliment behaviors of children with autism during athletic group play. *Journal of Autism and Developmental Disorders, 45*, 3836–3845.

McCoy, K., & Hermansen, E. (2007). Video modeling for individuals with autism: A review of model types and effects. *Education and Treatment of Children, 30*, 183–213.

Meltzoff, A. N., & Moore, M. K. (1977). Imitation of facial and manual gestures by human neonates. *Science, 198*, 75–78.

Miltenberger, C., & Charlop, M. H. (2015). The comparative effectiveness of portable video modeling vs. traditional video modeling interventions with children with autism spectrum disorder. *Journal of Developmental and Physical Disabilities, 45*, 341–358.

Minshew, N. J., Goldstein, G., & Siegel, D. J. (1997). Neuropsychologic functioning in autism: Profile of a complex information processing disorder. *Journal of the International Neuropsychological Society, 3*, 303–316.

Nikopoulos, C. K., & Keenan, M. (2003). Promoting social initiation in children with autism using video modeling. *Behavioral Interventions, 18*, 87–108.

Nikopoulos, C. K., & Keenan, M. (2004). Effects of video modeling on social initiations by children with autism. *Journal of Applied Behavior Analysis, 37*, 93–96.

Nikopoulos, C. K., & Keenan, M. (2007). Using video modeling to teach complex social sequences to children with autism. *Journal of Autism and Developmental Disorders, 37*, 678–693.

Ozonoff, S., Pennington, B. F., & Rogers, S. J. (1991). Executive function deficits in high-functioning autistic individuals: Relationship to theory of mind. *Journal of Child Psychology and Psychiatry, 32*, 1081–1105.

Plavnick, J. B., & Ferren, S. J. (2011). Establishing verbal repertoires in children with autism using function-based video modeling. *Journal of Applied Behavior Analysis, 44*, 747–766.

Ploog, B. O. (2010). Stimulus overselectivity four decades later: A review of the literature and its implications for current research in autism spectrum disorder. *Journal of Autism and Developmental Disorders, 40*, 1332–1349.

Quill, K. A. (1997). Instructional considerations for young children with autism: The rationale for visually cued instruction. *Journal of Autism and Developmental Disorders, 27*, 697–714.

Rumsey, J. M., & Hamburger, S. D. (1988). Neuropsychological findings in high-functioning men with infantile autism, residual state. *Journal of Clinical and Experimental Neuropsychology, 10*, 201–221.
Shane, H. C., & Albert, P. D. (2008). Electronic screen media for persons with autism spectrum disorders: Results of a survey. *Journal of Autism and Developmental Disorders, 38*, 1499–1508.
Shane, H. C., Laubscher, E. H., Schlosser, R. W., Flynn, S., Sorce, J. F., & Abramson, J. (2012). Applying technology to visually support language and communication in individuals with autism spectrum disorders. *Journal of Autism and Developmental Disorders, 42*, 1228–1235.
Sherer, M., Pierce, K. L., Paredes, S., Kisacky, K. L., Ingersoll, B., & Schreibman, L. (2001). Enhancing conversation skills in children with autism via video technology: Which is better,"self" or "other" as a model? *Behavior Modification, 25*, 140–158.
Shipley-Benamou, R., Lutzker, J. R., & Taubman, M. (2002). Teaching daily living skills to children with autism through instructional video modeling. *Journal of Positive Behavior Interventions, 4*, 166–177.
Simpson, A., Langone, J., & Ayres, K. M. (2004). Embedded video and computer based instruction to improve social skills for students with autism. *Education and Training in Developmental Disabilities, 39*, 240–252.
Stokes, T. F., & Baer, D. M. (1977). An implicit technology of generalization. *Journal of Applied Behavior Analysis, 10*, 349–367.
Taylor, B. A., Levin, L., & Jasper, S. (1999). Increasing play-related statements in children with autism toward their siblings: Effects of video modeling. *Journal of Developmental and Physical Disabilities, 11*, 253–264.
Thelen, M. H., Fry, R. A., Fehrenbach, P. A., & Frautschi, N. M. (1979). Therapeutic videotape and film modeling: A review. *Psychological Bulletin, 86*, 701.
Tryon, A. S., & Keane, S. P. (1986). Promoting imitative play through generalized observational learning in autistic-like children. *Journal of Abnormal Child Psychology, 14*, 537–549.
Varni, J. W., Lovaas, O. I., Koegel, R. L., & Everett, N. L. (1979). An analysis of observational learning in autistic and normal children. *Journal of Abnormal Child Psychology, 7*, 31–43.
Wert, B. Y., & Neisworth, J. T. (2003). Effects of video self-modeling on spontaneous requesting in children with autism. *Journal of Positive Behavior Interventions, 5*, 30–34.

Chapter 6
Visualizing Success: Visual Schedules and Script Strategies for Teaching Play and Social Skills

Background

The chapter on video modeling discusses the superiority and preference for visually based teaching strategies for many children with ASD. We explained why video modeling is a viable and effective treatment for play and social skills and gave a number of examples. To further explain why visually based interventions are effective for the children, specifically related to visual activity schedules and scripts, let's take a look at what these interventions represent.

Interventions for children with ASD can be presented in one of three modalities (see table below). The first is the auditory-temporal modality where information is provided in a transient mode and is perceived by hearing. This is when teaching is presented via verbal instructions that the children need to listen to. These verbal instructions are momentary, can be repeated, but do not stay permanently in the environment. That is, once they are spoken, these instructions are gone. An example of this is "Put in" when teaching puzzle play. Once the instruction is given to the child, the instruction has ended. The second modality is visual-temporal, where treatment is provided in a transient mode and is perceived by seeing. An example of this may be modeling. When teaching the child to put in a puzzle piece, the instruction may be given as a model or demonstration of "putting in the puzzle piece" for the child to imitate. With this modality, the child sees the demonstration, but the demonstration is fleeting. The third type of modality is visual-spatial where presentation of treatment is provided as a permanent product and is perceived by seeing (Charlop-Christy & Jones, 2006; Quill, 1997). With this modality, the treatment is seen, but it is permanent in the child's environment. A good example of this is the Picture Exchange Communication System (PECS) where picture cards are used for communication. These cards are a permanent fixture in the environment. Other examples include the picture activity schedules and scripts that will be discussed in this chapter. Any permanent product teaching material would be included here.

M.H. Charlop et al., *Play and Social Skills for Children with Autism Spectrum Disorder*, Evidence-Based Practices in Behavioral Health,
https://doi.org/10.1007/978-3-319-72500-0_6

Modalities of Presentation of Intervention

While visual-temporal and visual-spatial modalities both put treatment into the visual realm for children with ASD, and video modeling has been shown to be effective for a wide number of play and social skills, it is still considered transient, although the advantage of video modeling is that the video itself is a permanent product and can be played over until learning has occurred. However, for visual spatial modalities, such as visual activity schedules and scripts, we have a permanent product from the start. Choosing a visual activity schedule over a video would depend, however, on a number of variables. Visual activity schedules are generally for children who do not reach the prerequisite skills for video modeling (see Video Modeling Chap. 5). Some are better suited for each intervention. Some basic rules of thumb for choosing visual strategies and a comparison of visual activities and video modeling are presented in Tables 6.1 and 6.2, respectively.

Studies have directly compared static photo activity schedules to video modeling to mixed results (Mechling & Gustafson, 2008). So, at this point, we do not have conclusive evidence that one works better than the other. We recommend that therefore the above considerations be taken into account when determining which treatment procedure to use. Below is a discussion of visual activity schedules and scripts with concomitant fading. The reader is reminded to check out the Video Modeling chapter as well for additional visual strategies. Likewise, the reader should keep in mind that treatment should be motivating, and since children with ASD have shown preferences for visual stimuli, there may be some initial motivation to engage in the process.

Table 6.1 Presentation of treatment and examples of auditory-temporal, visual-temporal, and visual-spatial

	Auditory-temporal	Visual-temporal	Visual-spatial
Presentation of treatment	Transient, hearing	Transient, seeing	Permanent, seeing
Examples	Speech/verbal	Video modeling	PECS Visual activity schedules Scripts

Table 6.2 Comparison of visual activity schedules and video modeling

Visual activity schedules	Video modeling
Few prerequisites	Meets prerequisites for VM
Preschool-aged and younger children; less verbal children	Elementary school-aged and older children; generally more verbal children
Simple play behaviors and independent/cooperative play	More complex behaviors such as independent, cooperative, pretend, and sociodramatic play Social verbal behaviors
Better for discrete, one or two step behaviors Examples: puzzles, stacking, matching, cause and effect toys	Good for continuous behaviors Examples: social initiations, conversational speech, pretend play—car wash, expression of emotions

Visual Activity Schedules

A *visual activity schedule* is a picture or set of pictures that cue the child with ASD to engage in a behavior or sequence of behaviors (McClannahan & Krantz, 2010). It is a look-then-do chain of behavior (Banda & Grimmett, 2008). The pictures can be actual photographs, or they can be drawings or clip art. They can contain written words on them (if the child can read or for later use as with PECS cards). They can be used for the moment's activity (e.g., playing with blocks in the present) or consist of a Velcro string, notebook, rolodex, or even iPad series of pictures to represent a schedule of behaviors for the child (e.g., the child's morning's classroom activities, the child's nighttime routine). A visual activity schedule can be inexpensive and easy to make, can be easily transportable across settings, and, importantly, provides constant visual cues.

There are a few prerequisite skills for visual activity schedules, but there are some. These consist of the child being able to match to sample, such as being able to match the picture or photograph with an actual toy or object. Also, the child should be able to respond to manual prompts that may be needed in the beginning while learning how to use the schedules. Finally, the child should display independence with individual skills. However, it is also fairly easy to teach these prerequisite skills during visual activity schedule use or before the actual training of using the schedules. Therefore, it is usually quite easy to use visual activity schedules with a majority of children with ASD.

Photographic activity schedules are generally preferred over other forms of pictures because they have the most iconicity with the actual toys. There is a strong evidence base for these schedules (e.g., Krantz & McClannahan, 1993, 1998; Stevenson, Krantz, & McClannahan, 2000). Visual activity schedules have been used most often for an individual child, but a joint activity schedule also works in terms of teaching peers to play together.

Visual activity schedules can be made in a variety of sizes, shapes, and colors and tailored to you and the child's specific needs and situations. Most visual activity schedules have one picture per page, but that can depend on the child. Table 6.3 offers steps for making several variations of visual activity schedules as well as some helpful tips for preparation implementation.

Scripts

Do you struggle when you attempt to teach a child with ASD to say a specific phrase and the child gets quite confused? Sometimes, the child might repeat exactly what you tell him. For example, you might model a phrase for him such as "Say, may I have the ball" which results with the response, "Say, may I have the ball." Or, maybe the child responds with your instruction "Tell Johnny you want to play" while either looking at Johnny or looking at you. Perhaps the child says, "You want to play" or "you want a turn." Sometimes the child may think that you are talking to him/her

Table 6.3 How to make visual activity schedules

How to make a visual activity schedule—easy version
1. Take pictures with a digital camera or smartphone and download to your computer.
2. Print the pictures.
3. Cut out the pictures and glue or tape them to paper. You may make a written label if you want and paste (tape) to the paper.
4. Laminate the pictures. If you don't have a laminator, use any kind of plastic covering (pocket in notebooks, photo-books).
5. Put Velcro on the back of the pictures.
6. Laminate a larger piece of paper or put in plastic pocket of notebook. This will be the background for the visual activity schedule.
How to use a visual activity schedule for independent play
1. Make sure you prepare your photos and paste them or Velcro them to your schedule book ahead of time (or download them to your iPad).
2. Have your play items available near the child.
3. Present the visual activity schedule (e.g., notebook) and provide your instruction "Time to play!"
4. Prompt the child to open the schedule (book) and look at the first play activity (e.g., puzzle).
5. Wait for the child to get the puzzle (or point to the puzzle as a prompt) and wait as the child completes the puzzle. (Note: When first using a visual activity schedule, make sure you have selected highly preferred play items and ones that the child can do independently; the lesson here is to use the activity schedule, not to learn how to do the puzzle).
6. Have the child return play item.
7. After completion of the first play activity, prompt a page turn.
8. On the next page either a picture of a reinforcer appears for the child to be awarded, or the next play item.
9. Continue until you are done.
Tips for easy use of visual activity schedules
1. Make sure you have done a preference assessment for preferred play items.
2. Have a reinforcer appear in the schedule.
3. Have the reinforcer provided after every one or two play activities.
4. Fade out all of your prompts as soon as possible—remember that a main purpose of the activity schedule is for the child to engage in the play behavior independently.
5. Fade yourself back and out of the immediate setting as soon as it is possible.
6. Initially keep the play activities of short duration.

and not prompting a conversational phrase. You may model just the phrase, such as "It's my turn to go, Johnny," to which the child is utterly confused because he knows it is his turn. At this point, the child is not likely to say anything at all. I am reminded of a time when I was interviewing a teen with ASD who had early intervention. One of many things she told me was that when she was young and her speech was getting better, she couldn't figure out why sometimes she repeated phrases and she received praise, while at other times her therapists responded with "no echoing." She couldn't tell the difference between imitation and immediate echolalia and under what conditions it was acceptable to repeat a verbalization and what conditions it was not.

After hearing this, I became much more aware of how difficult language training is for a child with ASD.

Engaging in conversational phrases is the core of social verbal behavior. Asking questions, giving answers, making comments, and the to-and-fro, give-and-take nature of talking with someone are the basic of social dialogue. We can prompt, but our prompts tend to get in the way and confuse the child with ASD as to whom the verbalization is for. Is the verbal prompt a statement for the child, or is it a modeled phrase that needs to be imitated? For those children with ASD who can read, a *script* can become a prompt, an indispensable technique to use (e.g., Krantz & McClannahan, 1993). Scripts can be delivered via a number of different media such as audio recordings, written on paper, or accessed via technology (e.g., Charlop-Christy & Kelso, 2003; Ramdoss et al., 2012; Raulston et al., 2013). Scripts are usually written out, and therefore they are visual strategies, and we have already discussed that visual strategies tend to work better. Scripts can be faded out so they typically do not create prompt dependency (Wong et al., 2013).

In general, *scripts* are defined as an intervention in which pre-written statements serve as a cue to enhance social communication. Scripts are typically written on paper (white boards, etc.) and are not verbally modeled by adults or peers. Thus, they do require basic literacy skills. With scripts, the children basically "read and then say" what is on the script, and what is on the script is a social verbal statement. Scripts enable children with ASD to engage in a number of verbal social behaviors such as conversations, initiations, greetings, asking questions, social commenting, and play-related statements, to name a few (Brown, Krantz, McClannahan, & Poulson, 2008; Goldstein & Cisar, 1992; McClannahan & Krantz, 2005). As the children start to use the scripted phrases with others, the script is typically faded out, word by word, from the last word or statement learned to the first. For instance, "Let's play with the Legos" would be faded to "Let's play with the" to "Let's play with" and so on until the entire script is removed. In terms of feasibility, written scripts are inexpensive and easy to develop and implement.

Previous research has demonstrated the efficacy of script strategies in many different ways. First, systematically fading scripts can occasion an increase in unscripted or novel verbal phrases (Brown et al., 2008; Krantz & McClannahan, 1998; Ledbetter-Cho et al., 2015; Stevenson et al., 2000). Second, research has shown that script use and subsequent fading have improved peer-to-peer communication (Krantz & McClannahan, 1993; Sarokoff, Taylor, & Poulson, 2001; Wichnick, Vener, Pyrtek, & Poulson, 2010). Third, while the majority of studies have addressed using a script to teach a one word to one phrase initiation (e.g., Krantz & McClannahan, 1993, 1998; Sarokoff et al., 2001; Woods & Poulson, 2006), scripts have also been used to teach conversational statements to children with ASD (Brown et al., 2008; Goldstein & Cisar, 1992). In a study by Brown et al. (2008), the authors used a script fading procedure during simulated shopping trips to teach three children with autism how to initiate and sustain verbal interactions through conversational statements.

While individual conversational statements have been taught using scripts (e.g., Goldstein & Cisar, 1992), scripts can also be used to teach that to-and-fro, back-

and-forth nature required with conversations. This requires continued script reading and saying of more than one line of script. Charlop-Christy and Kelso (2003) conducted a study that used scripts as a method to teach children with ASD to engage successfully in full conversations. Conversational scripts were composed of seven lines, each consisting of a statement plus a question, with the exception of the first and last lines that were statements to initiate and conclude the conversation. The topics of conversation were abstract and related to activities familiar to the children including school, favorite pastimes, and watching shows. Conversations were presented to the children on cue cards which each contained one line of the conversation (i.e., an answer to the previous question and a continuation question). During training, the therapist asked the initial conversational question then immediately presented the child with the appropriate cue card. The child was told to read the cue card. Once the child read it, they were told to repeat the scripted line to the therapist while maintaining eye contact. This procedure was repeated for each of the child's three lines of conversation. Once training on the entire conversation was completed, the child was given reinforcement for good reading, sitting, and attending. All the children with ASD in this study quickly met training criteria and maintained correct responding without the cue cards. In addition, the children demonstrated generalization to untrained topics and across conversational partners and settings.

How to Do Scripts

The previous literature discussed has shown you that scripts are generally a one phrase proposition. Alternatively, they can also consist of several phrases that can be used by the child in a checklist fashion where he/she checks off which phrase out of the list has been spoken (it is assumed that he will say each phrase in order as they appear on the list). Also, some script literature shows us that scripts can consist of several phrase (typically three) for a sustained conversation. So, depending on length of your desired social communication, the type of script presentation format you choose will come into play. Also, the amount of verbal behavior an individual child has in his repertoire and reading ability are all important factors. Remember to consider all of this when creating your script intervention.

Pre-assessments Two important pre-assessments need to be done before you create your script treatment program. First, a *verbal pre-assessment* needs to take place. Any observational assessment would be helpful for you to determine the length, the sophistication, and the type of script intervention you are planning. For example, if your target child is not very verbal, then you would not want to make your scripts longer than one phrase and you would want to keep your phrases short. If you are thinking about a child with a strong verbal repertoire, then you may want to use a script protocol for conversation training (Charlop-Christy & Kelso, 2003). The main social skill you are trying to rectify is social communication, so you do not have to worry about speech skills, per se.

The second pre-assessment you need to do is a *reading pre-assessment.* Again, here you may do a formal reading assessment (as in a standardized test) or just do an informal reading analysis. Make sure the child can read the words you are likely to use in the script. Many studies pre-trained the children to read the words before they put them in the scripts. Here is a bit of a dilemma: if the child cannot read the word, and you have not heard him say the word, then maybe he does not know the word; therefore, he would *not know* what he is saying during the scripted interaction. The child should not merely verbalize content when he does not know what he is saying because that is not true social communication. Also, you are not likely to get content generalization as we discussed earlier in this book.

Script Formats Script formats can be *pre-written for verbal models* for later use, such as in *video modeling*, when the script is not the center of the intervention, but a very important component of the treatment. Here, the format would be considered *modeling* (it could be in vivo or video). Another form of script could be *written,* and it is directly off this written script that the child will read and then speak. Such direct written scripts can be typed, printed, on paper, on white boards, and so on. There are many ways to present these written scripts. They may be presented all at once in a school binder (McClannahan & Krantz, 2005), or they may have each phrase pre-typed on an individual cue card (Charlop-Christy & Kelso, 2003) and presented one cue card at a time. Finally, a written phrase may be attached to a picture cue. Guidelines are offered in Table 6.4.

Writing a Script A one phrase script should be easy to write as long as you remember the pre-assessments. Do not use words that the child does not know, cannot say, or cannot read. Remember that an environmental stimulus needs to be in the setting to be associated with the content of the script for later after the script is faded. Script checklists are a little more difficult to write up so it is helpful to stay on the same subject each day. That way, you are more likely to get the child to remember to check for script phrases as he/she knows that there needs to be discussion about that topic. Conversational scripts are the most difficult to write. Remember to have each line follow from each other and stay with the same content. Also, to keep the to-and-fro nature of a conversation, it is recommended that after the first phrase of the script (typically spoken by the adult or peer), each phrase contains an answer plus a question so that the conversational partner needs to respond to the previous verbalization (Charlop & Milstein, 1989). Table 6.5 contains several example scripts that can be used or modified to meet your needs.

Table 6.4 Guidelines for determining scripts

Guidelines for determining scripts
1. Do pre-assessments to determine the verbal and reading levels of the child.
2. Decide what type of occasion do you want the scripts for?
A. One-phrase utterance—social greeting, initiation, social commenting
B. Throughout-the-day social phrases—check list of several phrases
C. Sustained conversation—several phrases in script consisting of questions and answers

Table 6.5 Example scripts

Type and purpose of script	Example script
Greeting script	Hi, I'm home! Good morning, Ms. Jones What's up, Dude?
Initiation script samples	Let's play with cars! Watch me play! What's your favorite video game? Who's your teacher? I like chips for snack.
Social commenting	I like your tower. That was a good kick! You made a basket!
Throughout-the-day scripted phrases sample	I went to Disneyland on Saturday. I went on the Storybook ride at Disneyland. I ate a frozen banana at Disneyland. I had a great weekend. I got a Disneyland T-shirt.
Conversational script	Peer's phrase: Do you like cars? Child's phrase: Yes. Do you like trucks? Peer: Yes. What color cars and trucks do you like? Child: I like blue cars. Do you like garbage trucks? Peer: I like dump trucks. Do you like to dump sand? Child: I like playing with sand. Do you like playing with dirt? Peer: No, that's messy. Let's play with these cars.

Signaling Script Use After a script is written, there needs to be a way to signal the use of the script. Often, the best way to signal the use of a script is an environmental stimulus such as the presence of a toy, another person, a certain setting, and so on. So, if a script is written as an initiation as a bid for attention, person should approach the child, and the child should then be presented with the script, and the child would read the script "Watch me play." If a script was a conversation for about toys, the child would be brought into the environment where the toys about which the script was written appear, and the first line of the script should be provided. Or, if already in place, the toy can be brought to the forefront and then the script can be presented. The important point to remember here is that the scripts need to be associated with some environmental stimulus so that when they are faded out (discussed below), they will continue to be spoken when coming into contact with the environmental stimulus (toy, person, setting) and not relying on the therapist or the script for prompts.

Script Fading As with any intervention support provided to children with autism, the goal is to remove the instructional components without the newly acquired target behavior returning to levels before intervention. To accomplish this goal, it is often necessary to gradually remove elements of the intervention package until the child is performing the target skill without the additional support. This process is referred to as fading and steps for script fading are presented in Table 6.6.

Table 6.6 Script fading procedures

For one-phrase scripts, script fading steps are the following:
1. Last word of phrase is removed (faded) from the script first
2. Last two words are removed (faded) from the script
3. Last three words are removed from the script
4. All but the first word are removed
5. Half of the first word is removed from the script
6. A blank card/sheet of paper is presented

Note that if script fading is not going well, you may fade out partial words, especially if you are using a short phrase with an early reader. For example, if you are fading out "Watch me," you may want to fade out "Watch m," then "Wat m," then "Wa m," and so on. You can individualize the fading. However, in our experience, fading backward, one word at a time works well. Also, we have learned that many children do not need much fading at all and you can jump ahead in the fading protocol.

For longer scripts, you do the same fading procedure, but for each line of the script. So, for a conversational script, the last line of the child's in the conversation would be faded back word by word. Then, you resume fading with the second to the last line of the child's starting with the last word in this line. However, when using longer scripts, you are working with more verbal, and stronger readers to the children are likely to be faded off their scripts rapidly. Sometimes they can be faded off their scripts line by line as opposed to word by word. You may try this first to see if this is possible.

Putting scripts on common technology has only recently begun to be studied. Grosberg and Charlop (2017) implemented a text message script intervention using smartphones to increase the number of conversational phrases and responses in real time during play sessions for children with ASD. A multiple baseline design across dyads of playmates assessed the efficacy of a text message intervention to teach conversational speech with typically developing peers. The participants were trained in their homes on how to retrieve and read messages on an iPhone. Pre-assessments of reading on a smartphone were taken, and once that was established, only a brief amount of training on the smartphone was needed to teach the children with ASD to read their incoming texts and then say what they read to their peer during the play session. Thus, the child had a smartphone by his side, and conversational phrases were texted to him while in a play session with a friend for him to read and say. The therapist was sitting from outside the play session but within hearing distance and sending in text messages to keep the conversation going. This way, the conversation could change and be adapted as in situ. The smartphone and the script texts were faded out. A sample script with fading might look like what is pictured in Fig. 6.1.

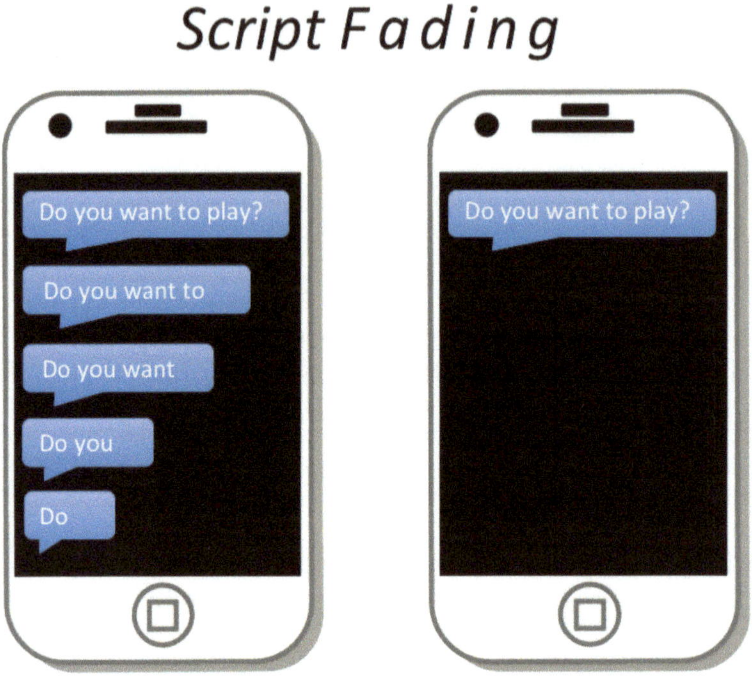

Fig. 6.1 Script fading on smartphone

Conclusion

Visual strategies focusing on visual activity schedules and scripts are important procedures to use with children with ASD to teach play and social skills. They take advantage of their visual strengths and visual preferences and for these reasons often work when many other intervention do not. They are easy to implement and portable enough to be used in a variety of settings, including natural play settings and community settings.

References

Banda, D. R., & Grimmett, E. (2008). Enhancing social and transition behaviors of persons with autism through activity schedules: A review. *Education and Training in Developmental Disabilities*, *2008*(*43*), 324–333.

Brown, J. L., Krantz, P. J., McClannahan, L. E., & Poulson, C. L. (2008). Using script fading to promote natural environment stimulus control of verbal interactions among youths with autism. *Research in Autism Spectrum Disorders*, *2*, 480–497.

Charlop, M. H., & Milstein, J. P. (1989). Teaching autistic children conversational speech using video-modeling. *Journal of Applied Behavior Analysis*, *22*, 276–285.

Charlop-Christy, M. H., & Jones, C. (2006). Picture Exchange Communication System (PECS) for autism and other related disorders. In R. McCauley & M. Fey (Eds.), *Treatment of language disorders*. Pacific Grove, CA: Brookes-Cole.

Charlop-Christy, M. H., & Kelso, S. E. (2003). Teaching children with autism conversational speech using a cue card/written script program. *Education and Treatment of Children, 26*, 108–127.

Goldstein, H., & Cisar, C. L. (1992). Prompting interaction during sociodramatic play: Teaching scripts to typical preschoolers and classmates with disabilities. *Journal of Applied Behavioral Analysis, 25*, 265–228.

Grosberg, D., & Charlop, M. H. (2017). Teaching conversational speech to children with autism spectrum disorder using a test-messaging prompting intervention. *Journal of Applied Behavior Analysis, 50*, 789–804.

Krantz, P. J., & McClannahan, L. E. (1993). Teaching children with autism to initiate to peers: Effects of a script-fading procedure. *Journal of Applied Behavior Analysis, 26*, 121–132.

Krantz, P. J., & McClannahan, L. E. (1998). Social interaction skills for children with autism: A script-fading procedure for beginning readers. *Journal of Applied Behavior Analysis, 31*, 191–202.

Ledbetter-Cho, K., Lang, R., Davenport, K., Moore, M., Lee, A., Howell, A., … O'Reilly, M. (2015). Effects of script training on the peer-to-peer communication of children with autism spectrum disorder. *Journal of Applied Behavior Analysis, 48*, 785–799.

McClannahan, L. E., & Krantz, P. J. (2005). *Teaching conversation to children with autism*. Bethesda, MD: Woodbine House.

McClannahan, L. E., & Krantz, P. J. (2010). *Activity schedules for children with autism: Teaching independent behavior*. Bethesda, MD: Woodbine House.

Mechling, L. C., & Gustafson, M. R. (2008). Comparison of static picture and video prompting on the performance of cooking-related tasks by students with autism. *Journal of Special Education and Technology, 23*, 31–45.

Quill, K. A. (1997). Instructional considerations for young children with autism: The rationale for visually cued instruction. *Journal of Autism and Developmental Disorders, 27*, 697–714.

Ramdoss, S., Machalicek, W., Rispoli, M., Mulloy, A., Lang, R., & O'Reilly, M. (2012). Computer-based interventions to improve social and emotional skills in individuals with autism spectrum disorders: A systematic review. *Developmental Neurorehabilitation, 15*, 119–135.

Raulston, T., Carnett, A., Lang, R., Tostanoski, A., Lee, A., Machalicek, W., … Lancioni, G. E. (2013). Teaching individuals with autism spectrum disorder to ask questions: A systematic review. *Research in Autism Spectrum Disorders, 7*, 866–878.

Sarokoff, R. A., Taylor, B. A., & Poulson, C. L. (2001). Teaching children with autism to engage in conversational exchanges: Script fading with embedded textual stimuli. *Journal of Applied Behavior Analysis, 34*, 81–84.

Stevenson, C. L., Krantz, P. J., & McClannahan, L. E. (2000). Social interaction skills for children with autism: A script-fading procedure for nonreaders. *Behavioral Interventions, 15*, 1–20.

Wichnick, A. M., Vener, S. M., Pyrtek, M., & Poulson, C. L. (2010). The effect of a script-fading procedure on responses to peer initiations among young children with autism. *Research in Autism Spectrum Disorders, 4*, 290–299.

Wong, C., Odom, S. L., Hume, K., Cox, A. W., Fettig, A., Kucharczyk, S., … Schultz, T. R. (2013). *Evidence-based practices for children, youth, and young adults with autism spectrum disorder*. Chapel Hill, NC: University of North Carolina/Frank Porter Graham Child Development Institute/Autism Evidence-Based Practice Review Group.

Woods, J., & Poulson, C. L. (2006). The use of scripts to increase the verbal initiations of children with developmental disabilities to typically developing peers. *Education and Treatment of Children, 29*, 437–457.

Chapter 7
Want to Play? Peer-Mediated Intervention for Young Children with Autism Spectrum Disorder

Background and Theoretical Constructs

Peer-mediated interventions (PMI) are strategies to promote positive social interactions between children with ASD and their neurotypical peers. PMI allows children with ASD to learn from their peers who are "natural experts" in age-appropriate social interactions (Bambara, Cole, Kunsch, Tsai, & Ayad, 2016). In PMI, typically developing peers are trained to use specific strategies to interact with children with ASD. PMI has been found to improve play skills, communication skills, and social skills, to increase task engagement, and to increase friendships for children with ASD (Carter et al., 2015; Chang & Locke, 2016). PMI creates multiple opportunities for children to interact with their peers, which makes it easier for new skills to generalize into other situations (Barber, Saffo, Gilpin, Craft, & Goldstein, 2016). Indeed, teaching social interaction skills directly with peers, rather than with adults, can make it easier for children with ASD to interact and to learn socially appropriate behaviors (Boudreau, Corkum, Meko, & Smith, 2015).

Children naturally practice, refine, and become fluent in social interaction and play skills as they play with one another. This development of social skills is based on social learning theory (Bandura, 1989) in which social and communicative skills are developed through ongoing social interaction within a social environment. However, children with ASD have deficits in social communication behaviors including coordinating joint attention, responding to social bids, and initiating social interactions (Bass & Mulick, 2007; Kamps et al., 2014). Deficits in social skills can lead to a host of negative short- and long-term outcomes including social isolation, peer rejection, and engagement in challenging behavior (Katz & Girolametto, 2013). To prevent these negative outcomes, children with ASD often require specially designed interventions to develop appropriate social skills.

The push for inclusive education in which children with disabilities are educated in their natural environments alongside their neurotypical peers seemed to be one

M.H. Charlop et al., *Play and Social Skills for Children with Autism Spectrum Disorder*, Evidence-Based Practices in Behavioral Health,
https://doi.org/10.1007/978-3-319-72500-0_7

way to increase opportunities for children with ASD to interact with same-age peers. Yet, research has shown that simply placing children with ASD in the same environment with neurotypical peers does not necessarily produce gains in social interaction skills (Katz & Girolametto, 2013; Laushey & Heflin, 2000). Children with ASD have specific needs and require systematic instruction to meet those needs (e.g., Strain, Shores, & Timm, 1977).

Interventions based on the science of applied behavior analysis have the strongest empirical support and the best outcomes for treating core features of ASD (National Autism Center, 2015; National Research Council, 2001; Wong et al., 2014). Applied behavior analysis is based within behavioral psychology and utilizes operant conditioning and careful arrangement of the environment to teach new behaviors. This approach involves systematic instruction with clear instructions, prompting and prompt fading, error correction, and reinforcement. Usually applied behavior analytic interventions are implemented by adult interventionists (Knapczyk, 1989). This reliance on adults can lead to issues in simulating authentic social interactions with young children and can create barriers for skill generalization to same-age peers (Radley, Dart, Furlow, & Ness, 2015). This is particularly an issue for children with ASD who have difficulties generalizing learned behaviors across people, contexts, and materials (Laushey & Heflin, 2000; Watkins et al., 2015).

If we want children to engage in particular social, communicative, or play behaviors, we must intentionally teach them to use these skills across a variety of people, places, and materials (Kamps et al., 2014; Laushey & Heflin, 2000). In other words, placing children near neurotypical peers is not sufficient; we must also provide instruction to the children and their peers. Involving peers in teaching new behaviors to children with ASD can promote generalization of new behaviors by "training loosely" in the child's natural environment (Stokes & Baer, 1977), rather than in a highly structured one-on-one session with an adult.

Research has shown that to promote child engagement in a behavior over time, we should teach that behavior in the context in which the child will use the behavior. In addition, involving peers in intervention may promote skill generalization through the use of "multiple exemplars" (Stokes & Baer, 1977). That is, children with ASD have multiple opportunities across repeated social interactions and across multiple peers to learn and practice new behaviors. In traditional adult-directed instruction, the adult teaches a new behavior to the child and then teaches that child to use the new behavior in a different setting or with different people. Teaching new skills directly with peers in the child's natural environment may reduce the number of teaching phases needed by eliminating this transfer phase (Bass & Mulick, 2007). Given these potential advantages over adult-delivered intervention, research studies began to evaluate more intentional, systematic means of involving peers in social skill interventions (Katz & Girolametto, 2013).

Research into instructional practices which involve neurotypical peers led to the development of the peer-mediated intervention (PMI) approach. The first study in which peers were enlisted to teach social skills to children with disabilities was conducted by Strain et al. (1977). In that study six young children with social communication delays and challenging behavior were divided into two groups of three. Each group was partnered with a typically developing peer who was taught to engage the children in social interactions by making statements such as "Come play!" or modeling how to play with toys such as trucks, balls, and blocks. Results showed that the children's social initiations and responses improved with the peer-mediated intervention. Today, PMI has been established as an evidence-based practice for teaching social interaction and communication skills to young children with ASD (Chang & Locke, 2016; Fettig, 2013; Wong et al., 2014).

In PMI trained peers serve as intervention agents and are taught various behaviors such as delivering instructions, modeling socially appropriate behaviors, responding to social attempts of students with ASD, and reinforcing target behaviors. PMI is typically implemented within classroom routines such as free play centers, outdoor play, and snack time (Prizant, Wetherby, & Rydell, 2000). Peers may be taught to support a child with ASD in a specific activity, to engage in conversation with the child with ASD, and to partner with the child during play (Chan et al., 2009; Disalvo & Oswald, 2002; Katz & Girolametto, 2013; Mason et al., 2014). Peers may form one-on-one dyads with the child with ASD or interact with the child within a small group setting (Mason et al., 2014). Peers are usually the same age as or slightly older than the child with ASD (Chan et al., 2009). PMI research has taken place in a variety of settings including during recess on the playground (Mason et al., 2014), during lunch in the school cafeteria (Koegel et al., 2012), and in special education classrooms (e.g., Radley et al., 2015), general education classrooms (e.g., Ganz & Flores, 2008), and inclusive preschools (e.g., Watkins et al., 2015).

Previous studies have suggested PMI can be a beneficial program for individuals with ASD for several reasons. First, peers are readily accessible within school and community settings. With peers serving as interventionists, the number of teaching opportunities increases beyond those which the teacher is able to offer alone. In addition, peers can serve as age-appropriate models of desired social behaviors. PMI may also facilitate a positive inclusive classroom environment. Through direct training and coaching, peers are able to learn how they can socially communicate and interact with their classmates with ASD. Trained peers are also more likely to initiate social interactions and to develop social relationships as a result of these repeated social interactions with children with ASD. These repeated social interactions allow children with ASD to have ongoing opportunities not only to practice learned social skills in natural settings but also to generalize their acquired skills across different peers and contexts.

PMI may also be beneficial for the neurotypical peers.

Although PMI may involve removing the peer from some of their own instruction time, particularly in grade school settings, peers may develop important social skills themselves. In particular, previous research has found that PMI can lead to increased empathy, friendship skills, and leadership qualities (Carter, Cushing, Clark, & Kennedy, 2005; Kamps et al., 1998; Kamps, Barbetta, Leonard, & Delquadri, 1994). Elementary school children who have served as peer interventionists have reported increased acceptance of children with disabilities and more favorable expectations for future interactions with children with ASD (Kamps et al., 1998).

PMI Improves Outcomes for Children with ASD

Research has shown that PMI improves a variety of outcomes for children with ASD including reduction of challenging behavior (Chung et al., 2007; Lee, Odom, & Loftin, 2007), improved communicative behaviors (e.g., Trembath, Balandin, Togher, & Stancliffe, 2009), and turn-taking and sharing (Harper, Symon, & Frea, 2008). PMI has been applied with older children with ASD to improve academic behaviors such as reading fluency (e.g., Kamps et al., 1994), reading comprehension (e.g., Kamps, Leonard, Potucek, & Garrison-Harrell, 1995), sight word recognition (e.g., Kamps, Dugan, Potucek, & Collins, 1999), and math skills (e.g., Hunt, Staub, Alwell, & Goetz, 1994). However, the primary outcomes targeted with PMI include social interaction and play skills (Chan et al., 2009; Chang & Locke, 2016; Watkins et al., 2015).

Social Interaction Skills Given their deficits in social communication skills, children with ASD are less likely to engage with their peers. Compounding this issue, when peers do initiate social interactions, the child with ASD may not respond to those initiations, thereby decreasing the chance the peer will initiate again in the future. PMI lends itself most naturally to teaching social interaction behaviors between children with ASD and their peers. Indeed, the majority of studies evaluating PMI have targeted improvement in children's social interaction skills (Chan et al., 2009; Chang & Locke, 2016). Social interaction skills have included initiating social interaction (Banda & Hart, 2010), responding to social bids from peers (Radley et al., 2015), conversational turn-taking (Harper et al., 2008), and engaging in joint attention (Schleien, Mustonen, & Rynders, 1995). Overall, research results have shown improvements in both the quality and quantity of social interactions of children with ASD following PMI (Chang & Locke, 2016; Katz & Girolametto, 2015; Watkins et al., 2015).

PMI has been implemented as part of a structured approach, such as pivotal response training, through arranging class-wide social structures such as peer buddies or peer networks, or in specially selected dyads or small groups of children with ASD and a peer. Pivotal response training involves the application of applied behavior analysis in natural interactions. When pivotal response training is implemented through PMI, peers are taught to gain the child's attention, provide the child with choices, model appropriate behaviors, acknowledge the child when he/she engages in appropriate behavior, such as engaging and extending conversations, taking turns, and narrating play activities (Pierce & Schreibman, 1995). For example, Harper et al. (2008) taught typically developing peers to use pivotal response training with two 8- and 9-year-old boys with ASD. The peers were taught to prompt and reinforce the child with ASD to initiate social interactions and to take turns.

Laushey and Heflin (2000) evaluated a class-wide peer-buddy intervention "stay, play, and talk" (English, Goldstein, Kaczmarek, & Shafer, 1996) to teach two 5-year-old boys with ASD and their typically developing classmates to play together during free play center time. The children in the class were assigned to a peer buddy for the day. Peers were taught to stay in the same center as their buddy, to play with their buddy, and to talk to their buddy. Data were collected on four social and play behaviors: requesting toys, gaining a peer's attention appropriately, taking turns, and looking at the person who is speaking. Results showed that the children with ASD engaged in more appropriate social interactions with their peers during the "stay, play, and talk" intervention. Teachers reported that the intervention was feasible to implement in their classrooms and that the children with and without disabilities appeared to enjoy the peer-buddy system.

Katz and Girolametto (2013) evaluated PMI using a small triad approach across three inclusive daycare classrooms. In each classroom, a child with ASD and two typically developing peers participated. Observations of social interaction (initiations and responses) were conducted during free play centers. The peers were taught to initiate and maintain play interactions with the child with ASD. Results showed that the number of social interactions between the child with ASD and both his/her peers increased during the PMI condition for children in all three classrooms and maintained during 1-month follow-up observations.

PMI is one of the most successful approaches for improving social skills in children with ASD (Bass & Mulick, 2007; Chang & Locke, 2016). Some research suggests that PMI is more effective in teaching social responding rather than social initiations (Rogers, 2000). One reason for this could be that initiating social interaction is a more difficult skill than responding for children with ASD (Conroy, Boyd, Asmus, & Madera, 2007; Katz & Girolametto, 2015). A second explanation may be that it is more difficult to teach peers to provide opportunities for a child with ASD to initiate than it is to teach peers to provide opportunities for the child with ASD to respond (Bass & Mulick, 2007).

Play Skills Peers are natural models of developmentally appropriate play behaviors. Typically developing children play with one another, engage in novel play behaviors, and develop creative themes to guide their play (Kamps et al., 2002; Mason et al., 2014). In contrast, children with ASD often play alone and engage with materials in a repetitive fashion (Chang & Locke, 2016; Mason et al., 2014). Intervention is often required to increase interaction during play between children with ASD and their peers and to create a larger repertoire of play behaviors. To promote maintenance and generalization of play skills, it makes sense to have peers model and teach play behaviors, rather than having adults teach these play behaviors to children with ASD and hoping those play skills transfer to peers. PMI has been used to teach toy play (e.g., Kamps et al., 2014; Odom & Strain, 1986; Pierce & Schreibman, 1997), to teach toy sharing (e.g., Odom & Watts, 1991), and to teach cooperative play (e.g., Knapczyk, 1989).

Pierce and Schreibman (1997) implemented PMI to increase cooperative play skills of two 10-year-old boys with ASD. Each boy with ASD was paired with a typically developing 10-year-old-boy. Peers were taught to model appropriate play and conversation behaviors, to praise the child with ASD when he engaged in appropriate play behaviors, to encourage and extend conversations (e.g., "What is your favorite food?"), to take turns with the child with ASD, and to narrate play (e.g., "I'm going to cook the pizza."). The authors measured play behaviors including play initiation (e.g., "Let's play blocks"), toy engagement (e.g., driving a toy car), and coordinated joint attention (e.g., alternating eye gaze from toy to peer). They found that the cooperative play and social interaction behaviors improved with the PMI intervention and maintained at a 2-month follow-up assessment.

Peer Training

A critical component of PMI is the selection and training of peers. While some studies have matched peers to the age and gender of the focus child (e.g., Roeyers, 1996), other studies have found positive outcomes when gender (e.g., Odom & Watts, 1991) or age (e.g., Owen-DeSchryver, Carr, Cale, & Blakeley-Smith, 2008) were not matched. Instead, key considerations for selecting peers are their social and communication skills, their ability to follow directions, and their attendance record (Bass & Mulick, 2007; Chan et al., 2009).

Although the format and content of peer training vary across the research base, several themes have emerged. Most studies trained peers separately from children with ASD (Chang & Locke, 2016). In other cases, target social skills were taught to the focus child and the participating peers simultaneously (Strasberger & Ferreri, 2014). Following this initial training, the focus child and his/her peers were encouraged to use those new social skills in the context of classroom activities and routines (Laushey & Heflin, 2000). Some peer training sessions have been conducted immediately prior to PMI sessions (Ganz & Flores, 2008). In these cases, the training sessions may serve to "prime" target peer behaviors.

Peers have been trained in various formats. Some studies trained peers in a single session (e.g., Strasberger & Ferreri, 2014), while others held multiple training sessions (Storey, Smith, & Strain, 1993). It may be beneficial to hold multiple training sessions in order to ensure peers are fluent in implementing the target strategies (Bass & Mulick, 2007). For example, Katz and Girolametto (2013) held five 30-min social skill lessons in a separate room at the child care center with the focus child with ASD and the two participating peers. During the first two sessions, the instructor read a book about friendship, and the children created a puppet show to summarize what had happened in the story. In the third and fourth sessions, the instructor provided written and verbal instruction on how to initiate and maintain play. Children then role played these play interaction behaviors and received coaching and feedback.

Across these varied peer training formats and structures, there are common, recommended training components based on direct instruction. First, most research studies have used direct verbal instruction to explain the rationale and importance of the intervention in combination with other strategies (Chan et al., 2009). For example, Kalyva and Avramidis (2005) taught 25 preschoolers to participate in the "Circle of Friends" curriculum with five children with ASD. During the training the teachers explained to the peers (without the focus child present) that the purpose of the program was to help the child learn to ask a friend to play.

In some studies, peers were given an overview of ASD to help them anticipate behaviors the focus child might engage in and to help set expectations for interactions. Roeyers (1996) incorporated videos of three children with ASD into the peer training session to expose peers to children with varying levels of support needs. Rather than focusing on a specific disability or child, Laushey and Heflin (2000) conducted a 15-min lesson with the entire kindergarten classroom prior to the PMI. In the lesson children were asked to reflect on their own unique characteristics, to consider that all people share similarities and have differences, and to understand the importance of interacting with people who have different characteristics.

Teachers may engage the peers in discussion to brainstorm ways to initiate interaction with the focus child, topics to discuss with the child, or toys and games to play with the child. Though discussion has most commonly been applied with children who are in elementary school or older (e.g., Brady, Shores, McEvoy, Ellis, & Fox, 1987; Lee et al., 2007; Thiemann & Goldstein, 2004), some studies (e.g., Odom & Strain, 1986) have implemented discussion with preschool-aged peers.

Peer training also typically includes live or video modeling of strategies. Storey et al. (1993) taught 16 typically developing preschoolers to initiate social interaction with a child with ASD. The teachers first verbally described how the peers should obtain the focus child's attention (e.g., "One way to get your friend's attention is to hand him a toy and say, 'here'"). The teachers then modeled how to get a child's attention (e.g., "Watch me share with Bobby. First I get his attention by handing him a toy and saying, 'here'"). Strasberger and Ferreri (2014) used video modeling to teach peers to use a communication device with a child with ASD. Following a model of the appropriate behaviors, many studies incorporate opportunities for practice and role play. This allows the peer to practice the skills in a simulated environment and to receive performance feedback before interacting with the focus child. Role play also allows the peers to encounter and work through potential challenges, such as an unresponsive focus child (Bass & Mulick, 2007). Kamps et al. (2014) trained kindergarten and first-grade peers to initiate and respond to social interactions with children with ASD during structured play activities. The training sessions included verbal instruction of target social interaction skills followed by child and peer practice sessions with adult feedback. During the practice sessions, the adults prompted the peers to use the previously taught skills and provided reinforcement and feedback immediately after each session.

In addition to training peers prior to PMI, teachers should prepare the environment to support peers' use of target strategies and to oversee peer behavior during the PMI sessions. Preparing the environment may include presenting visual cues to remind the peers of the behaviors they should be implementing. For example, Storey et al. (1993) placed posters of photos that illustrate children engaging in target social skills around the room. In some studies, teachers delivered verbal or gestural cues to the peers to prompt them to engage in specific behaviors (Goldstein, Schneider, & Thiemann, 2007). For instance, a teacher might approach a peer and quietly say, "Now would be a good time to ask Timmy to play blocks with you."

Teachers should offer praise and reinforcement for desired peer behaviors and offer redirection and error correction when peers stray from the target strategies.

Praise may be sufficient for some children without the addition of a tangible reinforcer (Kamps et al., 2002). In other cases, peers may benefit from token economy systems in which points are earned for engaging in desired behaviors during the PMI session. Odom and Strain (1986) designed a token economy system in which peers earned happy faces on an index card each time the peer responded to an extended focus child's social interaction. Once each circle on the card was filled with a happy face, the peer could exchange the card for a backup reinforcer, such as a sticker, a crayon, or a small toy.

PMI requires careful planning in terms of peer selection and peer training. Selecting peers based on their history of interacting with the focus child with ASD, their attendance, and their social and communication skills is a critical first step. While peer training can take multiple sessions and carefully planned instruction, research shows that a variety of training components can be successfully applied to teaching peers to implement strategies with children with ASD.

PMI Strategies

Peers have been taught to implement many different strategies within PMI. The most common strategies include (a) peer proximity, (b) peer initiation, (c) prompting and reinforcing, and (d) comprehensive programs (DiSalvo & Oswald, 2002; Watkins et al., 2015). Below we provide an overview of each of these strategies along with recent research example.

Proximity A hallmark of inclusive education and a prerequisite for PMI is proximity between children with ASD and typically developing children. Proximity interventions do not usually require specific peer training, but do require careful planning and implementation. In proximity-based PMI, the teacher carefully arranges the environment so that peers with good social, communication, and/or play skills are in the same area or group as the focus child. Preparing the environment in this way is designed to promote social interaction between the selected peers and the focus child with ASD. In addition to placing peers in proximity of the child with ASD, the teacher also alters the materials or context. For example, the focus child and his/her peers may be placed in an area of the preschool classroom with the focus child's favorite activities. The presence of preferred materials has been shown to create more opportunities for social interaction (Koegel et al., 2012; Koegel, Kim, Koegel, & Schwartzman, 2013).

For example, Roeyers (1996) paired children with ASD with peers of similar age, height, and sex in an effort to reduce social isolation. Using verbal instruction and role play, the peers were taught ways to get the attention of the focus child and ways to respond if the focus child engaged in challenging behavior. Following this training, the peers and the focus children were taken to a playroom with toys and told to do their best to play together. No additional feedback or prompting was provided to the peers. Results showed that peer proximity led to increased responsiveness, increased time spent in social interactions, and more frequent social initiations. Although this study highlights the benefits of peer proximity, it is important to note that while proximity is always a component of PMI, additional peer training and supports may be necessary to lead to positive outcomes for the child with ASD (e.g., Watkins et al., 2015).

Peer Initiation In order to teach social skills to students with ASD, teachers and professionals can train typically developing peers to initiate conversation and play activities with their friends with ASD. Peer training for initiation includes direct instruction, modeling, prompting, and reinforcing of appropriate social interaction format. Various types of peer training can be implemented depending on the age group of students, and additional cues for performing their roles (e.g., picture card, script, self-monitoring sheet) can be provided as well.

Ganz and Flores (2008) examined the effects of the use of visual strategies with preschool children with ASD and their peers in a play group setting. They trained four typically developing peers to initiate talk and play by introducing peer instruction cards. The peer instruction cards included the following components: (a) to get your friends' attention, talk to him and hand him a toy, (b) play with the toys your friend is playing with, and (c) when your friend talks, you say something too. Peers were asked to verbally repeat and role play the instruction with an adult. The students with ASD were also trained to verbally interact with peers by using individualized scripts (e.g., "Do you see the purple fish?," "Let's decorate the cake."). During the intervention phase, the peer instruction card was presented on the wall in the play area, and peers were reminded of the directions on the card during 5-min play sessions. Results showed that PMI with visual scripts led to increases in the frequency of communication and in the use of context-related statements for the children with ASD.

Prompting and Reinforcement Peer prompting refers to offering a physical, verbal, or gestural prompt to guide students with ASD to engage in desired social behaviors. For example, in order to promote verbal requesting skills of a child with ASD in a free play setting, the peer can be trained to deliver a verbal prompt (e.g., "Do you want to play with Legos™? You can say, 'I want Legos™'"). Peers can also be trained to provide reinforcement by responding to the focus child when the focus child makes an appropriate social interaction bid. Thus, PMI allows newly acquired target social skills to be met with natural social reinforcement including access to peer attention or access to preferred materials or activities. Creating opportunities for behaviors to meet natural sources of reinforcement is one of the most powerful tools we have for promoting maintenance of newly learned behaviors (Stokes & Baer, 1977).

Katz and Girolametto (2013) investigated the effects of PMI on social initiations and responses of preschoolers with ASD. First the researchers trained the teachers in strategies to support play and to provide performance feedback to peers during social interactions with the focus child. Then the researcher and teachers co-led five social skill training sessions for both the children with ASD and two peers. During these sessions the children were read a book which discussed ways of playing together and developing friendships. Following the book, the children were asked to reenact the story using puppets. After this training, the teacher supervised six play sessions in the classroom. During the play sessions, the teacher paired a focus child with a trained peer for 20 min of free play. At the beginning of the free play session, the teacher reviewed the desired social interaction behaviors using a communication board. The communication board included illustrations of a target social interaction behavior, such as initiation, responding, or turn-taking. During the play session, the teacher provided verbal prompts to peers as needed to encourage them to prompt or reinforce the focus child's social behaviors. For example, if no interaction between the children occurred, the teachers might say to the peer, "Joey is not playing with you. Ask him to help." The teacher also provided specific verbal praise to the peers when they initiated or responded to the focus child. Results showed that with PMI, social initiations and responses improved for all three preschoolers with ASD, maintained 4 weeks after the intervention, and generalized to untrained peers.

Comprehensive Intervention Wong et al. (2014) defined a comprehensive intervention model for autism as a coordinated set of practices with the goal of having a broad impact on learning and development associated with core features of ASD (p. 9). Comprehensive intervention models are based on a conceptual framework, include manualized procedures, state a recommended length of time and intensity with which the program should be implemented, and address many learning outcomes (Odom, Boyd, Hall, & Hume, 2009). Examples of comprehensive intervention models which have involved PMI include the LEAP model (Strain & Hoyson, 2000) and pivotal response training (Koegel et al., 2012).

One comprehensive intervention model which involves PMI is the LEAP (Learning Experiences and Alternative Program for Preschoolers and their Parents) program (Strain, Kohler, & Goldstein, 1996). Within the LEAP model, preschool-aged children with ASD are taught in an inclusive program with typically developing peers. In the LEAP model, peers are taught to model appropriate social behaviors, to take turns with children with ASD, to encourage and provide social reinforcement to children with ASD, and to persist in attempts to engage and respond to children with ASD in their classroom (Kohler & Strain, 1999). Results of a recent randomized control trial study (Strain & Bovey, 2011) found significant differences in cognitive, social, communication skills among children in the LEAP program versus children in the control group. Positive social outcomes of this comprehensive intervention model included increased social participation, ability to generalize learned behaviors across settings and time periods, and greater frequency of social interactions.

In summary, PMI is an effective model for promoting positive social interaction, communication, and play behavior between young children with ASD and typically developing peers. Though PMI involves peers as the primary intervention agent, teachers and other adults are critically involved in planning the PMI intervention, in training and coaching peers, and in monitoring the effectiveness of the intervention.

How to Implement Peer-Mediated Interventions

Although peers are the interventionists in PMI, adults play a critical role in this intervention as well. The adult's role is generally "behind the scenes" as they plan, implement, and evaluate PMI. That is, the adult identifies peers who would be effective interventionists, designs and implements lessons to teach the peers how to implement PMI, coaches and provides feedback to the peers during PMI, and monitors the focus child's progress toward the target outcomes. Below we outline interventionist behaviors for planning, implementing, and evaluating PMI.

Planning

Interventionists are, by definition, interested in changing behaviors and may be inclined to jump right in to PMI. However, before implementing PMI, the interventionist must take time to carefully plan the design and the implementation of PMI. Before implementing PMI, the adult interventionist should address the six questions in Box 7.1

Box 7.1 Planning for Peer-Mediated Intervention
Questions to ask during PMI planning

1. What skills will be targeted using PMI?
2. Where and when will PMI take place?
3. How will peers be selected?
4. How will peers be trained?
5. How will peers be provided feedback?
6. How will PMI be evaluated?

What Skills Will Be Targeted Using PMI? Though PMI has been shown to improve a variety of target behaviors, the target behaviors with the most research support are social interaction and play skills. When selecting a target behavior, be sure the new behavior is developmentally appropriate and socially important for the child and the child's family. One way to determine what skills are developmentally appropriate is to administer developmental assessments, such as the Hawaii Early Learning Profile for Preschoolers (HELP), the Battelle Developmental Inventory, or the Preschool Language Scale with the focus child. It may also be helpful to observe the social interaction and play behaviors of typically developing peers. This can be done anecdotally or with an ecological congruence assessment (see Table 7.1). This allows the interventionist to compare the focus child's skills to those of his/her peers

Table 7.1 Sample ecological congruence assessment

Activity/routine	Observation	Interpretation	Notes
Arrival	Is the child doing the same thing as the peers?	Does the child require assistance in this activity?	
	What are the peers doing?	Potential target behaviors include:	
	What is the focus child doing?		
Free play centers	Is the child doing the same thing as the peers?	Does the child require assistance in this activity?	
	What are the peers doing?	Potential target behaviors include:	
	What is the focus child doing?		

in order to identify developmentally appropriate areas for improvement. Interventionists should always consult with the child's family to determine what behaviors the family values and would like their child to improve.

The interventionist should collect pre-intervention (baseline) data on the focus child's use of the target skills before implementing PMI. This will enable the interventionist to select an achievable goal and to set the stage for evaluating the effects of PMI on the target behavior. Collecting baseline data involves assessing the child at his/her present state, before presenting any form of intervention. The data collection process does not need to be complicated or time-consuming in any way. Simply tallying the occurrence of a behavior or timing its duration may be sufficient. The interventionist can collect baseline data by observing the focus child and making a mark each time the child engages in the target behavior. When the target behavior is a response to a peer's behavior, it can be helpful to take data on both the peer and the focus child's behaviors. For example, if the target behavior is responding to peer initiations, then the number of initiations the peer makes should be counted along with the number of the focus child's responses to those initiations. These can then be converted to a percentage of initiations with responding by dividing the number of responses by the total number of initiations (see Table 7.2). Because responding can vary from day to day, the interventionist should collect baseline data across several days to obtain a more accurate picture of the child's pre-intervention behaviors. Baseline is the starting point before PMI has been implemented, so expect low levels of the target behavior.

Where and When Will PMI Take Place? After the target behavior has been chosen, the interventionist must plan where and when PMI will take place. The activity and setting should be based on where the child would naturally engage in the target behavior. If the target behavior is imitating peers' gross motor play behaviors, then the playground would be a logical setting to conduct PMI. If the target behavior is requesting preferred materials, then conducting PMI during snack or free play would be appropriate.

The interventionist should also examine the child's daily schedule to determine when motivation to engage in the target behavior would be high. For example, if

Table 7.2 Sample PMI data sheet for responding to peer initiations

Date	Peer initiations	Child responses	Percent of initiations with responses (%)
Monday March 10	///////	///	43
Wednesday March 12	////////	/////	62
Monday March 17	////////	///////	87

PMI is being used to help the focus child request preferred toys from peers, then it would make sense to hold the PMI sessions at a time when the child has not had recent access to their favorite toys so that they will be more motivated to ask for the toys. Similarly, if the target behavior is imitating peers' gross motor play behaviors on the playground, then it makes sense to pick a time when the child has not had recent access to gross motor activities.

Once the setting and time for implementing PMI have been determined, the interventionist should prepare the environment to promote successful peer interactions. For young children, selecting predictable routines within which to implement PMI may help to facilitate social interaction with peers (Prizant et al., 2000). The physical environment should be structured to allow children to access materials and be in close proximity to one another but with sufficient space to move, interact, and play appropriately. Including the focus child's preferred toys or activities will also help increase motivation to stay, play, and interact in the designated area.

How Will Peers Be Selected? Selecting peers is one of the most important parts of PMI. Interventionists should consider peers who have good, consistent school/daycare attendance, strong social skills, age-appropriate language skills, who usually follows directions, and who may have a history or interest in interacting or have positive previous interactions with the focus child (Bass & Mulick, 2007; Battaglia & Radley, 2014; Chan et al., 2009; Chang & Locke, 2016; Kamps et al., 2014; Katz & Girolametto, 2013; Mason et al., 2014; Watkins et al., 2015). Peers can be the same age as the focus child or older than the focus child (Zhang & Wheeler, 2011). However, to provide multiple opportunities for interaction between the focus child and the peers, it makes sense to select peers who are in the same class as the focus child. Research studies have found that finding shared topics of interest may help create more opportunities for positive social interactions between the child with ASD and his/her peers (Koegel et al., 2012, 2013). If the interventionist is consulting or providing related services in a different classroom or center, they should ask the teacher for nomination of peers. The teacher will be familiar with the peers' attendance patterns, social skills, communication skills, and compliance with directions. The interventionist should also obtain parent permission in advance, particularly if the peer will miss instructional time in the classroom to participate in PMI Box 7.2.

Box 7.2 Selecting Peers

- Strong social skills
- Age-appropriate language skills
- Follows directions
- Good attendance
- Positive history with focus child

How Will Peers Be Trained? Once you have selected the outcome(s) targeted for intervention and the peers to be involved in the intervention, it is time to plan for and design the peer training procedures. This involves deciding what will be taught during the training, selecting instructional strategies, and determining when peers will be trained, by whom, and in what setting. In some cases, beginning the training with an overview of ASD may be helpful for teaching peers what to expect when they interact with the focus child. For younger children, it may be helpful to be specific to the focus child, rather than talking in broad or abstract terms. The interventionist may conduct a discussion session during which peers consider their own strengths and areas of growth, as well as strengths and areas of growth for the focus child. For example, the interventionist can say, "Sean loves playing with Legos™. He can build really tall towers!" The interventionist can then ask the peers to brainstorm their own areas of strength, "What are some things that you do well?" Then the interventionist can focus the discussion on areas for growth, "Sean sometimes needs help talking to his friends, especially asking his friends to play with him. What are some things that you need help doing?" In this way, the interventionist is focused on developing empathy between the peers and the focus child, rather than taking an approach that solely focuses on the differences or deficits of the focus child.

Following this overview, the interventionist can help prepare the peers for what they should do or say to help the focus child. Research shows peers can be effectively trained using a combination of verbal instruction, discussion, modeling, and role play. Verbal instruction should include a clear statement of the rationale for the intervention and why the peer intervention is important. The interventionist may provide direct instruction and tell the peers exactly what to do. For example, "You can help Sean learn how to talk to his friends by asking Sean to play Legos™ with you during center time. You can say, 'Let's play Legos™, Sean!'" Alternatively, the interventionist may incorporate a discussion-based approach. In this approach, the interventionist can ask peers to brainstorm ways to initiate social interaction or play with the focus child, topics to discuss with the focus child, or activities or toys to engage in with the focus child.

Following verbal instruction or discussion, it is critical to show the peers the behaviors they will engage in as part of PMI by modeling the behaviors. The interventionist can model the behaviors, ask peers to model the behaviors, or show video examples of children engaged in the target behaviors. Peers should also be given an opportunity to practice or role play. The interventionist should provide feedback including behavior-specific praise of behaviors the peers engaged in correctly and corrective feedback for errors the peers made. For example, "You did a great job walking over to Sean and asking him to play with you. Remember to give him a few seconds to answer you before you begin playing."

Interventionists will need to determine when the peer training will take place. Peers can be trained in advance of the PMI sessions, coached during the sessions, or a combination of these two. If the interventionist decides to provide PMI training in advance, the time between the training and the actual PMI session should be minimized. If training is conducted well in advance of the PMI session, the interventionist should provide a brief booster session to help prime the peer behaviors to be used in PMI. This could be a quick role play session with performance feedback or simply a verbal reminder of what the peer should do during the session.

It may also be helpful to offer cues during the PMI sessions. Using visual supports to prompt peer behaviors is one way to provide cues without disrupting the interactions between peers and the focus child. Visual supports could include a picture schedule illustrating the sequence of behaviors the peer should engage in, a written script, or a reminder card with a picture of two children interacting (see Fig. 7.1). For some children, more intrusive prompts may be necessary for them to implement PMI correctly. In those cases, the interventionist may verbally cue the peer to engage in a specific behavior with the focus child. For example, the interventionist may lean over to the peer and say, "Remember to stay, play, and talk with Charlie during centers." A list of initial training procedures is provided in Box 7.3.

Box 7.3 Initial Training Procedures

- Overview of ASD and the focus child
- Purpose of PMI
- Clearly define what peers will do
- Model peer behaviors
- Role play and feedback

How Will Peers Be Provided with Feedback? It is important to remember that just like adult interventionists, children may require ongoing support and feedback as they gain experience implementing PMI. This means the interventionist should observe all PMI sessions and provide praise when peers implement PMI well, prompts to remind peers of what they should do during the sessions, and error correction when the peers make a mistake during the session. Providing behavior-specific praise to peers will help peers learn exactly what they are doing well and what they should continue to do during PMI. For example, rather than making a general praise statement such as "Nice work, Jorge," the interventionist would describe exactly what Jorge did well by saying, "Jorge, you did a great job showing Charlie how to play with the blocks today!" For some children, it may also be helpful to include additional reinforcement, such as tokens that the peer can exchange for a backup reward. For example, the interventionist may ask the peer to initiate

Fig. 7.1 Sample visual supports

with the focus child ten times during the session. Each time the peer initiates, the teacher places a sticker on a note card. Once the card has ten stickers, the peer can pick a prize from the class treasure box or can earn a privilege, such as being the class line leader or feeding the class pet.

If the peer does make a mistake, the error correction procedure should be brief and should include a more intrusive prompt or model of what the peer should do. For instance, "Jorge, remember to make sure Charlie is looking at you before you ask him a question." When the peer corrects the error, even with a prompt, he/she should receive specific praise from the interventionist.

How Will PMI Be Evaluated? The first step in evaluating any intervention is to create a measurable goal for the target behavior. A measurable goal includes a clear description of the target behavior, the conditions or supports that should be in place for the behavior, and the criteria for determining when the objective has been met. For example, "Charlie will vocally respond within 5 s to 75% of peer initiations during a 20-min free play session for 5 consecutive days." The behavior is "vocally respond within 5 s," the condition is "during a 20-min free play session," and the criterion is 75% of initiations for 5 consecutive days. This way, the interventionist can easily determine when Charlie has met his goal.

Once PMI is introduced, the interventionist will use the same data collection procedures used in baseline to monitor the child's response to PMI. It may not be feasible, or necessary, to collect data on the child's behavior for every PMI session. Instead, the interventionist may select 1–3 days per week to monitor the child's progress toward the goal.

To interpret the collected data, it is important to plot the data on a graph. This allows stakeholders to see changes in the focus child's behavior (see Fig. 7.2). Graphs can lead to one of three data-driven decisions: (a) the focus child's target skills are improving, so continue implementing PMI, (b) it is difficult to determine if target skills are improving, so continue PMI until a pattern emerges, or (c) the child's target skills are not improving, so modify the PMI. If target skills are not improving, the interventionist should check to see if peers are implementing PMI

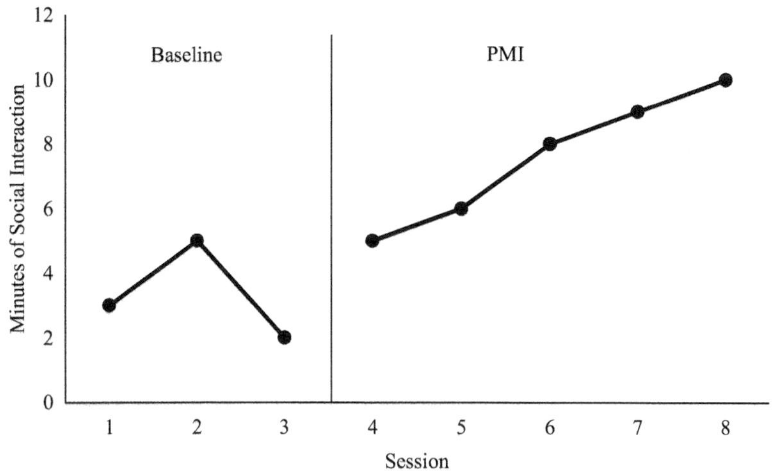

Fig. 7.2 Sample progress monitoring graph

accurately. If needed, the peers should be given a booster training session. If the peers are implementing PMI accurately, then the interventionist may need to adjust the timing and structure of the session to allow for more opportunities to practice the target skills, to include more preferred materials, or to occur at a different time of day or location. In some cases, the match between the peer and the focus child may not be strong. In that case, it may be important to select different peers who have a more positive history of social interaction with the focus child.

References

Bambara, L. M., Cole, C. L., Kunsch, C., Tsai, S., & Ayad, E. (2016). A peer-mediated intervention to improve the conversational skills of high school students with autism spectrum disorder. *Research in Autism Spectrum Disorders*, *27*, 29–43. https://doi.org/10.1016/j.rasd.2016.03.003

Banda, D. R., & Hart, S. L. (2010). Increasing peer-to-peer social skills through direct instruction of two elementary school girls with autism. *Journal of Research in Special Education Needs*, *10*, 124–132.

Bandura, A. (1989). Human agency in social cognitive theory. *American Psychologist*, *44*(9), 1175.

Barber, A. B., Saffo, R. W., Gilpin, A. T., Craft, L. D., & Goldstein, H. (2016). Peers as clinicians: Examining the impact of Stay Play Talk on social communication in young preschoolers with autism. *Journal of Communication Disorders*, *59*, 1–15. https://doi.org/10.1016/j.jcomdis.2015.06.009

Bass, J. D., & Mulick, J. A. (2007). Social play skill enhancement of children with autism using peers and siblings as therapists. *Psychology in the Schools*, *44*(7), 727–735. https://doi.org/10.1002/pits.20261

Battaglia, A. A., & Radley, K. C. (2014). Peer-mediated social skills training for children with autism spectrum disorder. *Beyond Behavior*, *23*, 4–13.

Boudreau, A. M., Corkum, P., Meko, K., & Smith, I. M. (2015). Peer-mediated pivotal response treatment for young children with autism spectrum disorders: A systematic review. *Canadian Journal of School Psychology, 30*, 218–235. https://doi.org/10.1177/0829573515581156

Brady, M. P., Shores, R. E., McEvoy, M. A., Ellis, D., & Fox, J. J. (1987). Increasing social interactions of severely handicapped autistic children. *Journal of Autism and Developmental Disorders, 17*, 375–390.

Carter, E. W., Cushing, L. S., Clark, N. M., & Kennedy, C. H. (2005). Effects of peer support interventions on students' access to the general curriculum and social interactions. *Research and Practice for Persons with Severe Disabilities, 30*, 15–25.

Carter, E. W., Moss, C. K., Asmus, J., Fesperman, E., Cooney, M., Brock, M. E., … Vincent, L. B. (2015). Promoting inclusion, social connections, and learning through peer support arrangements. *Teaching Exceptional Children, 48*(1), 9–18. https://doi.org/10.1177/0040059915594784

Chan, J. M., Lang, R., Rispoli, M., O'Reilly, M., Sigafoos, J., & Cole, H. (2009). Use of peer-mediated interventions in the treatment of autism spectrum disorders: A systematic review. *Research in Autism Spectrum Disorders, 3*, 876–889. https://doi.org/10.1016/j.rasd.2009.04.003

Chang, Y., & Locke, J. (2016). A systematic review of peer-mediated interventions for children with autism spectrum disorder. *Research in Autism Spectrum Disorders, 27*, 1–10.

Chung, K.-M., Reavis, S., Mosconi, M., Drewry, J., Matthews, T., & Tasse, M. J. (2007). Peer-mediated social skills training program for young children with high-functioning autism. *Research in Developmental Disabilities, 28*, 423–436.

Conroy, M. A., Boyd, B. A., Asmus, J. M., & Madera, D. (2007). A functional approach for ameliorating social skills deficits in young children with autism spectrum disorders. *Infants & Young Children, 20*, 242–254.

Disalvo, C. A., & Oswald, D. P. (2002). Peer-mediated interventions to increase the social interaction of children with autism: Consideration of peer expectancies. *Focus on Autism and Other Developmental Disabilities, 17*, 198–207. https://doi.org/10.1177/10883576020170040201

English, K., Goldstein, H., Kaczmarek, L., & Shafer, K. (1996). Buddy skills for preschoolers. *Teaching Exceptional Children, 28*, 62.

Fettig, A. (2013). *Peer-mediated instruction and intervention (PMII) fact sheet.* Chapel Hill, NC: The University of North Carolina, Frank Porter Graham Child Development Institute, The National Professional Development Center on Autism Spectrum Disorders.

Ganz, J. B., & Flores, M. M. (2008). Effects of the use of visual strategies in play groups for children with autism spectrum disorders and their peers. *Journal of Autism and Developmental Disorders, 38*, 926–940. https://doi.org/10.1007/s10803-007-0463-4

Goldstein, H., Schneider, N., & Thiemann, K. (2007). Peer-mediated social communication intervention: When clinical expertise informs treatment development and evaluation. *Topics in Language Disorders, 27*, 182–199.

Harper, C. B., Symon, J. B., & Frea, W. D. (2008). Recess is time-in: Using peers to improve social skills of children with autism. *Journal of Autism and Developmental Disorders, 38*, 815–826.

Hunt, P., Staub, D., Alwell, M., & Goetz, L. (1994). Achievement by all students within the context of cooperative learning groups. *Journal of the Association for Persons with Severe Handicaps, 19*, 290–301.

Kalyva, E., & Avramidis, E. (2005). Improving communication between children with autism and their peers through the 'circle of friends': A small-scale intervention study. *Journal of Applied Research in Intellectual Disabilities, 18*, 253–261.

Kamps, D., Royer, J., Dugan, E., Kravits, T., Gonzalez-Lopez, A., Garcia, J., & Kane, L. G. (2002). Peer training to facilitate social interaction for elementary students with autism and their peers. *Exceptional Children, 68*, 173–187. https://doi.org/10.1177/001440290206800202

Kamps, D., Thiemann-Bourque, K., Heitzman-Powell, L., Schwartz, I., Rosenberg, N., Mason, R., & Cox, S. (2014). A comprehensive peer network intervention to improve social communication of children with autism spectrum disorders: A randomized trial in kindergarten and first grade. *Journal of Autism and Developmental Disorders, 45*(6), 1809–1824. https://doi.org/10.1007/s10803-014-2340-2.

Kamps, D., Mason, R., Thiemann-Bourque, K., Feldmiller, S., Turcotte, A., & Miller, T. (2014). The use of peer networks to increase communicative acts of students with autism spectrum disorders. *Focus on Autism and Other Developmental Disabilities, 29*, 230–245.

Kamps, D. M., Barbetta, P. M., Leonard, B. R., & Delquadri, J. C. (1994). Classwide peer tutoring: An integration strategy to improve reading skills and promote peer interactions among students with autism and general education peers. *Journal of Applied Behavior Analysis, 27*, 49–61.

Kamps, D. M., Dugan, E., Potucek, J., & Collins, A. (1999). Effects of cross-age peer tutoring networks among students with autism and general education students. *Journal of Behavioral Education, 9*, 97–115.

Kamps, D. M., Kravits, T., Lopez, A. G., Kemmerer, K., Potucek, J., & Harrell, L. G. (1998). What do the peers think? Social validity of peer-mediated programs. *Education and Treatment of Children, 21*, 107–134.

Kamps, D. M., Leonard, B., Potucek, J., & Garrison-Harrell, L. (1995). Cooperative learning groups in reading: An integration strategy for students with autism and general classroom peers. *Behavioral Disorders, 28*, 89–109.

Katz, E., & Girolametto, L. (2013). Peer-mediated intervention for preschoolers with ASD implemented in early childhood education settings. *Topics in Early Childhood Special Education, 33*, 133–143. https://doi.org/10.1177/0271121413484972

Katz, E., & Girolametto, L. (2015). Peer-mediated intervention for pre-schoolers with ASD: Effects on responses and initiations. *International Journal of Speech-Language Pathology, 17*, 565–576. https://doi.org/10.3109/17549507.2015.1024166

Knapczyk, D. R. (1989). Peer-mediated training of cooperative play between special and regular class students in integrated play setting. *Education and Training in Mental Retardation, 24*, 255–265. Retrieved from http://www.jstor.org/stable/23878489

Koegel, R., Fredeen, R., Kim, S., Danial, J., Rubinstein, D., & Koegel, L. (2012). Using perseverative to improve interactions between adolescents with autism and their typical peers in school settings. *Journal of Positive Behavior Interventions, 14*, 133–141. https://doi.org/10.1177/1098300712437043

Koegel, R., Kim, S., Koegel, L., & Schwartzman, B. (2013). Improving socialization for high school students with ASD by using their preferred interests. *Journal of Autism and Developmental Disorders, 43*, 2121–2134. https://doi.org/10.1007/s10803-013-1765-3

Kohler, F. W., & Strain, P. S. (1999). Maximizing peer-mediated resources integrated preschool classrooms. *Topics in Early Childhood Special Education, 19*, 92–102. https://doi.org/10.1177/027112149901900203

Laushey, K. M., & Heflin, L. J. (2000). Enhancing social skills of kindergarten children with autism through the training of multiple peers as tutors. *Journal of Autism and Developmental Disorders, 30*, 183–193. https://doi.org/10.1023/a:1005558101038

Lee, S., Odom, S. L., & Loftin, R. (2007). Social engagement with peers and stereotypic behavior of children with autism. *Journal of Positive Behavior Interventions, 9*, 67–79.

Mason, R., Kamps, D., Turcotte, A., Cox, S., Feldmiller, S., & Miller, T. (2014). Peer mediation to increase communication and interaction at recess for students with autism spectrum disorders. *Research in Autism Spectrum Disorders, 8*, 334–344. https://doi.org/10.1016/j.rasd.2013.12.014

National Autism Center. (2015). *Findings and conclusions: National standards project, phase 2*. Randolph, MA: National Autism Center.

National Research Council. (2001). In C. Lord & J. P. McGee (Eds.), *Educating children with autism*. Washington, DC: National Academy Press.

Odom, S. L., Boyd, B. A., Hall, L. J., & Hume, K. (2009). Evaluation of comprehensive treatment models for individuals with autism spectrum disorders. *Journal of Autism and Developmental Disorders, 40*(4), 425–436. https://doi.org/10.1007/s10803-009-0825-1

Odom, S. L., & Strain, P. S. (1986). A comparison of peer-initiation and teacher-antecedent interventions for promoting reciprocal social interaction of autistic preschoolers. *Journal of Applied Behavior Analysis, 19*, 59–71.

Odom, S. L., & Watts, E. (1991). Reducing teacher prompts in peer-mediated interventions for young children with autism. *The Journal of Special Education, 25*, 26–43.

Owen-DeSchryver, J. S., Carr, E. G., Cale, S. I., & Blakeley-Smith, A. (2008). Promoting social interactions between students with autism spectrum disorders and their peers in inclusive school settings. *Focus on Autism and Other Developmental Disabilities, 23*, 15–28.

Pierce, K., & Schreibman, L. (1995). Increasing complex social behaviors in children with autism: Effects of peer-implemented pivotal response training. *Journal of Applied Behavior Analysis, 28*, 285–295.

Pierce, K., & Schreibman, L. (1997). Multiple peer use of pivotal response training to increase social behaviors of classmates with autism: Results from trained and untrained peers. *Journal of Applied Behavior Analysis, 30*, 157–160.

Prizant, B. M., Wetherby, A. M., & Rydell, P. J. (2000). Communication intervention issues for children with autism spectrum disorders. In A. M. Wetherby, B. M. Prizant, A. M. Wetherby, B. M. Prizant (Eds.), *Autism spectrum disorders: A transactional developmental perspective* (pp. 193–224). Baltimore, MD, US: Paul H Brookes Publishing.

Radley, K. C., Dart, E. H., Furlow, C. M., & Ness, E. J. (2015). Peer-mediated discrete trial training within a school setting. *Research in Autism Spectrum Disorders, 9*, 53–67. https://doi.org/10.1016/j.rasd.2014.10.001

Roeyers, H. (1996). The influence of nonhandicapped peers on the social interactions of children with a pervasive developmental disorder. *Journal of Autism and Developmental Disorders, 26*, 303–320. https://doi.org/10.1007/BF02172476

Rogers, S. J. (2000). Interventions that facilitate socialization in children with autism. *Journal of Autism and Developmental Disorders, 30*, 399–409.

Schleien, S. J., Mustonen, T., & Rynders, J. E. (1995). Participation of children with autism and nondisabled peers in a cooperatively structured community art program. *Journal of Autism and Developmental Disorders, 25*, 397–413.

Stokes, T. F., & Baer, D. M. (1977). An implicit technology of generalization. *Journal of Applied Behavior Analysis, 10*, 349–367.

Storey, K., Smith, D. J., & Strain, P. S. (1993). Use of classroom assistants and peer-mediated intervention to increase integration in preschool settings. *Exceptionality, 4*, 1–16.

Strain, P. S., & Bovey, E. I. (2011). Randomized, controlled trial of the LEAP model of early intervention for young children with autism spectrum disorders. *Topics in Early Childhood Special Education, 31*, 133–154. https://doi.org/10.1177/0271121411408740

Strain, P. S., & Hoyson, M. (2000). The need for longitudinal, intensive social skill intervention: LEAP follow-up outcomes for children with autism. *Topics in Early Childhood Special Education, 20*, 116–122.

Strain, P. S., Kohler, F. W., & Goldstein, H. (1996). LEAP: Peer-mediated intervention for young children with autism. In E. Hibbs & P. Jensen (Eds.), *Psychosocial treatments for child and adolescent disorders* (pp. 573–587). Washington, DC: American Psychological Association.

Strain, P. S., Shores, R. E., & Timm, M. A. (1977). Effects of peer social initiations on the behavior of withdrawn preschool children. *Journal of Applied Behavior Analysis, 10*, 289–298.

Strasberger, S. K., & Ferreri, S. J. (2014). The effects of peer assisted communication application training on the communicative and social behaviors of children with autism. *Journal of Developmental and Physical Disabilities, 26*, 513–526.

Thiemann, K. S., & Goldstein, H. (2004). Effects of peer training and written text cueing on social communication of school-age children with pervasive developmental disorder. *Journal of Speech, Language, and Hearing Research, 47*, 126–144.

Trembath, D., Balandin, S., Togher, L., & Stancliffe, R. J. (2009). Peer-mediated teaching and augmentative and alternative communication for preschool-aged children with autism. *Journal of Intellectual and Developmental Disability, 34*, 173–186.

Watkins, L., O'Reilly, M., Kuhn, M., Gevarter, C., Lancioni, G. E., Sigafoos, J., & Lang, R. (2015). A review of peer-mediated social interaction interventions for students with autism in inclusive settings. *Journal of Developmental Disorder*, *45*, 1070–1083. https://doi.org/10.1007/s10803-014-2264-x

Wong, C., Odom, S. L., Hume, K., Cox, A. W., Fettig, A., Kucharczyk, S., … Schultz, T. R. (2014). *Evidence-based practices for children, youth, and young adults with autism spectrum disorder*. Chapel Hill, NC: The University of North Carolina/Frank Porter Graham Child Development Institute/Autism Evidence-Based Practice Review Group.

Zhang, J., & Wheeler, J. J. (2011). A meta-analysis of peer-mediated interventions for young children with autism spectrum disorders. *Education and Training in Autism and Developmental Disabilities*, *46*, 62–77.

Chapter 8
The Power of Parents: Parent-Implemented Interventions for Young Children with Autism

Parents play a critical role in their child's development. As parents coo and smile at their infant, the infant is exposed to the reciprocal nature of social interaction. As parents point to something flying above them and say "Bird!" the toddler learns to associate the word "bird" with the flying creature. Indeed, young children's social-emotional and language development are greatly influenced through these daily interactions with their parents (Hart & Risley, 1995). Typically developing children and their parents may be able to create these learning opportunities with ease and require little, if any, external assistance. Yet, children with ASD often require explicit instruction to develop social interaction and communication skills. Such intentional and explicit instruction may not already be within parents' skill sets.

Parent-implemented intervention refers to at least one primary caregiver being taught by a professional to serve as an interventionist for their child (Beaudoin, Sébire, & Couture, 2014; Hong, Ganz, Neely, Gerow, & Ninci, 2016). Parent-implemented intervention is based on the theory that changing parent behavior can lead to changes in child behavior (Kashinath, Woods, & Goldstein, 2006). Parent-implemented intervention is cost-effective (Wainer & Ingersoll, 2015) and usually non-intensive instruction that is implemented within everyday activities and routines (McConachie & Diggle, 2007). Parent-implemented intervention has been shown to be beneficial for the child with ASD and also for the entire family unit. When parents implement interventions, their children can access intervention at a very young age (Hancock & Kaiser, 2002; Wetherby & Prizant, 1992), which, in turn, can lead to responsive parent-child interactions and improved language development (Siller, Hutman, & Sigman, 2013).

Parent-implemented interventions have been shown to improve outcomes for young children with ASD. When parents implement interventions, the child is able to access learning opportunities in their natural environment (e.g., home, community settings) and may be able to benefit from intervention beyond the clinical

M.H. Charlop et al., *Play and Social Skills for Children with Autism Spectrum Disorder*, Evidence-Based Practices in Behavioral Health,
https://doi.org/10.1007/978-3-319-72500-0_8

treatment setting (Koegel, Bimbela, & Schreibman, 1996). Furthermore, when parents and professionals implement interventions consistently, children are able to acquire new skills more efficiently and successfully (Kaiser & Hancock, 2003).

Background and Theoretical Constructs

Family-Centered Approach

When a pebble is tossed into the center of a pond, a small splash is made, and a small ripple of water develops. This small ripple gradually travels from the center of the pond all the way to the pond's edges. Though the pebble entered only one spot of the pond, the entire pond was impacted. Like the pebble in the pond, when something occurs with one family member, all family members become affected through an interconnected system. This is known as family systems theory (Bowen, 1974) and is a foundation for a family-centered approach to intervention.

To observe the family as an interconnected system, let's examine the communication interactions between parents and their children with ASD. Children with ASD often have difficulty initiating and responding to social interactions. As a result, a child with ASD may not respond to his/her parents' bids for social interaction. When parents' bids for social interaction are unsuccessful, they will be less likely to make social bids in the future. Thus, the number and quality of parent-child interactions remain low or may even decrease. These limited interactions can lead to parents feeling stress and even feeling disconnected from their child. Simultaneously, the child remains socially and communicatively isolated from the family (Zaidman-Zait et al., 2014). However, when parents are taught specific interventions to gain their child's attention and to interact with their child, the child will be more likely to respond, and the parents' social interaction bids will be met with positive social interaction (Norton & Drew, 1994). This strengthens, or reinforces, parents' attempts to interact with their child, and parents will be more likely to initiate interaction in the future. More social bids from the parent mean more opportunities for the child to practice and improve their social interaction skills (Shire, Gulsrud, & Kasari, 2016). In addition to the development of reciprocal social interactions, parents have reported less stress and more confidence once they are equipped with the tools and strategies they need to help their child (Cidav, Marcus, & Mandell, 2012).

Family systems theory shows us that when we changed the parents' behavior, we also changed the child's behavior as well as the relationships between parent and child. Since the early 1990s, the Division for Early Childhood of the Council for Exceptional Children has recognized the family-centered approach as an ideal early childhood intervention model (Odom, McLean, Johnson, & LaMontagne, 1995). In this model, the contribution of other family members impacts the achievement of the children (Bott, 1994). In alignment with the family-centered approach, Part C of the Individuals with Disabilities Education Act (IDEA, 2004) requires that early intervention services focus on family support through consultation, training, and coaching. Involving parents in early intervention for ASD is critical (National Research Council [NRC], 2001).

Early Intervention

Parent-implemented interventions may be particularly beneficial for young children with or at risk for ASD. Research shows that children's short- and long-term outcomes improve with early intervention services (Diggle, McConachie, & Randle, 2003; NRC, 2001; Smith, Klorman, & Mruzek, 2015) which address the core features of autism (social skills, communication skills, restrictive and repetitive patterns of behaviors and interests; *Diagnostic and Statistical Manual of Mental Disorders* [5th ed.; *DSM-5*; American Psychiatric Association, 2013]). Unfortunately, many families experience difficulty in accessing early intensive intervention services (Rivard et al., 2017). The Individuals with Disabilities Education Act (IDEA, 2004) requires that early intervention services be provided to children with disabilities between birth and 3 years of age. Once the child turns 3 years, the local education agency (typically the local public schools) takes over providing intervention services. However, for those infants and toddlers with developmental delays or ASD, services are often brief with as few as 1 h of direct intervention per week (IDEA Infant and Toddler Coordinators Association, 2016). To compound this issue, there is a critical shortage of early intervention specialists across the United States (Edwards & Gallagher, 2016). One way to address the shortage of early intervention services is through parent training. By providing parents with knowledge and skills in early intervention strategies, children can gain additional exposure to intervention (Hoffman, 2016).

Promoting Generalization and Maintenance of Learning

Children with ASD who receive early intensive behavioral intervention have been shown to have better outcomes (Estes et al., 2015). However, often these intensive behavioral interventions are provided in highly structured clinical settings with little to no carryover to life outside the clinic. In some cases, parents may be unaware of what interventions are being implemented with their child and thus unable to continue to implement those interventions outside of the clinic. In other cases, parents may actually be using practices that conflict with the intervention. This disconnect between the clinic setting and the child's natural environment can be detrimental to child outcomes (Cosbey & Muldoon, 2017).

Teaching parents to implement effective interventions with their child outside of clinical settings is a critical component of early autism intervention (Wetherby et al., 2014). We know from decades of behavioral research that children with ASD have difficulty using new skills or behaviors outside of the original instructional context (Crone & Mehta, 2016; Simpson, de Boer-Ott, & Smith-Myles, 2003). In other words, the child with ASD who has been taught to label photographs of 30 different animals in a clinical setting with a therapist may not be able to label those animals on a trip to the zoo with their family. The behavior has not generalized. Interventionists must intentionally plan instruction to teach the child to generalize their newly acquired skills across settings, stimuli, and people. We can promote generalization by teaching in multiple environments, by teaching with a variety of stimuli, and by creating opportunities for their child to learn from a variety of people (Stokes & Baer, 1977).

Parents are with their child in multiple environments and can be key players in promoting generalization and maintenance of their child's newly acquired behaviors across these settings (Oono, Honey, & McConachie, 2013). For example, if a child is learning to request preferred items such as juice, cookie, or banana during intervention sessions with a trained therapist, his parent may be taught how to create opportunities and help the child request for these items in other settings as well. Now, when the child and his father go to the grocery store, the father can walk the child down the aisles that contain juice, cookies, and bananas, draw the child's attention to those items (e.g., Dad points to the bananas and says "Ooh! I see something yummy!"), prompt the child to request the item by name (e.g., Dad says "say, banana"), and, when the child requests correctly, deliver the item to the child while expanding on the child's request (e.g., Dad hands the banana to the child and models the sentence "I want banana"). Research shows that with specialized instruction, children with ASD and their parents can be taught to use new skills in a variety of environments (e.g., Crockett, Fleming, Doepke, & Stevens, 2007; Crone & Mehta, 2016; Gianoumis & Sturmey, 2012).

Brief Literature Review

Types of Parent-Implemented Interventions

Though mothers have served as the interventionists in most research studies (Barton & Fettig, 2013), both mothers and fathers have been taught to implement a variety of interventions with their children with ASD. These interventions can be grouped into two main categories: focused intervention practices and multicomponent approaches. A focused intervention practice refers to a specific set of steps to improve a target outcome (Wong et al., 2014). For example, to improve the child's language skills, a parent can be taught to create opportunities for their child to speak. The mother may sing "The itsy-bitsy…." and then pause and provide 10 s of silence while looking expectantly at the child. This allows the child to have the opportunity to fill in the word "spider" to their mother's song. The mother has been taught a specific strategy to produce a specific child outcome. Parent-implemented focused interventions usually include modeling, shaping, prompting, and reinforcement. Many of these interventions are designed to produce improvements in children's social, communication, and play behaviors (Meadan, Ostrosky, Zaghlawan, & Yu, 2014). For example, Kashinath et al. (2006) taught the parents of five preschoolers with ASD to implement four focused interventions: (a) arranging the environment to promote interaction, (b) using natural reinforcement, (c) time delay prompting, and (d) imitating the child's actions. The result showed that with parent-implemented intervention, all five preschooler's communication skills improved.

Parents have also been taught to implement multicomponent intervention approaches with their child. A multicomponent approach refers to comprehensive interventions designed to impact a variety of target outcomes by incorporating many different strategies. Examples of multicomponent approaches for young children with ASD include KidTalk Tactics Project (Brown & Woods, 2015), the Early Start Denver Model (ESDM; Rogers et al., 2012), pivotal response training (PRT; Schreibman, Kaneko, & Koegel, 1991), Project ImPACT (Ingersoll & Wainer, 2013), and Enhanced Milieu Teaching (EMT; Hancock & Kaiser, 2002). EMT consists of three components: (a) environmental arrangement to create opportunities for the social and communicative interactions, (b) responsive interactions between the interventionist (or parent) and the child, and (c) milieu teaching which includes behavioral strategies such as modeling, prompting, and providing natural reinforcement (Hemmeter & Kaiser, 1994). These naturalistic teaching strategies lend themselves to parent implementation as they can be seamlessly embedded into ongoing home activities and routines.

Parents have been successfully taught to implement multicomponent intervention approaches. Gengoux et al. (2015) found children with ASD whose parents participated in a 12-week group training for PRT had better language and social outcomes 3 months after the intervention than did children with ASD whose parents were not trained in PRT. Kaiser, Hancock, and Nietfeld (2000) taught six parents of preschoolers with ASD to implement EMT first in a clinical setting and then in their homes. In a clinical setting with a trained interventionist, parents were taught each EMT component one at a time until they reached a specified criterion of implementation (e.g., 80% of steps correct). Data on the parents' implementation of EMT and their child's communication behaviors were recorded in both the clinical setting and in the families' home. Results showed that with parent training, all six parents learned to implement EMT in the clinical setting with their child which led to improvements in child communication. Five of the six parents were able to then use EMT in their homes with their child, and again, child communication for these five families improved. Parents reported they were highly satisfied with the parent training and the EMT approach.

Dawson and colleagues (2010) conducted a study in which 48 children with ASD between 1 and 3 years of age went through either the parent-implemented ESDM or commonly available community-based interventions over 2 years. In the ESDM intervention, therapists used a manual and curriculum to train parents to implement

ESDM strategies within daily activities such as play, feeding, and bathing. The intervention sessions were conducted 2 h per session, twice a day, and 5 days per week. Parents could choose goals that they deemed as high priority and implement corresponding strategies. At the end of the 2-year intervention, significant increases in cognitive, communication, and socialization abilities were observed in children in the ESDM treatment group as compared to those in the business-as-usual group.

Rogers and colleagues (2006) compared two models of parent-implemented communication intervention and evaluated their impact on children between 1 and 6 years of age. One model is the Denver Model, which employs a combination of behavioral, developmental, and relationship-oriented approaches, while the other is the Prompts for Restructuring Oral Muscular Phonetic Targets (PROMPT) model, which employs a neurodevelopmental approach to enhance speech production (Rogers et al., 2006). Parents were given the autonomy to decide the daily routines in which they would like to incorporate intervention strategies and spent approximately 30 min per day to implement the strategies they learned via videos and interactive sessions with the therapists. Both treatments resulted in similar outcomes possibly due to their common features such as the focus on shared attention, use of naturalistic communication, matching activities to child's developmental level, and highly structured and active involvement of parents in the treatment procedures. The child participants in both treatment groups displayed improvement in integrated use of both verbal and nonverbal communication (i.e., imitation, functional play).

Teaching and Supporting Parents to Implement Interventions

Before parents can implement interventions, training in specific practices must be provided (Lane et al., 2016). Though parent training models vary across the literature, they share some common features such as focusing on a specific intervention or small set of interventions, opportunities for parents to practice the target intervention and receive feedback, and coaching (Kaiser & Hancock, 2003). In this section we provide an overview of research-based parent training practices.

Training Structure

Parent training can occur in the family's home, at a location in the community, at an intervention clinic or school, or across a combination of these locations (Brown & Woods, 2015). Much of the parent training research has focused on teaching parents in their homes (Barton & Fettig, 2013). Decades of behavioral research show that we should teach a skill in the setting in which the skill is to be used. Since parents will implement interventions within the context of family routines at home, it makes sense that parent training occurs in the home as well. In some cases, travel to the family's home may not be feasible or welcomed. In those instances, parent training may need to take place in a clinical setting with a plan to help the parents generalize their new skills to their home routines (Grahame et al., 2015).

Traditionally, parents have been trained by professional in a face-to-face format in which both parties meet at a specific location. However, with advances in online learning and video conferencing technology, recent research has explored online parent training (McDuffie et al., 2013). Meadan et al. (2016) taught three mothers of young children with ASD to implement naturalistic interventions with their child. The researchers and the mothers met via Skype. During these training sessions, the researcher provided verbal instructions, shared written files with directions for implementing the interventions, shared video demonstrations of the interventions, and helped the mother to create a plan for how she would implement the intervention that week. The mothers were given an iPad and were told to video record themselves implementing the interventions with their child in their home. The mothers then uploaded the videos to an online secure file sharing service. The researcher and the mother bet via Skype twice a week to view and discuss the videos.

Parents have been successfully taught to implement interventions with their child with ASD via individual training and coaching sessions or in a group format that can be trained individually or in a small group (Barton & Lissman, 2015). Individual parent training is a training format often utilized by home-based service providers, who meet with parents one to two times per week over 2–6 months (Suppo, 2012). While training procedures vary from family to family, common procedures include direct instruction of intervention strategies using written handouts (Elder, Valcante, Won, & Zylis, 2003; Kashinath et al., 2006; Nunes & Hanline, 2007), modeling of appropriate intervention techniques (Kashinath et al., 2006), and feedback on parent's implementation of intervention (Shire et al., 2016; Solomon, Necheles, Ferch, & Bruckman, 2007). For example, Shire et al. (2016) provided individual weekly coaching to help parents implement a social communication intervention. In the training sessions, trained clinicians modeled the intervention strategies and provided verbal feedback as each parent practiced specific strategies with the child. The training package produced increases in the children's social communication and play skills during the intervention and at 6-month follow-up.

Group training typically involves weekly group instruction sessions for parents at local early intervention agencies (Barton & Lissman, 2015; Gengoux et al., 2015; Hardan et al., 2015). For instance, Hardan et al. (2015) implemented 12 weekly sessions of group parent training to teach pivotal response training strategies to improve their children's functional communications skills. A strategy manual, video examples, and supplemental handouts were used for training. Parents were also given the opportunity to practice at home and received feedback on their implementation of the strategies after viewing their own video recordings of in-home practice sessions. Results indicated that majority of the parents were able to implement pivotal response training strategies with fidelity after 12 weeks (Hardan et al., 2015). A 3-month follow-up indicated that the children maintained their significant gains in the frequency of functional utterances.

Training Duration

The length of time required to train parents varies across the literature. Most training durations are measured with respect to the number of meetings between the professional and the parent. Barton and Fettig (2013) reviewed the research on parent training across disabilities and found most studies conducted between one and four training sessions followed by frequent observations or coaching sessions. It is likely that parents may require mores training on comprehensive or complex interventions than on focused interventions. For example, Hardan et al. (2015) trained parents over 12 weeks to implement a comprehensive intervention called pivotal response training, while Tellegen and Sanders (2012) implemented four brief training sessions (i.e., 15–30 min) with each parent to address one or two specific problems such as noncompliance and aggression.

Training Procedures

Parent training generally consists of an initial training session(s) to provide parents with an overview and rationale of the procedures followed by ongoing observation, coaching, and feedback sessions. For the initial training, parents are often provided with written and verbal directions, modeling, either live or from videos, practice, self-reflection, and performance feedback (Barton & Fettig, 2013). Written materials can include a training manual for complex interventions or a simple one-page handout with reminders and tips for implementing the intervention. After going over the written materials, the professional provides a model demonstration of the intervention. In some cases, the professional may role-play the procedures. In other cases, the professional may show the parent a video recording of the intervention. Research studies have shown that parents also need an opportunity to practice implementing the intervention. This practice could be in a role-play fashion with the professional or with the child with ASD. In either case, the parent should be provided with an opportunity to reflect on his/her implementation and to obtain feedback from the professional.

Following the initial training session(s), parents should be provided with ongoing feedback and support (e.g., Rivard et al., 2017). This support is often achieved through coaching. Coaching typically involves setting performance goals, building action plans to help the parent meet the goal(s), creating opportunities for the parent to practice the intervention, observing the parent implementing the intervention, and providing opportunities for coach feedback and parent self-reflection on progress toward the goal based on those observations. Coaching usually takes place after the parent implements the intervention (Wainer, Pickard, & Ingersoll, 2017) or, in some cases, while the parent implements the intervention (Lequia, Machalicek, & Lyons, 2013). This is often called in vivo coaching. When in vivo coaching is provided during the session, the professional may interrupt the parent if there is an error in implementation, may praise the parent when a step is implemented correctly, or may prompt the parent when it is time to implement a specific step. Lane et al. (2016) combined initial parent training with two types of coaching: in vivo coaching and coaching following the observations. During the 4-min in vivo parent coaching sessions, the coach provided the parent with praise when they implemented a strategy correctly and cued the parent to attend to opportunities when they could use the strategies. Following these sessions, the coach met with the parent to provide additional performance feedback and to allow the parent the opportunity to engage in self-reflection of their use of the strategies and their child's response to those strategies.

Advances in technology have helped professionals provide live coaching in a more discrete fashion. Lequia et al. (2013) taught three parents to implement strategies to decrease their child's challenging behavior. The parent training consisted of written and verbal instruction followed by opportunities for practice. The parents practiced the strategies with their child in a room at the research center. The researchers observed the parent and child through a one-way mirror and provided verbal prompts and performance feedback to the parents using wireless headphones. The use of wireless technology allowed the researchers to unobtrusively coach the parents. Other studies have shown that wireless technology paired with videoconferencing technology (e.g., Machalicek et al., 2016; Simacek, Dimian, & McComas, 2017) is an effective means for professionals to feasibly provide parents with coaching, practice, and performance feedback without having to travel from home to home.

Additional Considerations

In addition to teaching parents how to implement the specific interventions, parent training may also involve helping the parent to create an environment that will enable successful and sustainable intervention implementation. Barton and Fettig (2013) reviewed the research literature and found parent training themes related to *planning*, *motivation*, and *problem solving*. Specifically, research has shown that when parents are involved in planning how the intervention can be incorporated into their family life, they are more likely to implement the intervention, and the intervention is more likely to be successful in improving their child's target outcomes (Moes & Frea, 2000). Lucyshyn et al. (2007) taught the parents of a 5-year-old girl with ASD to implement interventions to reduce their daughter's challenging behavior. Prior to teaching the parents the intervention procedures, the researchers met with the family to plan which four daily routines were important to the family and in which the child engaged in challenging behavior. Once the parents have been taught when and how to implement the intervention, steps must be taken to build the family's motivation to use their newly learned strategies in between coaching sessions. This may include setting goals for the number of times the parents will implement the intervention before the next coaching session. For example, Brown and

Woods (2015) asked the parents they were training to plan three activities during which they could implement their newly learned interventions without receiving coaching or performance feedback. Finally, parents may also need to be taught how to engage in problem solving when the intervention is not successful or when they make errors while implementing the intervention (Moes & Frea, 2002).

Parent-Implemented Intervention Improves Child Outcomes

The majority of research studies on parent-implemented interventions have focused on improving child social communication skills (Bottema-Beutel, Yoder, Hochman, & Watson, 2014; Igersoll & Gergans, 2007; Shire et al., 2016; Vernon, 2014) and play skills (Besler & Kurt, 2016; Pierucci, 2016). In this section, we highlight some of the research focusing on each of these child outcome areas.

Social Communication

Joint Attention In recent years, researchers have begun to focus a great deal of work on teaching parents to help their child to develop the foundational skills required for communication. These foundation skills are sometimes referred to precursors (Mundy, Sigman, & Kasari, 1990). One of these precursors to communication is the development of joint attention. Joint attention is the state of shared attention with another individual regarding an object or event in the environment. Joint attention is established through initiating a common focus (e.g., showing or pointing to objects) or responding to others' initiation of a common focus (e.g., following another person's eye gaze or point) (Kasari, Freeman, & Paparella, 2006; Kasari, Gulsrud, Paparella, Hellemann, & Berry, 2015; Schertz & Odom, 2007). When a child is able to exhibit joint attention, he or she knows how to alternate eye gaze between a person and an object (Kaale, Smith, & Sponheim, 2012), point to objects to engage another individual's attention, and develop mutually sustained state of engagement with others (Kasari, Gulsrud, Wong, Kwon, & Locke, 2010). Given that joint attention skills are critical for building language and social abilities in later years (Kasari et al., 2006), there has been an increasing amount of research focusing on developing joint attention skills for children with ASD through parent mediated interventions. However, the results have been mixed (Kasari et al., 2015). Here we would like to introduce some parent-implemented early interventions that have worked in very young children with ASD.

Kasari et al. (2010) investigated the effect of a play routine intervention with 19 children with ASD aged between 1 and 3 years. The intervention consisted of 24 sessions implemented over 8 weeks, with approximately three sessions per week. The main goal was to encourage prolonged engagement in a play topic. In each session, the interventionist coached the caregiver and the child as they were engaging in play routines. The caregiver had naturalistic opportunities to practice intervention strategies such as following the child's interest in activities, imitating the child's actions, expanding on the child's verbal comments, making eye contact, etc. By the end of the intervention, the caregivers could carry out the intervention with high accuracy. More importantly, the children developed better joint attention skills by shifting their focus from objects to both objects and people. In addition, a follow-up measurement at 1 year after the intervention showed that the levels of joint attention continued to increase.

JASPER (Joint Attention, Symbolic Play, Engagement, and Regulation) is another treatment approach developed at the University of California in Los Angeles to develop and sustain joint engagement and increase joint attention gestures and play skills for toddlers and preschoolers (Kasari et al., 2015). In one JASPER study, Kasari et al. (2015) coached parents to implement several strategies not only to engage children in play but at the same time facilitate the use of social communication gestures and spoken words. The intervention was conducted two sessions per week, over 10 weeks. At the beginning, parents received coaching on identifying the child's development level of play and use of social communication gestures. In each 30-min coaching sessions, parents interacted with the child while receiving coaching from the interventionist. As a result of the intervention, the children showed significant growth in joint attention skills as well as in developmental level; there was an approximately 17-month gain in receptive language and 10-month gain in expressive language over a period of 9 months.

Verbal Communication Parent-implemented intervention fits nicely with naturalistic teaching strategies to improve their child's communication skills (see Chap. 4 of this book for more on naturalistic teaching strategies). Parents have successfully implemented interventions to improve their children's verbal communication skills (Kashinath et al., 2006). Often interventions have focused on teaching children to request for desired objects or activities, to comment or label items in the environment, or to engage in appropriate communication to replace challenging behaviors. Kaiser et al. (2000) taught six parents how to implement EMT in order to increase their child's spontaneous verbal communication as well as the complexity of the child's verbal communication. Following individual training sessions at a clinic, the parents generalized their use of EMT to their home routines with their child. With the parent-implemented EMT intervention, all six children increased the spontaneous communication and the diversity of their utterances. These results generalized to the home environment and maintained at follow-up observations for four of the six participants.

Simacek et al. (2017) taught three families to replace their child's challenging behavior with appropriate communication. The families participated in online training and coaching. The parents were taught to complete an assessment to determine what their child was communicating through challenging behavior. Then the parents were taught to implement functional communication training (Carr & Durand, 1985) to teach their child an appropriate way to communicate that served the same purpose as their challenging behavior. For all three families, parents learned to implement the intervention accurately, challenging behavior decreased, and the children's appropriate communication increased.

Augmentative and Alterative Communication For children with no or limited verbal language, parents have been taught to implement augmentative and alternative communication systems including speech generating devices (Sigafoos et al., 2004), manual sign (Casey, 1978), and picture exchange systems (Chaabane, Alber-Morgan, & DeBar, 2009). Park, Alber-Morgan, and Cannella-Malone (2011) trained parents to implement the Picture Exchange Communication System (PECS; Bondy & Frost, 1994) to increase independent communicative behaviors of their children with ASD aged 2–3. Parents in this study were trained to 90% accuracy before implementing the intervention independently with their children. Parents learned to initiate communication with their children by presenting preferred objects and pictures, prompting their child to exchange the corresponding picture to request the item, and then responded to their children's actions accordingly (e.g., delivering the requested item, correcting error). The children in the study mastered communication with PECS after 14–22 parent-implemented intervention sessions and continued to use PECS consistently to communicate after the study.

Social Interaction A number of studies have examined ways to improve social interaction skills in young children with ASD (Adams et al., 2012; Kroeger, Schultz, & Newsom, 2007; Williams, Gray, & Tonge, 2012), and many studies have involved parents to different extents in the treatment process (Jull & Mirenda, 2011; Koegel, Koegel, Frea, & Fredeen, 2001; McConachie & Diggle, 2007; Morrison, Sainato, Benchaaban, & Endo, 2002; Stahmer, 1995; Wolfberg, Bottema-Beutel, & DeWitt, 2012; Yang, Wolfberg, Wu, & Hwu, 2003). However, the primary focus of past research has been on clinician-child curricula instead of parent implementation (Wetherby et al., 2014). With this in mind, we would like to briefly describe some successful examples of parent-implemented interventions targeting their children's social and communication skills.

Jull and Mirenda (2011) taught parents to serve play date facilitators for their child with ASD and their typically developing peers. Prior to intervention, the researchers visited the homes a few times to train parents in reinforcing play activities and structure them such that both the child with ASD and the typical peer were required to participate and enjoyed doing so. A manual with key play date strategies and specific examples was also provided to the parents. The parents implemented several intervention sessions with researcher support before attempting independent implementation. Throughout the intervention, a continuous increase in social interaction with playmates was observed in the children with ASD (Jull & Mirenda, 2011).

Play Skills Parents have been taught to implement interventions to increase specific play skills with their child, to increase verbal behaviors during play, and to serve as facilitators for peer play. Pierucci (2016) taught parents of children with ASD between 1 and 3 years of age to implement a play intervention to improve their child's pretend play skills. The parents participated in group training sessions twice a week for 9 weeks. Targeted intervention techniques include commenting on a toy (e.g., "I bet your doll is hungry"), requesting specific play behavior (e.g., "Why don't you scramble an egg for your doll?"), and prompting visually or physically (e.g., showing a toy, using child's hand to perform a play action). With parent-implemented play intervention, the children developed more complex pretend play skills after 17–18 intervention sessions.

Reagon and Higbee (2009) taught three mothers of children with ASD to implement a visual script intervention to increase their child's verbal initiations during play. Using verbal and written instruction, role-play, and performance feedback, the mothers were taught to develop, implement, and fade visual supports during play in their homes. Results showed that the mothers implemented the intervention accurately and that their child's verbal initiations improved and maintained after the visual supports were withdrawn.

How to Use Parent-Implemented Intervention (Fig. 8.1)

Evaluating the Fit of Parent-Implemented Intervention with Individual Families

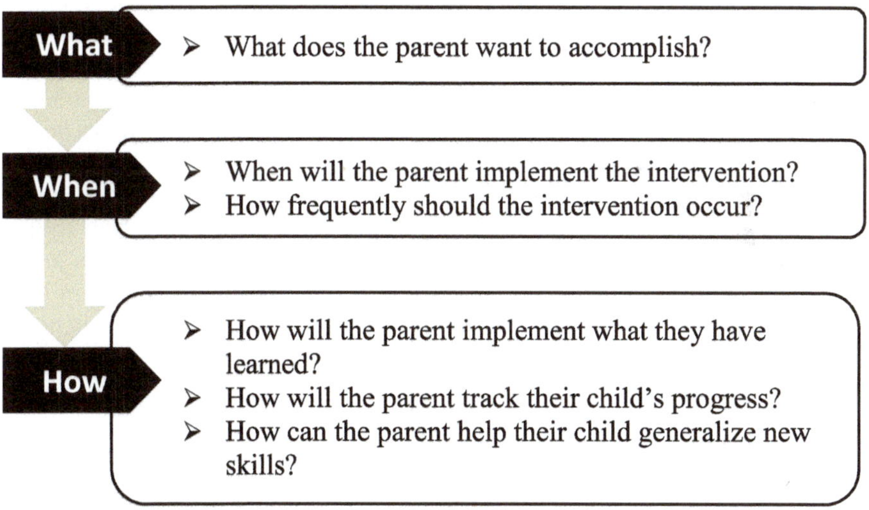

Fig. 8.1 Planning for parent-implemented intervention

Parent-implemented intervention begins with joint planning between the professional and the family. The professional should meet with the child's family to describe what parent-implemented intervention is and how it could be implemented within daily family routines. It is up to the family to decide if this approach will fit with their values, culture, and home life. While parent-implemented intervention has strong research support, it is not necessarily a good fit for every family (Barton & Lissman, 2015). Some parents may be eager to learn as much as they can about serving as an interventionist for their child. Other parents may see their role as a caretaker, and not as an interventionist, or may be under such stress that learning how to implement an intervention may feel overwhelming (Kaiser et al., 2000). Working with families to determine how a parent-implemented intervention could be made more feasible, acceptable, and less stressful for the family is essential.

Selecting Child Outcomes

If a family is open to parent-implemented intervention, then the professional can begin conversations with the family to identify child outcomes which are important to the family and which may align well with interventions implemented by the parent. When selecting an outcome or outcomes for intervention, the professional and the family should consider behaviors that the child would have multiple opportunities to engage in within the context of their daily routines. Potential child outcomes may relate to increased communication skills, increased social interaction skills, improved play skills, or decreases in challenging behaviors. Professionals should pay careful attention to the family's desires and concerns about their child's development. Then, the professional can help take the family's desire for their child and convert it into a measurable objective so that the child's progress toward that goal can be assessed. For example, a parent may be interested in increasing their child's ability to ask for things they want. The professional could translate that goal into a measurable objective such as "During mealtimes when a preferred food item is in sight but out of reach, Amy will say, 'I want_' followed by the desired food item for 12 consecutive meals" (Fig. 8.2).

Identifying Routines

One of the greatest strengths of parent-implemented intervention is the potential to embed intervention within daily family routines. Asking families to create a time in their day to work one-on-one with their child in a structured setting may not be feasible for families, can increase parental stress, and can take time away from other tasks, activities, and priorities the family has (Koegel, 2000). By embedding instruction into daily routines, the parent is able to implement the intervention with their child while continuing with their own daily routines and tasks.

How to Identify Child Outcomes which are IMPORTANT to FAMILY

- Questions to ask -

- ✓ What are the family's desires?
- ✓ What are the family's concerns?
- ✓ Are there at least 5 times each day when the child could engage in this behavior?
- ✓ Are there at least 2 routines per day when the parents could target this outcome?

*icon: https://goo.gl/images/IGkK60

Fig. 8.2 Selecting a target outcome

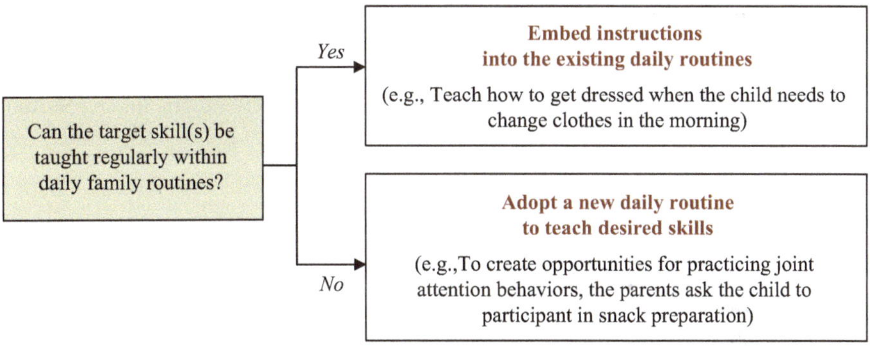

Fig. 8.3 Identifying a routine for intervention

Additionally, the child is able to practice behaviors in a natural setting with naturally occurring materials and consequences which promotes maintenance and generalization of their new skills. In most cases, the professional and parents may work to identify existing routines into which intervention can be implemented. Daily routines might include getting dressed in the morning, mealtimes, going to the park, grocery shopping, or playing with toys. In some cases, the professional may encourage the family to adopt a new daily routine to encourage the desired behavior. For example, instead of preparing a snack for the child, the parent may be encouraged to involve the child in food preparation routines. Within this new routine, the parent can create opportunities for the child to practice joint attention behaviors, to request missing ingredients, to label utensils, and to practice turn-taking. These opportunities would not be present if the parent prepared the snack independently from the child (Fig. 8.3).

Training Parents

Once the child's outcome(s) and targeted routines are selected, the professional can begin to teach the parents how to implement an evidence-based intervention for that target outcome. Again, to improve the contextual fit of the intervention with the family's home life, the professional should collaborate with the family to ensure the intervention aligns with the family's values and culture. Families must have access to training and coaching opportunities before they can be expected to implement an intervention. Professionals can train parents individually, in groups, in person, or through the use of online technology. Professionals should work with the families they serve to identify the training format and training schedule that is most feasible and acceptable. For families whose children are in need of particularly intensive interventions and supports, individualized training sessions may be necessary (Fig. 8.4).

Regardless of the format, there are some key components that should be included in the training. These include written instructions, verbal instruction, models of the intervention being implemented, opportunities for the parent to practice the intervention, and performance feedback. When providing parents with written instructions, professionals should avoid jargon or terms that may not be familiar to the family. Written instructions could be as complex as a manual for complex or multi-component interventions or as simple as a single page handout for more focused interventions. All written instructions should include a step-by-step guide for

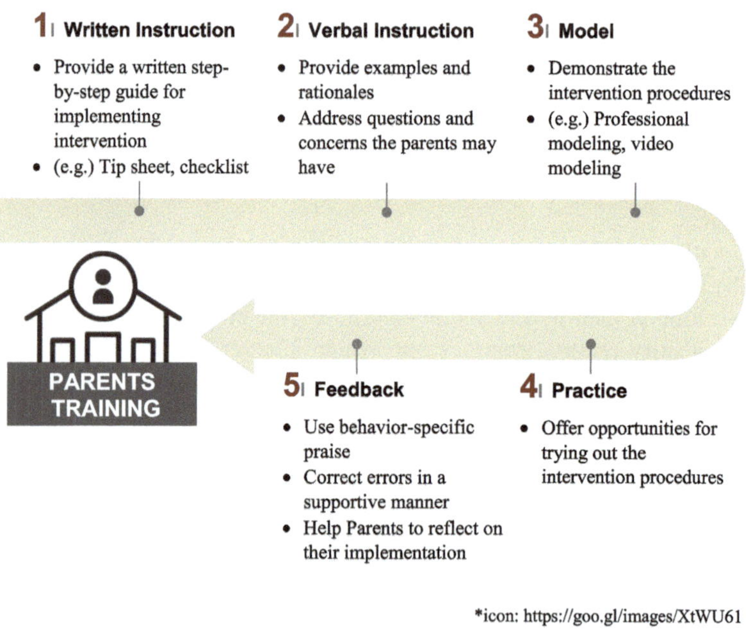

Fig. 8.4 Key elements of parents training

implementing the intervention. This can serve as either a tip sheet or a checklist for the parent to refer back to during the intervention. Written instructions also allow the parent to mentally rehearse the steps for implementing the intervention (Kashinath et al., 2006) (Fig. 8.5). Verbal instruction should parallel and expand upon what is provided in writing to the family. During verbal instruction, the professional should provide some examples of the intervention, should provide a rationale for why and how the intervention is designed to impact child outcomes, and should address any questions or concerns the parents may have.

Functional Communication Training (FCT) for Chris

- Preferred Item: Puzzles
- Challenging Behavior: Screaming, hitting, biting, dropping down the floor
- Appropriate Response: Saying, "I want puzzles"

Basic Concept

Purpose	Behavior		Consequence
Getting preferred item (i.e., puzzles)	Chris engages in challenging behaviors (e.g., screaming, hitting)	→	Mom does not give Chris the item
	Chris says, "I want puzzles"	→	Mom gives Chris the item

Specific Training Procedures

1	Provide access to puzzles for 30s	
2	Tell Chris "*It's my turn*" and remove the puzzles	
3	Do not respond to challenging behavior	
4	If Chris says, "I want the puzzle" ↓ ➢ Say, "*Great job asking for puzzles*" ➢ Provide access to puzzles for 30s	If Chris does NOT say, "I want puzzle" ↓ ➢ Wait 5s ➢ Ask Chris to repeat, "*I want puzzles*" ➢ Provide access to puzzles immediately after Chris emits the appropriate response

Fig. 8.5 Examples of written instructions

It is important for the parents to see a demonstration of the intervention procedures. This demonstration could consist of the professional modeling the procedures or could include prerecording video models. If possible, the professional should demonstrate the intervention with the child so that the parent can see exactly how the intervention applies to and can be used with their child. If a prerecording video model is provided during training, the professionals should ensure that the video captures each of the parent behaviors clearly and that the child pictured in the video mirrors as many characteristics of the focus child as possible. Video models should be brief and should focus specifically on the intervention the parent is learning to implement. The professional should "set up" the video example by letting the parent know what she is about to observe. For example, "In this video, you'll see a mom interacting with her son during a shared book reading routine. Notice how the mom creates opportunities for her son to communicate, how she prompts him to communicate, and how she responds to him when he communicates." Then, following the video model, the professional should ask the parent some open-ended questions about the video, such as "What did you notice? How did the mom create opportunities for communication?" The professional may also want to assess the parent's understanding of the intervention by asking him/her to explain the intervention procedures in their own words. This can help the professional to identify points of confusion or to determine whether it is time to move forward to the next phase of training.

Practice and Performance Feedback After the parent has read about, heard about, and seen the intervention, it is time to offer opportunities for practicing the intervention. This practice is part of the learning process, and the professional and the parent should anticipate that there will be implementation errors. As such, the professional should create a safe space where the parent feels comfortable trying out the intervention and making mistakes. This can be achieved by telling the parent that at first she will likely make many errors, and that's perfectly fine and even expected. If she makes a mistake, she can correct herself, or the professional may offer some guidance. The professional should be encouraging, use behavior-specific praise when the parent implements a step correctly, and correct errors in a constructive and supportive manner. Helping parents to reflect on their own implementation may facilitate parent learning. For example, the professional may ask "What do you think went well this time? What is something that you thought could be better?" Setting a goal for mastery criterion for parent implementation helps to add structure to the training and allows the parent and professional to track parent progress. For example, the professional may say "Once you have implemented each of the four steps of the intervention correctly and you feel comfortable with the procedures, then you should be ready to implement the intervention on your own at home."

Coaching Parents

The professional and the family should develop a coaching schedule once the parent has met mastery criteria for implementing the intervention (Fig. 8.6). The purpose of coaching sessions is to observe the implementation of the intervention and the child's progress. Coaching sessions also enable the professional to continue to support the parent's learning through additional performance feedback, joint reflection, and action planning. Coaching sessions should be frequent enough that the parent can continue to refine their use of the intervention. In some cases, coaching sessions may be quite frequent at the beginning, and, as the parent's implementation improves, can gradually be spaced further apart. When travel to the family's home is a barrier to holding coaching sessions, online technology can be a powerful tool. Parents can either video record themselves implementing the intervention and share the video with the professional. Alternatively, video conferencing software can be used to allow the professional to observe the intervention "live." As in the practice and performance feedback phase, the coach should help the parent to reflect on his/her own implementation, should provide behavior-specific praise, and should offer support and additional examples and resources to help correct errors the parent may have made during the observation. In addition to providing verbal performance feedback, professionals may want to provide parents with a written evaluation form or a self-report form so that the parent can refer back to the feedback at a later time, perhaps immediately before the next opportunity to implement the intervention.

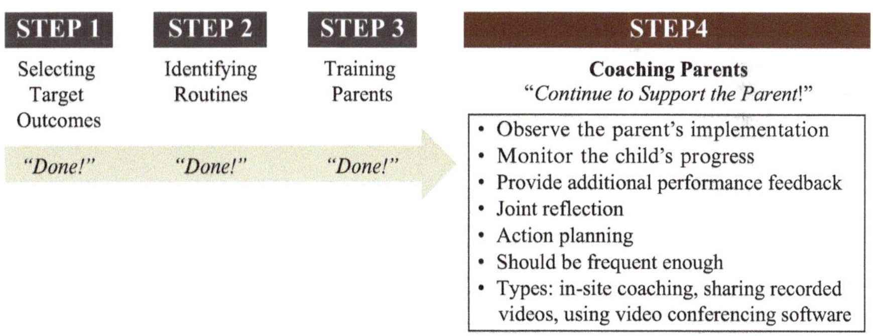

Fig. 8.6 Coaching parents

Conclusion

In summary, parent-implemented intervention is an effective practice for improving child communication, social, play, and challenging behavior outcomes. Parent-implemented intervention also has been shown to decrease parental stress and improve the quality and quantity of parent-child interactions. Research shows that with quality training and coaching, parents can be taught to implement a variety of evidence-based interventions within the context of their daily routines. As noted throughout this chapter, parents play a vital role in early intervention. As parents' intervention skills increase, their children are able to benefit from increased opportunities to practice communication, social, and play behaviors across a range of environments and routines already present in their daily lives.

References

Adams, C., Lockton, E., Freed, J., Gaile, J., Earl, G., McBean, K., ... Law, J. (2012). The social communication intervention project: A randomized controlled trial of the effectiveness of speech and language therapy for school-age children who have pragmatic and social communication problems with or without autism spectrum disorder. *International Journal of Language & Communication Disorders/Royal College of Speech & Language Therapists, 47*(3), 233–244. https://doi.org/10.1111/j.1460-6984.2011.00146.x.

American Psychiatric Association. (2013). *Diagnostic and statistical manual of mental disorders: DSM-5*. Washington, DC: American Psychiatric Association.

Barton, E. E., & Fettig, A. (2013). Parent-implemented interventions for young children with disabilities. *Journal of Early Intervention, 35*(2), 194–219. https://doi.org/10.1177/1053815113504625

Barton, E. E., & Lissman, D. C. (2015). Group parent training combined with follow-up coaching for parents of children with developmental delays. *Infants and Young Children, 28*(3), 220–230. https://doi.org/10.1097/IYC.0000000000000036

Beaudoin, A. J., Sébire, G., & Couture, M. (2014). Parent training interventions for toddlers with autism spectrum disorder. *Autism Research and Treatment, 2014*, 1–15. https://doi.org/10.1155/2014/839890

Besler, F., & Kurt, O. (2016). Effectiveness of video modeling provided by mothers in teaching play skills to children with autism. *Educational Sciences: Theory & Practice, 16*(1), 209–230. 10.12738/estp.2016.1.0273

Bott, D. (1994). A family systems framework for intervention with individuals. *Counselling Psychology Quarterly, 7*(2), 105–115. https://doi.org/10.1080/09515079408254139

Bondy, A., & Frost, L. (1994). The picture exchange communication system. *Focus on Autistic Behavior, 9*, 1–19.

Bottema-Beutel, K., Yoder, P. J., Hochman, J. M., & Watson, L. R. (2014). The role of supported joint engagement and parent utterances in language and social communication development in children with autism spectrum disorder. *Journal of Autism and Developmental Disorders, 44*(9), 2162–2174. https://doi.org/10.1007/s10803-014-2092-z

Bowen, M. (1974). Alcoholism as viewed through family systems theory and family psychotherapy. *Annals of the New York Academy of Sciences, 233*(1), 115–122. https://doi.org/10.1111/j.1749-6632.1974.tb40288.x

Brown, J. A., & Woods, J. J. (2015). Effects of a triadic parent-implemented home-based communication intervention for toddlers. *Journal of Early Intervention, 37*(1), 44–68. https://doi.org/10.1177/1053815115589350

Carr, E. G., & Durand, V. M. (1985). Reducing behavior problems through functional communication training. *Journal of Applied Behavior Analysis, 18*(2), 111–126. https://doi.org/10.1901/jaba.1985.18-111

Casey, L. O. (1978). Development of communicative behavior in autistic children: A parent program using manual signs. *Journal of Autism and Childhood Schizophrenia, 8*(1), 45–59. https://doi.org/10.1007/BF01550277

Chaabane, D. B., Alber-Morgan, S. R., & DeBar, R. M. (2009). The effects of parent-implemented PECS training on improvisation of mands by children with autism. *Journal of Applied Behavior Analysis, 42*(3), 671–677. https://doi.org/10.1901/jaba.2009.42-671

Cidav, Z., Marcus, S. C., & Mandell, D. S. (2012). Implications of childhood autism for parental employment and earnings. *Pediatrics, 129*(4), 617–623. https://doi.org/10.1542/peds.2011-2700

Cosbey, J., & Muldoon, D. (2017). EAT-UP™ family-centered feeding intervention to promote food acceptance and decrease challenging behaviors: A single-case experimental design replicated across three families of children with autism spectrum disorder. *Journal of Autism and Developmental Disorders, 47*(3), 564–578. https://doi.org/10.1007/s10803-016-2977-0

Crockett, J. L., Fleming, R. K., Doepke, K. J., & Stevens, J. S. (2007). Parent training: Acquisition and generalization of discrete trials teaching skills with parents of children with autism. *Research in Developmental Disabilities, 28*(1), 23–36. https://doi.org/10.1016/j.ridd.2005.10.003

Crone, R. M., & Mehta, S. S. (2016). Parent training on generalized use of behavior analytic strategies for decreasing the problem behavior of children with autism spectrum disorder: A data-based case study. *Education & Treatment of Children, 39*(1), 64–94.

Dawson, G., Rogers, S., Munson, J., Smith, M., Winter, J., Greenson, J., … Varley, J. (2010). Randomized, controlled trial of an intervention for toddlers with autism: The Early Start Denver Model. *Pediatrics, 125*(1), e17–e23. https://doi.org/10.1542/peds.2009-0958

Diggle, T., McConachie, H. R., & Randle, V. R. (2003). Parent-mediated early intervention for young children with autism spectrum disorder. *Cochrane Database of Systematic Reviews.* https://doi.org/10.1002/14651858.cd003496.pub2

Edwards, N. M., & Gallagher, P. A. (2016). Early intervention special instructors and service coordinators in one state. *Infants & Young Children, 29*(4), 299–311. https://doi.org/10.1097/IYC.0000000000000074

Elder, J. H., Valcante, G., Won, D., & Zylis, R. (2003). Effects of in-home training for culturally diverse fathers of children with autism. *Issues in Mental Health Nursing, 24*(3), 273–295. https://doi.org/10.1080/01612840305276

Estes, A., Munson, J., Rogers, S. J., Greenson, J., Winter, J., & Dawson, G. (2015). Long-term outcomes of early intervention in 6-year-old children with autism spectrum disorder. *Journal of the American Academy of Child and Adolescent Psychiatry, 54*(7), 580–587. https://doi.org/10.1016/j.jaac.2015.04.005

Gengoux, G. W., Berquist, K. L., Salzman, E., Schapp, S., Phillips, J. M., Frazier, T. W., … Hardan, A. Y. (2015). Pivotal response treatment parent training for autism: Findings from a 3-month follow-up evaluation. *Journal of Autism and Developmental Disorders, 45*, 2889–2898. https://doi.org/10.1007/s10803-015-2452-3

Gianoumis, S., & Sturmey, P. (2012). Generalization procedures in training interventionists for individuals with developmental disabilities. *Behavior Modification, 36*(5), 619–629. https://doi.org/10.1177/0145445511432920

Grahame, V., Brett, D., Dixon, L., McConachie, H., Lowry, J., Rodgers, J., … Le Couteur, A. (2015). Managing repetitive behaviours in young children with autism spectrum disorder (ASD): Pilot randomised controlled trial of a new parent group intervention. *Journal of Autism and Developmental Disorders, 45*(10), 3168–3182. https://doi.org/10.1007/s10803-015-2474-x

Hancock, T. B., & Kaiser, A. P. (2002). The effects of trainer-implemented enhanced milieu teaching on the social communication of children with autism. *Topics in Early Childhood Special Education, 22*(1), 39–54. https://doi.org/10.1177/027112140202200104

Hardan, A. Y., Gengoux, G. W., Berquist, K. L., Libove, R. A., Ardel, C. M., Phillips, J., … Minjarez, M. B. (2015). A randomized controlled trial of Pivotal Response Treatment Group for parents of children with autism. *Journal of Child Psychology and Psychiatry and Allied Disciplines, 56*(8), 884–892. https://doi.org/10.1111/jcpp.12354

Hart, B., & Risley, T. R. (1995). *Meaningful differences in the everyday experience of young American children*. Baltimore, MD: Paul H. Brookes.

Hemmeter, M. L., & Kaiser, A. P. (1994). Enhanced milieu teaching: Effects of parent-implemented language intervention. *Journal of Early Intervention, 18*(3), 269–289. https://doi.org/10.1177/105381519401800303

Hoffman, T. K. (2016). An exploration of service delivery in early intervention over the last two decades. *International Journal of Early Childhood Special Education, 8*(2), 107–112. 10.20489/intjecse.284568

Hong, E. R., Ganz, J. B., Neely, L., Gerow, S., & Ninci, J. (2016). A review of the quality of primary caregiver-implemented communication intervention research for children with ASD. *Research in Autism Spectrum Disorders, 25*, 122–136. https://doi.org/10.1016/j.rasd.2016.02.005

IDEA Infant and Toddler Coordinators Association. (2016). ITCA tipping points part C implementation: State challenges and responses. Retrieved from http://ideainfanttoddler.org/pdf/2016-ITCA-State-Challenges-Report.pdf

Igersoll, B., & Gergans, S. (2007). The effect of a parent-implemented imitation intervention on spontaneous imitation skills in young children with autism. *Research in Developmental Disabilities, 28*(2), 163–175. https://doi.org/10.1016/j.ridd.2006.02.004

Individuals with Disabilities Education Act, 20 U.S.C. § 1400 (2004).

Ingersoll, B., & Wainer, A. (2013). Initial efficacy of project ImPACT: A parent-mediated social communication intervention for young children with ASD. *Journal of Autism and Developmental Disorders, 43*(12), 2943–2952. https://doi.org/10.1007/s10803-013-1840-9

Jull, S., & Mirenda, P. (2011). Parents as play date facilitators for preschoolers with autism. *Journal of Positive Behavior Interventions, 13*(1), 17–30. https://doi.org/10.1177/1098300709358111

Kaale, A., Smith, L., & Sponheim, E. (2012). A randomized controlled trial of preschool-based joint attention intervention for children with autism. *Journal of Child Psychology and Psychiatry and Allied Disciplines, 53*(1), 97–105. https://doi.org/10.1111/j.1469-7610.2011.02450.x

Kaiser, A. P., & Hancock, T. B. (2003). Teaching parents new skills to support their young children's development. *Infants & Young Children, 16*(1), 9–22. https://doi.org/10.1097/00001163-200301000-00003

Kaiser, A. P., Hancock, T. B., & Nietfeld, J. P. (2000). The effects of parent-implemented enhanced milieu teaching on the social communication of children who have autism. *Early Education & Development, 11*(4), 423–446. https://doi.org/10.1207/s15566935eed

Kasari, C., Freeman, S., & Paparella, T. (2006). Joint attention and symbolic play in young children with autism: A randomized controlled intervention study. *Journal of Child Psychology and Psychiatry and Allied Disciplines, 47*(6), 611–620. https://doi.org/10.1111/j.1469-7610.2005.01567.x

Kasari, C., Gulsrud, A., Paparella, T., Hellemann, G., & Berry, K. (2015). Randomized comparative efficacy study of parent-mediated interventions for toddlers with autism. *Journal of Consulting and Clinical Psychology, 83*(3), 554–563. https://doi.org/10.1037/a0039080

Kasari, C., Gulsrud, A. C., Wong, C., Kwon, S., & Locke, J. (2010). Randomized controlled caregiver mediated joint engagement intervention for toddlers with autism. *Journal of Autism and Developmental Disorders, 40*(9), 1045–1056. https://doi.org/10.1007/s10803-010-0955-5

Kashinath, S., Woods, J., & Goldstein, H. (2006). Enhancing generalized teaching strategy use in daily routines by parents of children with autism. *Journal of Speech, Language and Hearing Research, 49*(3), 466–485. https://doi.org/10.1044/1092-4388

Koegel, L. K. (2000). Interventions to facilitate communication in autism. *Journal of Autism and Developmental Disorders, 30*(5), 383–391. https://doi.org/10.1023/A:1005539220932

Koegel, L. K., Koegel, R. L., Frea, W. D., & Fredeen, R. M. (2001). Identifying early intervention targets for children with autism in inclusive school settings. *Behavior Modification, 25*(5), 745–761. https://doi.org/10.1177/0145445501255005

Koegel, R. L., Bimbela, A., & Schreibman, L. (1996). Collateral effects of parent training on family interactions. *Journal of Autism and Developmental Disorders, 26*(3), 347–359. https://doi.org/10.1007/BF02172479

Kroeger, K. A., Schultz, J. R., & Newsom, C. (2007). A comparison of two group-delivered social skills programs for young children with autism. *Journal of Autism and Developmental Disorders, 37*(5), 808–817. https://doi.org/10.1077/s10803-006-0207-x

Lane, J. D., Ledford, J. R., Shepley, C., Mataras, T. K., Ayres, K. M., & Davis, A. B. (2016). A brief coaching intervention for teaching naturalistic strategies to parents. *Journal of Early Intervention, 38*(3), 135–150. https://doi.org/10.1177/1053815116663178

Lequia, J., Machalicek, W., & Lyons, G. (2013). Parent education intervention results in decreased challenging behavior and improved task engagement for students with disabilities during academic tasks. *Behavioral Interventions, 28*(4), 322–343. https://doi.org/10.1002/bin.136

Lucyshyn, J. M., Albin, R. W., Horner, R. H., Mann, J. C., Mann, J. A., & Wadsworth, G. (2007). Family implementation of positive behavior support for a child with autism: Longitudinal, single-case, experimental, and descriptive replication and extension. *Journal of Positive Behavior Interventions, 9*, 131–150. https://doi.org/10.1177/10983007070090030201

Machalicek, W., Lequia, J., Pinkelman, S., Knowles, C., Raulston, T., Davis, T., & Alresheed, F. (2016). Behavioral telehealth consultation with families of children with autism spectrum disorder. *Behavioral Interventions, 31*, 223–250. https://doi.org/10.1002/bin.1450

McConachie, H., & Diggle, T. (2007). Parent implemented early intervention for young children with autism spectrum disorder: A systematic review. *Journal of Evaluation in Clinical Practice, 13*(1), 120–129. https://doi.org/10.1111/j.1365-2753.2006.00674.x

McDuffie, A., Machalicek, W., Oakes, A., Haebig, E., Weismer, S. E., & Abbeduto, L. (2013). Distance video-teleconferencing in early intervention: Pilot study of a naturalistic parent-implemented language intervention. *Topics in Early Childhood Special Education, 33*(3), 172–185. https://doi.org/10.1177/0271121413476348

Meadan, H., Ostrosky, M. M., Zaghlawan, H. Y., & Yu, S. (2014). Using coaching with preschool teachers to support the social skills of children with and without Autism Spectrum Disorders. *International Journal of Early Childhood Special Education, 4*(8648). https://doi.org/10.20489/intjecse.107941

Meadan, H., Snodgrass, M. R., Meyer, L. E., Fisher, K. W., Chung, M. Y., & Halle, J. W. (2016). Internet-based parent-implemented intervention for young children with autism: A pilot study. *Journal Of Early Intervention, 38*, 3–23. https://doi.org/10.1177/1053815116630327

Moes, D. R., & Frea, W. D. (2000). Using family context to inform intervention planning for the treatment of a child with autism. *Journal of Positive Behavior Interventions, 2*, 40–46. https://doi.org/10.1177/109830070000200106

Moes, D. R., & Frea, W. D. (2002). Contextualized behavioral support in early intervention for children with autism and their families. *Journal of Autism and Developmental Disorders, 32*, 519–533. https://doi.org/10.1023/A:1021298729297

Morrison, R. S., Sainato, D. M., Benchaaban, D., & Endo, S. (2002). Increasing play skills of children with autism using activity schedules and correspondence training. *Journal of Early Intervention, 25*(1), 58–72.

Mundy, P., Sigman, M., & Kasari, C. (1990). A longitudinal study of joint attention and language development in autistic children. *Journal of Autism and Developmental Disorders, 20*(1), 115–128. https://doi.org/10.1007/BF02206861

National Research Council. (2001). *Educating children with autism*. Wasington, DC: The National Academy Press. https://doi.org/10.17226/10017

Norton, P., & Drew, C. (1994). Autism and potential family stressors. *American Journal of Family Therapy, 22*, 67–76. https://doi.org/10.1080/01926189408251298

Nunes, D., & Hanline, M. F. (2007). Enhancing the alternative and augmentative communication use of a child with autism through a parent-implemented naturalistic intervention. *International Journal of Disability, Development and Education, 54*(2), 177–197. https://doi.org/10.1080/10349120701330495

Odom, S. L., McLean, M. E., Johnson, L. J., & LaMontagne, M. J. (1995). Recommended practices in early childhood special education: Validation and current use. *Journal of Early Intervention, 19*(1), 1–17. https://doi.org/10.1177/105381519501900101

Oono, I. P., Honey, E. J., & McConachie, H. (2013). Parent-mediated early intervention for young children with autism spectrum disorders (ASD). *Cochrane Database System Review, 30*(4). https://doi.org/10.1002/14651858.CD009774.pub2

Park, J. H., Alber-Morgan, S. R., & Cannella-Malone, H. (2011). Effects of mother-implemented picture exchange communication system (PECS) training on independent communicative behaviors of young children with autism spectrum disorders. *Topics in Early Childhood Special Education, 31*(1), 37–47. https://doi.org/10.1177/0271121410393750

Pierucci, J. M. (2016). Mothers' scaffolding techniques used during play in toddlers with autism spectrum disorder. *Journal of Developmental and Physical Disabilities, 28*(2), 217–235. https://doi.org/10.1007/s10882-015-9459-8

Reagon, K. A., & Higbee, T. S. (2009). Parent-implemented script fading to promote play-based verbal initiations in children with autism. *Journal of Applied Behavior Analysis, 42*, 659–664. https://doi.org/10.1901/jaba.2009.42-659

Rivard, M., Morin, M., Mercier, C., Terroux, A., Mello, C., & Lépine, A. (2017). Social validity of a training and coaching program for parents of children with autism spectrum disorder on a waiting list for early behavioral intervention. *Journal of Child and Family Studies, 26*(3), 877–887. https://doi.org/10.1007/s10826-016-0604-5

Rogers, S. J., Estes, A., Lord, C., Vismara, L., Winter, J., Fitzpatrick, A., … Dawson, G. (2012). Effects of a brief Early Start Denver Model (ESDM)–based parent intervention on toddlers at risk for autism spectrum disorders: A randomized controlled trial. *Journal of the American Academy of Child and Adolescent Psychiatry, 51*(10), 1052–1065. https://doi.org/10.1016/j.jaac.2012.08.003

Rogers, S. J., Hayden, D., Hepburn, S., Charlifue-Smith, R., Hall, T., & Hayes, A. (2006). Teaching young nonverbal children with autism useful speech: A pilot study of the Denver model and PROMPT interventions. *Journal of Autism and Developmental Disorders, 36*(8), 1007–1024. https://doi.org/10.1007/s10803-006-0142-x

Schertz, H. H., & Odom, S. L. (2007). Promoting joint attention in toddlers with autism: A parent-mediated developmental model. *Journal of Autism and Developmental Disorders, 37*(8), 1562–1575. https://doi.org/10.1007/s10803-006-0290-z

Schreibman, L., Kaneko, W. M., & Koegel, R. L. (1991). Positive affect of parents of autistic children: A comparison across two teaching techniques. *Behavior Therapy, 22*(4), 479–490. https://doi.org/10.1016/S0005-7894(05)80340-5

Shire, S. Y., Gulsrud, A., & Kasari, C. (2016). Increasing responsive parent-child interactions and joint engagement: Comparing the influence of parent-mediated intervention and parent psychoeducation. *Journal of Autism and Developmental Disorders, 46*(5), 1737–1747. https://doi.org/10.1007/s10803-016-2702-z

Sigafoos, J., O'Reilly, M. F., Seely-York, S., Weru, J., Son, S. H., Green, V. A., & Lancioni, G. E. (2004). Transferring AAC intervention to the home. *Disability And Rehabilitation: An International, Multidisciplinary Journal, 26*, 1330–1334. https://doi.org/10.1080/09638280412331280235

Siller, M., Hutman, T., & Sigman, M. (2013). A parent-mediated intervention to increase responsive parental behaviors and child communication in children with ASD: A randomized clinical trial. *Journal of Autism and Developmental Disorders, 43*(3), 540–555. https://doi.org/10.1007/s10803-012-1584-y

Simacek, J., Dimian, A. F., & McComas, J. J. (2017). Communication intervention for young children with severe neurodevelopmental disabilities via telehealth. *Journal of Autism and Developmental Disorders, 47*, 744–767. https://doi.org/10.1007/s10803-016-3006-z

Simpson, R. L., de Boer-Ott, S. R., & Smith-Myles, B. (2003). Inclusion of learners with autism spectrum disorders in general education settings. *Topics in Language Disorders, 23*(2), 116–133. https://doi.org/10.1097/00011363-200304000-00005

Smith, T., Klorman, R., & Mruzek, D. W. (2015). Predicting outcome of community-based early intensive behavioral intervention for children with autism. *Journal of Abnormal Child Psychology, 43*(7), 1271–1282. https://doi.org/10.1007/s10802-015-0002-2

Solomon, R., Necheles, J., Ferch, C., & Bruckman, D. (2007). Pilot study of a parent training program for young children with autism. *Autism, 11*(3), 205–224. https://doi.org/10.1177/1362361307076842

Stahmer, A. C. (1995). Teaching symbolic play skills to children with autism using pivotal response training. *Journal of Autism and Developmental Disorders, 25*(2), 123–141.

Stokes, T. F., & Baer, D. M. (1977). An implicit technology of generalization. *Journal of Applied Behavior Analysis, 10*, 349–367. https://doi.org/10.1901/jaba.1977.10-349

Suppo, J. (2012). Parent training for families who have children with autism: A review of the literature. *American Council on Rural Special Education, 31*(2), 12–26. https://doi.org/10.1007/bf02178500

Tellegen, C. L., & Sanders, M. R. (2012). Using primary care parenting interventions to improve outcomes in children with developmental disabilities: A case report. *Case Reports in Pediatrics, 2012*, 1–5. https://doi.org/10.1155/2012/150261

Vernon, T. W. (2014). Fostering a social child with autism: A moment-by-moment sequential analysis of an early social engagement intervention. *Journal of Autism and Developmental Disorders, 44*(12), 3072–3082. https://doi.org/10.1007/s10803-014-2173-z

Wainer, A. L., & Ingersoll, B. R. (2015). Increasing access to an ASD imitation intervention via a telehealth parent training program. *Journal of Autism and Developmental Disorders, 45*(12), 3877–3890. https://doi.org/10.1007/s10803-014-2186-7

Wainer, A. L., Pickard, K., & Ingersoll, B. R. (2017). Using web-based instruction, brief workshops, and remote consultation to teach community-based providers a parent-mediated intervention. *Journal of Children and Family Studies, 26*(6), 1592–1602. https://doi.org/10.1007/s10826-017-0671-2

Wetherby, A., & Prizant, B. (1992). Profiling young children's communicative competence. In S. Warren & J. Reichle (Eds.), *Perspective on communication and language intervention: Development, assessment, and intervention* (pp. 217–251). Baltimore, MA: Paul H. Brookes.

Wetherby, A. M., Guthrie, W., Woods, J., Schatschneider, C., Holland, R. D., Morgan, L., & Lord, C. (2014). Parent-implemented social intervention for toddlers with autism: An RCT. *Pediatrics, 134*(6), 1084–1093. https://doi.org/10.1542/peds.2014-0757

Williams, B. T., Gray, K. M., & Tonge, B. J. (2012). Teaching emotion recognition skills to young children with autism: A randomised controlled trial of an emotion training programme. *Journal of Child Psychology and Psychiatry and Allied Disciplines, 53*(12), 1268–1276. https://doi.org/10.1111/j.1469-7610.2012.02593.x

Wolfberg, P., Bottema-Beutel, K., & DeWitt, M. (2012). Including children with autism in social and imaginary play with typical peers: Integrated play groups model. *American Journal of Play, 5*(1), 55–80.

Wong, C., Odom, S. L., Hume, K., Cox, A. W., Fettig, A., Kucharczyk, S., et al. (2014). *Evidence-based practices for children, youth, and young adults with autism spectrum disorder.* Chapel Hill, NC: The University of North Carolina, Frank Porter Graham Child Development Institute, Autism Evidence-Based Practice Review Group. Retrieved from http://autismpdc.fpg.unc.edu/sites/autismpdc.fpg.unc.edu/files/2014-EBP-Report.pdf

Yang, T. R., Wolfberg, P. J., Wu, S.-C., & Hwu, P.-Y. (2003). Supporting children on the autism spectrum in peer play at home and school: Piloting the integrated play groups model in Taiwan. *Autism: The International Journal of Research and Practice, 7*(4), 437–453. https://doi.org/10.1177/1362361303007004009

Zaidman-Zait, A., Mirenda, P., Duku, E., Szatmari, P., Georgiades, S., Volden, J., … Thompson, A. (2014). Examination of bidirectional relationships between parent stress and two types of problem behavior in children with autism spectrum disorder. *Journal of Autism and Developmental Disorders, 44*(8), 1908–1917. https://doi.org/10.1007/s10803-014-2064-3

Chapter 9
Conclusion: Play and Social Skills as Behavioral Cusps

Childhood theorists are in agreement in that there are five important attributes of play: (1) play is motivating, (2) play activities are freely chosen, (3) play is pleasurable, (4) more advanced forms of play include an element of pretend, and (5) play is actively engaging (e.g., Wolfberg, 2003). For typically developing children, play develops in as a linear process, initially by exploring toys and objects, usually orally and then by touch and shaking. Subsequently, play includes others, initially by situating oneself near or side-by-side, parallel of another. At this point, children do not necessarily interact with each other, but may observe each other. From a very early age, typically developing children's play becomes social, first during infancy and toddler years with the primary caretaker and then with a peer or sibling. At this point, this social play is often referred to as associative or cooperative play (see Chap. 1). Although parents of children with ASD may take note that their toddlers are not playing with toys functionally (i.e., the way toys are meant to be played with), it is generally at this time when they become concerned that their children are not engaging socially. They see their children interacting with toys either immaturely (e.g., mouthing a toy after 3 years of age) or inappropriately (e.g., staring at the wheel of a toy truck). Parents of children with ASD may also become concerned when they see their children rubbing or flapping toys, lining items up, or organizing them according to some property of belongingness, such as type, color, size, shape, and so on, in the absence of more functional play.

However, for many parents, one major worry is that their child does not seem interested in playing with others. As the child gets older and interest still does not develop this deficit will become more obvious. While the child may interact better with adults, interactions are not qualitatively like typically developing children, and interactions with other children do not seem to be displayed. Interests tend to be restricted to specific items and concepts, and patterns of manipulation of play items (stereotypy) tend to be repetitive and quite unusual. As one mother put it, "I became

M.H. Charlop et al., *Play and Social Skills for Children with Autism Spectrum Disorder*, Evidence-Based Practices in Behavioral Health,
https://doi.org/10.1007/978-3-319-72500-0_9

concerned when it became obvious to me that I have a much better relationship and enjoyed playing with my friend's child more than my own child! That was when I knew I needed to get my son evaluated for autism."

Treatment Without Play and Social Skills

It has only been recently that a strong emphasis on play and social skills has been included in the course of treatment for children with ASD. While we may note that functional toy play might have appeared in early curricula for children, proportionally, little treatment time had been spent on the social aspect of play. We have collated, in this book, both the evidence-based literature on the play and social skills, as well as "how to" create programs which address these very important areas. In this chapter, we take a look at some children with ASD who did not have sufficient play and social skills treatment during their ABA programming or school programs.

The Case of Jake

Jake started his ABA treatment in the early 1990s. Jake started treatment when he was 4 years old and presented with a limited echoic verbal repertoire. He displayed problem behaviors such as tantrums, noncompliance, and aggression. He was preoccupied with animals and repetitively lined up animal figurines. When provided with other objects, Jake would line them up according to color, size, shape, and other similar characteristics. At the time, the zeitgeist in prognosis was speech before the age of 5 years. Fortunately, Jake was responsive to behavioral speech and language programming, and his echoic behavior was a starting point to introduce mand training and more sophisticated speech. Early treatment consisted of working through his escape-motivated tantrums and focusing his speech and language training on talking about animals. Jake would cry and yell "No!" That's a cow! No! That's a pig! No! I want the frog, please!" Soon, the crying and yelling subsided, and Jake could make up long stories about the animals and eventually talk about other subjects. Jake flourished in his ABA treatment and was fully mainstreamed into a regular education classroom by age 7 years. To all involved, he would be considered a "success story" because he scored 110 on his WISC IQ test and was placed in a regular education classroom. However, Jake was not taught to play with other children and was not presented with social skills as part of his curriculum.

As Jake aged, he and his siblings had less in common. He continued to be preoccupied with animals but his siblings and peers developed new more age-appropriate interests as they matured. Jake's preoccupation with dinosaurs persisted and took on a more sophisticated outlet, drawing them repetitively. He is a good artist. His parents supported his artwork, but this was something that he did solitarily. Jake becomes even more distant to his peers as he matriculated into middle and high school. During high school, it became evident that Jake, while doing adequate in his academic coursework, had few friends and no real occupation/vocation interests or skills. He had not joined any clubs, sports teams, community groups, and while he had speech skills, he did not know how to interact socially. Jake's art continued into sculpture and his parents hoped that maybe Jake's sculpting could be become a vocation. However, his sculpture turned out to be only of dinosaurs and his "sculptures" were in pipe cleaners. While dinosaurs are popular, Jake did not have any 3-D computer skills or other skills beyond this, and his parents were not sure what or where he would do/go after high school. The high school did have a social skills group, but progress was slow and arduous.

The Case of Richard

The first author employed Richard when he was around 23 years old after he graduated from college from a local prestigious university. Richard is very bright and did some data coding for us. That went well, and we attempted to keep him employed so offered him some office work. This required some social skills, which he had never received training in. A theoretically simple answer of the office phone was quite difficult for Richard. He did not learn to greet the person on the line. We attached a script to the phone, which he then read. However, when he needed to get the requested person and inform him/her that there was a call, he froze. When queried "what are you supposed to say?" he knew he was just to tell them they had a call. However, when asked "why are you not saying that," he would tell us he cannot tell them, get their attention, doesn't know what to say, and so on. The social aspects of interacting with people were interfering with his employment.

Now for the heartbreaking part of Richard's story. Richard eventually got a job for more money at a program in the mailroom sorting mail, a position way below Richard's competence level. At the mailroom, an older woman took Richard under her wing, explained the job, and was nice to Richard. He had his first friend, but he was never taught how to be a friend. As life happens, the woman's hourly shift changed and so Richard, and she no longer worked at the same time. However, Richard would wait for her by her car when she would leave work so he could talk to her. Unfortunately, Richard did not know how to start up a conversation so he would just wait for her to start it. This became annoying for the woman, so she gave Richard "hints" that she didn't want him to wait at her car. He didn't pick up on those hints so she told him directly. That didn't work either. Since the woman didn't understand autism, she thought she was being stalked. She filed a harassment suit against Richard with their human resources department as her last resort. Needless to say, this was a terrifying albeit unnecessary experience for Richard. He had also lost the "only friend" he had ever made.

The case stories of Jake and Richard may be more tragic than some, but they illustrate what can happen when programs and school IEPs do not take the need for play and social skills *as* seriously as other areas of treatment. If you ask a parent of a child with ASD what is the most important behavior they want us, as treatment providers to address, in general, they will answer, they want their child to speak (unless they child has a serious behavior problem such as self-injury). This is usually the first behavior, and we agree, communication is of utmost importance. But, usually, play and social skills are far down the line of treatment concerns of parents. Recent research and outcomes like Jake and Richard are changing this. Looking at the "big picture" of a child with ASD's life is also changing that. When we speak with parents, we try put play and social skills in the perspective of the child's life, and it is never too soon to start. It is of great importance for a child with ASD to grow up to have a life that is full, happy, social, and more like that of a typical child's.

Developmental Trajectories and Behavioral Cusps

Go to Preschool and Prevent Crime!

While you may be wondering what this topic has to do with play and social skills and ASD, if the above two case studies have not convinced you, this hopefully will illustrate how play and social skills lead to the further development and learning for the child with ASD. There is a sound body of literature that correlates the attendance of preschool with a decrease in violent crime in areas that are associated with higher rates of crime. So, while you may argue that a strong prison system and stiffer laws are what we need to fight crime, the data suggest that more preschools will also help a lot. How can that be? Does that even make sense? Go to preschool; decrease crime! How does this work?

Several longitudinal studies now show us that the behaviors taught in preschool can be viewed as so important that they put the children on developmental trajectories that lead them to much improved lives. For example, the Child-Parent Centers study (Temple & Reynolds, 2007) showed that attendance in preschool was associated with a decrease in behavior problems, a decrease in placement in special education, an increase in literacy rates, and an increase in high school retention, which ultimately led to the association with a decrease in crime, alcoholism, and addiction and an increase in income level. Other studies have corroborated these results.

But can attendance in preschool really lead to a reduction in crime so many years later? Sounds farfetched, and it is just correlation research (which does not indicate causation).

However, when you view it as a developmental trajectory, it makes much more sense. Behaviors that are learned in preschool help out children who will stay in school. These behaviors include the social skills (getting along with others, turn-taking, sharing, waiting your turn), pre-reading skills which will help the children with more academic areas later in school. Preschool interaction helps the young child learn self-regulation skills, and it is much easier to deal with behavior problems of young children who do not have an extensive history of the behavior. Children who can readily control themselves are less likely to be placed in special education classes. As the child develops, he is then able to learn other skills; learning the alphabet leads to advanced reading of science and social studies, learning basic math leads to opportunities of advanced classes, and so on. Importantly, success in school begets success in school later and lends itself more readily to success in the job market. Learning social skills early on increases the likelihood of socializing and recruiting many communities of reinforcement. Thus, each child in preschool is put on a more positive developmental trajectory than if he would not have gone. The results lead to a more productive citizen of the community as opposed to someone who did not have access to more and more skill sets and thus may have dropped out, taken drugs, and became affiliated in a gang or engaged in crime.

Preschool behaviors continue to "blossom" and give children the skills to put them on the trajectory that leads to further developmental milestones (Bijou & Baer, 1961). In the developmental psychology literature, these kinds of developmental trajectories open up the world to the youngster. They are referred to as milestones. In the behavioral literature, they are referred to as the behavioral cusp (Rosales-Ruiz & Baer, 1997).

Behavioral Cusps of Play and Social Skills

Behavioral cusps are behavior changes that will lead to the occurrence of many more behaviors, and these behaviors must be deemed as important (Rosales-Ruiz & Baer, 1997). That is, the behavioral cusps create new behaviors that are considered important because they are socially valid. Additionally, the behavioral cusps extend out into the environment and recruit new communities of reinforcement (both positive and negative; reinforcing and punishing) so that new behaviors are formed. This is a watered down definition of behavioral cusps (see Bosch & Fuqua, 2001 or Rosales-Ruiz & Baer, 1997). One important feature of behavioral cusps is that it leads to another cusp. Also, a behavioral cusp might compete and decrease other cusps (ones you do not want). Also, behavioral cusps, unlike developmental milestones, are learned behaviors. But it is easy to see how, in the preschool example above, literacy would be a good example of a behavioral cusp: learning the alphabet, a behavioral cusp that opens the door for further cognitive development, object identification, and so on. Most importantly (socially valid), it leads to the cusp of reading. Once reading, the child's world opens up to learning about many other subjects (it even helps in reading music). One cusp begets another. With literacy and doing well in school, a child will stay in school, and the chances of dropping out and getting involved in crime diminish.

When we teach play, we are creating a behavioral cusp. While we have already touted the importance of teaching play for plays' worth alone, the importance of play increases exponentially when we view play as a behavioral cusp. When viewed as a cusp, we can see that play opens up the child with ASD's world to more behavioral cusps, more socially valid behaviors, decreases unwanted behaviors, and ultimately expands the child's repertoire. Play behaviors lead to joint attention (e.g., Basso, Charlop, & Gumaer, 2017), language (e.g., Kasari, Gulsrud, Freeman, Paparella, & Hellemann, 2012), turn-taking (e.g., Laski, Charlop, & Schreibman, 1988), and social skills, to name a few. Each of these new behavioral cusps leads to other cusps; joint attention leads to language and further social skills (Kasari, Chang, & Patteson, 2013), language skills lead to cognitive development (Lillard et al., 2013) and social skills, and turn-taking leads to perspective-taking skills (Charlop-Christy & Daneshvar, 2003). Social skills lead to theory of mind skills (Baron-Cohen, Leslie, & Frith, 1985), reading comprehension, friendships and relationships, and employment/vocation skills. Importantly, studies have shown us that those children with ASD, who have more social skills, are less often bullying victims (Chen & Schwartz, 2012).

Behavioral cusps have long enduring positive effects upon the behavioral repertoires of children with ASD. While measuring collateral changes are important, such as decreasing stereotypy by increasing play, these gains tend to be temporary. Making sustainable changes in play and social skills has long-lasting positive effects upon the child's prognosis by means of creating behavioral cusps.

Treatment with Play and Social Skills

Amy was almost 4 when she started our early social skills groups. She scored in the severe range of ASD using the Childhood Autism Checklist, Second Edition (CARS2; Schopler, Van Bourgondien, Wellman, & Love, 2010). She had limited echoic speech but would communicate by one or two word phrases ("chips, No, potty!"). She seldom displayed any eye contact, spontaneously or upon request and engaged in problem behavior a large percentage of the day which prevented her from attending preschool. Many common sounds in the environment occasioned her to scream loudly and result in her running away. She was noncompliant with her parents for most requests and her parents described their life as "tiptoeing around Amy." Because Amy had a multitude of behavior problems, we needed to start there, although we had a social skills/play program going on at the same time so that Amy may get some joy out of her life instead of worrying about what noises she would come in contact with. Amy's mother requested that her two concerns were getting Amy to use the bathroom outside of the home bathroom and to decrease tantrums. As behavior problems usually go, they are quite easy to treat. Amy, void of her concerns of noises, using public bathrooms, and eager to learn, became a "different child." But it was in the milieu of play and social skills, where her mother had fewer expectations and concerns, that Amy began to shine. As Amy learned to play with toys, her speech and language developed in sophistication. She found something interesting to talk about others that what she didn't want to do. She then learned that her peers in her social skills group were important because many of her toys required others to be involved. She befriended another girl in the group but seemed happier with the more active boys. During athletic activities out on the yard, Amy excelled. She enjoyed running and learned that rules of a game made it more interesting, not confining. Soon, she was using her pretend skills to make up games.

While we do not have many years to report on Amy, we can state that Amy, after 6 months of her ABA program, inclusive with play and social skills, was enrolled into a local preschool and excelled. She learned her pre-K work with much gusto, and today she continues in second grade, partially mainstreamed due to reluctance of her school district and their budgetary problems. However, every morning, Amy greets her teacher with eye contact (which she now engages in most of the time), a smile, and says "Good morning, Mrs. Valdez" before Amy goes independently off to her desk to get her schedule for the day.

It is too soon to determine if Amy is a success story. By old-fashioned standards (with inherent problems), her IQ is not in the normal range (between 85 and 110), and she is not in a regular education class 100% of the time. It is difficult to predict whether either of these two will happen; we don't practice crystal ball prediction, and we are behaviorists, not psychics.

But Amy plays nicely with her sister and her cousins and is invited to play dates and birthday parties from friends at school. She loves going on camping trips with her large extended family, is on a soccer team, and will soon join the Brownies. Her favorite place to go is Disneyland—just like so many other little children. The procedures for Amy's play and social skills are summarized in Box 9.1.

Box 9.1 Amy's Play and Social Skills Program included the following procedures

Amy's play and social skills program included the following procedures:

1. Natural Language Paradigm (NLP) from Chap. 4 for speech and play
2. Reinforcement assessment with prompting, modeling, and reinforcement from Chap. 3 for functional toy play
3. General naturalistic teaching procedures from Chap. 3 for cooperative peer play
4. Multiple incidental teaching procedures (MITS) from Chap. 3 for verbal interactions with adults and peers (initiations, greetings, requests to go potty)
5. Peer modeling from Chap. 8 for athletic/outdoor activities
6. Social skills group–a combination of treatment procedures from peer modeling, teacher (modeling and naturalistic teaching strategies in Chaps. 3, 4, and 8)

Conclusion

Play and social skills have implications for much more far reaching consequences of positive gain. In this chapter, we presented play and social skills as behavioral cusps that continue to perpetuate their value by opening the world for to children with ASD and lead to other behavioral cusps that continue to widen the reinforcement communities for the children. Three brief case studies are provided for illustrative purposes. Toward this end, play and social skills are indeed of utmost importance when crafting the most positive prognosis a child can have.

References

Baron-Cohen, S., Leslie, A. M., & Frith, U. (1985). Does the autistic child have a "theory of mind"? *Cognition, 21*(1), 37–46.

Basso, T., Charlop, M. H., & Gumaer, C. (2017). *Using a play intervention to increase joint attention for School-aged, Non-verbal Children with Autism Spectrum Disorder (ASD).* Unpublished manuscript. Claremont, CA: Claremont McKenna College.

Bosch, S., & Fuqua, R. W. (2001). Behavioral cusps: A model for selecting target behaviors. *Journal of Applied Behavior Analysis, 34*(1), 123.

Bijou, S. W., & Baer, D. M. (1961). The nature of developmental theory. In *Child development: A systematic and empirical theory* (Vol. 1). East Norwalk, CT: Appleton-Century-Crofts.

Charlop-Christy, M. H., & Daneshvar, S. (2003). Using video modeling to teach perspective taking to children with autism. *Journal of Positive Behavior Interventions, 5*(1), 12–21.

Chen, P. Y., & Schwartz, I. S. (2012). Bullying and victimization experiences of students with autism spectrum disorders in elementary schools. *Focus on Autism and Other Developmental Disabilities, 27*(4), 200–212.

Kasari, C., Chang, Y., & Patteson, S. (2013). Pretending to play or playing to pretend: The case of autism. *American Journal of Play, 6*(1), 124–135.

Kasari, C., Gulsrud, A., Freeman, S., Paparella, T., & Hellemann, G. (2012). Longitudinal follow-up of children with autism receiving targeted interventions on joint attention and play. *Journal of the American Academy of Child & Adolescent Psychiatry, 51*(5), 487–495.

Laski, K. E., Charlop, M. H., & Schreibman, L. (1988). Training parents to use the natural language paradigm to increase their autistic children's speech. *Journal of Applied Behavior Analysis, 21*(4), 391–400.

Lillard, A. S., Lerner, M. D., Hopkins, E. J., Dore, R. A., Smith, E. D., & Palmquist, C. M. (2013). The impact of pretend play on children's development: A review of the evidence. *Psychological Bulletin, 139*, 1–34.

Rosales-Ruiz, J., & Baer, D. M. (1997). Behavioral cusps: A developmental and pragmatic concept for behavior analysis. *Journal of Applied Behavior Analysis, 30*, 533–544.

Schopler, E., Van Bourgondien, M. E., Wellman, G. J., & Love, S. R. (2010). *The childhood autism rating scale, (CARS2).* Los Angeles: WPS.

Temple, J. A., & Reynolds, A. J. (2007). Benefits and costs of investments in preschool education: Evidence from the Child–Parent Centers and related programs. *Economics of Education Review, 26*(1), 126–144.

Wolfberg, P. J. (2003). *Peer play and the autism spectrum: The art of guiding children's socialization and imagination*. AAPC Publishing.

Index

A
Amy's play and social skills program, 161
Applied behavior analysis (ABA), 1
Auditory-temporal treatment, 95, 96
Autism
  CARS2, 160
  children, 74–80
  core features of, 131
  definition, 9
  intervention model, 116
Autism spectrum disorder (ASD), 2, 3, 8–13, 53–55, 57, 59, 64–68

B
Behavioral cusp
  case of Jake, 156, 157
  case of Richard, 157, 158
  childhood theorists, 155
  children with ASD, 155, 162
  developmental trajectories, 158, 159
  play and social skills, 159, 160
  stereotypy, 155
  treatment, 156

C
Childhood
  play and social interaction, 1
  skill acquisition, 8
Childhood Autism Checklist, Second Edition (CARS2), 160
Child-Parent Centers study, 158
Cooperative play and turn-taking, 46

D
Development
  child, 2
  children with ASD, 2
  language, academics and motor skill, 1, 13
  play behavior, 5
  social and play, 3–8
  social skill acquisition and language, 13
Discrete trial training (DTT), 66

E
Early Start Denver Model (ESDM), 133, 134
Ecological congruence assessment, 117, 118
Education, PMI research, 109
Enhanced Milieu Teaching (EMT), 133
Evidence-based practice
  ABA, 17
  children with ASD
    Autism Evidence-Based Practice Review Group, 27
    classification, 20
    components, 22
    natural and social sciences, 20
    NPDC, 22, 26
    NSP, 26, 27
    treatments, 27, 28
  children with intellectual and developmental disabilities, 17
  early intervention studies, 17
  history of, 19, 20
  influence treatment selection, 28–30
  intervention, treatment, package and component, 21

M.H. Charlop et al., *Play and Social Skills for Children with Autism Spectrum Disorder*, Evidence-Based Practices in Behavioral Health,
https://doi.org/10.1007/978-3-319-72500-0

Evidence-based practice (*cont.*)
  National Autism Center's National Standards Project, 24
  National Professional Development Center, autism spectrum disorders, 23
  play and social skills, 18
  professional organizations, 17

F
Family-centered approach, 130, 131
Functional toy play, 44

G
Group games, target behaviors, 47

H
Hawaii Early Learning Profile for Preschoolers (HELP), 117

I
Incidental teaching (IT), 66
Individuals with Disabilities Education Act (IDEA), 131
Intervention
  children with ASD, 3, 34, 95
  conversation speech, 76
  play, 1, 43, 44
  prompting, 36
  PVMI, 79
  research-based teaching procedures, 12
  social and play skills, 1, 11
  social validity of, 80, 81
  teen with ASD, 98
  video modeling, 73, 75–77, 101

J
Joint Attention, Symbolic Play, Engagement, and Regulation (JASPER), 139

L
Learning Experiences and Alternative Program for Preschoolers and their Parents (LEAP) program, 116

M
Milieu teaching strategies, 65
Modeling, prompting, 42, 49
Multiple incidental teaching sessions (MITS), 66, 67

N
National Professional Development Center on Autism Spectrum Disorders (NPDC), 22, 23, 26, 27
National Standards Project (NSP), 24, 26, 27
Natural language paradigm (NLP), 61, 62, 64, 161
Naturalistic teaching strategies (NaTS)
  acquisition of, 67
  child choice, 58
  components of, 54–61
  description, 53
  generalization, 60
  Mand-model, 65, 66
  Milieu teaching strategies, 65
  MITS, 66, 67
  in natural environment, 53
  NLP, 61, 62
  PRT, 62–64
  self-management, 64, 65
  task variation, 56
Neurotypical children, 71, 72, 81

P
Parent-implanted intervention
  child behavior, 129
  child outcomes, 142
  children with ASD, 129
  coaching parents, 147, 148
  early intervention, 131
  family-centered approach, 130, 131
  generalization and maintenance of learning, 131, 132
  individual families, 141, 142
  parent-child interactions, 148
  planning, 141
  routines, 142–144
  social communication, 138–141
  social interaction, 129
  target outcome, 143
  teaching and supporting, 134–138
  training parents, 144–146
  types of, 132–134
  written instructions, 145

Peer-mediated interventions (PMI)
adult-directed instruction, 108
behavior analysis, 108
children with ASD, 107, 110–114
data sheet, 119
elementary school children, 109
individuals with ASD, 109
initial training procedures, 121
instructional practices, 108
intervention agents, 109
neurotypical peers, 107–109
planning, 117–123
progress monitoring graph, 123
research, 108
selection, 120
social and communicative skills, 107
social interactions, 109
strategies, 114–116
visual supports, 122
Peer training, 112–116
Picture Exchange Communication System (PECS), 73, 78
Pivotal response training (PRT), 62–64, 133
Play, 111, 112
acquisition of, 13
behavioral approach
children with ASD, 34–35
children's development, 34
individual parts of, 34
and nonplay items, 41, 42
car wash toy, 85, 86, 89
cause-effect toy, 84, 85
characteristics, ASD, 10
child-preferred toys, 38–42
children with ASD, 2, 8–11
considerations and trouble-shooting, 40, 41
cooperative, 46–47
developmental sequence, 5
foundational skills, 13
group games, 47
interventions, 43–44
JASPER study, 139
motor skill development, 13
parents and caregivers, 13
preference assessments, 38–40
pretend
associative and cooperative play, 37
games with rules, 37
solitary, 36, 37
reinforcement, 2
routine intervention, children with ASD, 138
skill development, 3–6
social skills (*see* Social skills)
teaching, 33, 34
toys
exploratory and functional, 35
imaginative and pretend, 36
Project ImPACT, 133
Prompting
exploratory behavior with toys, 35
procedures, 42, 43, 49
Prompts for Restructuring Oral Muscular Phonetic Targets (PROMPT) model, 134
Proximity, 114, 115
Pseudoscientific, 28, 29

R
Research-based, children with ASD, 20
Review, social interaction behaviors, 116

S
Script fading
procedures, 103
smartphone, 104
Script training, 100
Social communication
augmentative and alterative communication, 140
joint attention, 138, 139
play skills, 140, 141
social interaction, 140
verbal communication, 139
Social interaction skills, 110, 111
Social skills, 1, 3, 4, 7, 8, 11–13
acquisition of, 33
behavioral cusps, 159, 160
children with ASD, 64, 111
children with disabilities, 108
development, 3–8, 107
in intervention research, 8
NaTS, 53
play, 18, 28, 53, 59 (*see also* Play)
play and communication skills, 107
students with ASD, 115
target behavior, 82
treatment, 160, 161
Sociodramatic play, 33, 34, 36, 37, 49

T
Target behaviors, 82
Teaching independent play, 45

Treatment
child participants, 134
ESDM, 134
NaTS, 53
play and social skills, 95
visual-temporal and spatial modalities, 95, 96
VM, 74
Treatment of ASD, 11

U
The US Department of Education's Institute for Education Sciences, 19

V
Video modeling (VM)
adults, 86
advantages, 76
child motivation, 80, 87
children with ASD, 75
conversational skills, 75, 76
definition, 74
empirical support, 76–81
filming, 88, 89
intervention, 89, 90
model-less modeling, 87
pre-assessment criteria, 90
rationale, 71–73
readiness, 81, 82
scene setup, 87, 88
script, 86
social-communicative skills, 78–80
social validity of intervention, 80, 81
target behavior, 82–84
task analysis, 84–86
video footage, 75
visual activity schedules, 98
visual learning and ASD, 72, 73
visual strategies, 73–81
Visual activity schedules, 98, 104
Visual-spatial treatment, 96
Visual strategies
activity schedules, 97
advantage, 104
children with ASD, 95
modalities, 95, 96
pre-assessments, 100, 101
script fading, 102, 103
scripts, 97–104
signaling script use, 102
writing a script, 101
Visual-temporal treatment, 95, 96

FSC
www.fsc.org
MIX
Papier | Fördert
gute Waldnutzung
FSC® C083411

Kolibri 360 GmbH
Ferdinand-Jühlke-Straße 7
99095 Erfurt, Deutschland
produktsicherheit@kolibri360.de